RHETORIC AT ROME

This new edition of M. L. Clarke's classic study of Roman rhetoric incorporates corrections and a new introduction by D. H. Berry. A bibliography has also been provided for the first time.

Praise for the first edition:

'Professor Clarke's book presents both a reliable and a pleasant introduction to the subject. It should be read by every classical scholar.'

A. D. Leeman, *Mnemosyne*

admirably organized and documented ... marked by great clarity and good sense. Latinist and layman alike will enjoy and profit by this excellent book.'

Richard T. Bruère, *Classical Philology*

'It is ... a pleasantly written book, fully documented, and will be a useful text for anyone wishing an introduction to this branch of Latin literature.'

Harry M. Hubbell, *American Journal of Philology*

'The book will, one feels, hold its place as a standard work for some time to come.'

E. W. Bower, *Classical Review*

M. L. Clarke is Emeritus Professor of Latin at the University College of North Wales, Bangor. His other books include *The Roman Mind* (1956), *Higher Education in the Ancient World* (1971) and *The Noblest Roman* (1981). **D. H. Berry** is Lecturer in Classics at the University of Leeds and the editor of *Cicero: Pro P. Sulla Oratio* (1996).

RHETORIC AT ROME

A Historical Survey

M. L. CLARKE

Revised and with a new introduction by

D. H. Berry

London and New York

First published 1953
Second edition 1966
by Cohen & West Ltd

Third edition published 1996
by Routledge
11 New Fetter Lane, London EC4P 4EE

Simultaneously published in the USA and Canada
by Routledge
29 West 35th Street, New York, NY 10001

Printed and bound in Great Britain by
Redwood Books, Trowbridge, Wiltshire

British Library Cataloguing in Publication Data

A catalogue record for this book is available from the British Library

Library of Congress Cataloguing in Publication Data

Clarke, M. L. (Martin Lowther)
        Rhetoric at Rome: a historical survey/M. L. Clarke. – Rev. ed.
/rev. and with a new introduction by D. H. Berry.
            p.   cm. – (Routledge classical studies)
        Includes bibliographical references and index.
        ISBN 0–415–14155–9. – ISBN 0–415–14156–7 (pbk.)
            1. Speeches, addresses, etc., Latin–History and criticism–
Theory, etc.   2. Oral communication–Rome.   3. Rhetoric, Ancient.
4. Oratory, Ancient.   I. Berry, D. H.   II. Title.   III. Series.
PA6083.C6   1996
875′.0109–dc20
                                                                96-3816
                                                                CIP

CONTENTS

PREFACE TO THE FIRST AND SECOND EDITIONS

'THE AGE of Rhetoric,' wrote Thomas de Quincey over a century ago, 'like that of chivalry, has passed amongst forgotten things.' In a sense he was wrong. The art of persuasion is always with us, though it assumes new forms and is called by new names, such as advertising and propaganda. The spoken word is still a power, especially since broadcasting made us once more a listening rather than a reading people. But rhetoric as the ancients knew it, the systematic study of the art of argument and expression, has certainly passed away. The last substantial treatise on the subject published in this country, that of Archbishop Whately, appeared in 1828. Today we have only breezy little handbooks on after-dinner speaking—works which would have made Quintilian stare and gasp. In France rhetoric was banished from the secondary school curriculum in 1885. Only in America, with her professors of Rhetoric and University Departments of Speech, does something of the old tradition survive.

Yet anyone who studies the civilisation of Rome cannot fail to come up against rhetoric. The schoolboy reads speeches of Cicero in the Latin class while he reads plays or novels in the French class. The more advanced student comes upon the massive works of Cicero and Quintilian devoted to rhetoric, and discovers how large a part the subject played in Roman education. He observes too, perhaps with distaste, how the rhetorical manner spreads from oratory to other forms of literature. Some understanding of rhetoric is necessary for anyone who wishes to understand ancient Rome.

To assist such an understanding this book has been written. In it I have tried to show what rhetoric meant to the Roman world from its first introduction to the end of classical civilisation. I have not gone deeply into the technicalities of ancient rhetorical theory, knowing how few there are who can summon up any interest in them and remembering the scorn which one of the earliest Latin writers on rhetoric expressed for those who *ne parum multa scisse viderentur, ea conquisierunt quae nihil attinebant ut ars difficilior cognitu putaretur.*

I should like to acknowledge a particular debt to two works, Kroll's authoritative survey in Pauly-Wissowa's *Realencyclopädie*, Supplementband VII (cited in the notes as Kroll, *Rhetorik*) and Aubrey Gwynn's *Roman Education from Cicero to Quintilian*, which first aroused my interest in the subject. I am grateful to Dr. J. F. Lockwood, Master of Birkbeck College, London, for lending me an offprint of Kroll's article when the volume in which it has since appeared was not yet available in this country, and for reading and criticising my work in typescript. I have also profited by the criticisms of my colleague Dr. R. A. Browne. Finally I must thank the Board of the University of Wales Press for their generosity in making a grant towards the cost of publication.

1953

I have taken the opportunity of a new impression to alter a few passages where the original text seemed to me to be misleading and to add to the notes some references to recent work on the subject.

M.L.C.

1965

INTRODUCTION TO THE THIRD EDITION

THE TWO most important accomplishments a man in the ancient world could possess were generally agreed to be skill in the military sphere and skill in speaking. In the *Iliad* young heroes like Achilles are mighty warriors, while older ones, such as Nestor, are wise and impressive speakers. The elderly Phoenix was sent to Troy with Achilles to make him 'a speaker of words and a doer of deeds' (Hom. *Il.* 9.443). In democratic Athens, generals took their orders from the assembly, which reached decisions after listening to the arguments on either side; Thucydides acknowledged the importance of oratory by including speeches in his history. At Rome, L. Metellus, the consul of 251 and 247 B.C., was praised in the funeral speech given for him by his son as having been 'a first-class warrior, a brilliant orator and a very brave commander' (Plin. *Nat.* 7.140). To any Roman, military ability was, of course, more important than oratory: even Cicero conceded that (*Mur.* 30; *Brut.* 256; cf. *Off.* 2.45–8). Nevertheless, a good general would have to know how to address his troops, and if he was not an orator he would also, like Marius, find himself disadvantaged in the political arena. Marius and Cicero, both *novi homines* ('new men') from the same town, rose to the consulship by their own ability, Marius as a general, Cicero as an orator. Marius, however, viewed all forms of culture with distaste, and Cicero had no taste for soldiering. Caesar, by contrast, was an expert in both fields; but it was his oratory which first brought him to public notice (Plut. *Caes.* 3–5).

The political system at Rome under the republic was highly conducive to the practice of deliberative oratory.[1] Views on political questions were expressed orally by members of a body of elders, the senate, who remained senators for life; the consensus once agreed would be acted upon by magistrates who had been elected to serve for a year only and would not normally be re-elected. Unlike in modern political assemblies, senators had not necessarily decided in *is this due to use?*

advance which way they would vote, and so the debates were real: powerful speakers, regardless of their position in the hierarchy, had a chance of influencing the outcome. On 5 December 63 B.C., for instance, the senate debated what should be done with the five captured Catilinarian conspirators. Sixteen senators, asked for their opinion (*sententia*) in order of seniority, declared themselves in favour of execution. Then Caesar, who was praetor designate, proposed life imprisonment, and all the previous speakers but one changed their minds and agreed with him. Finally Cato, who as tribune designate was only a junior member of the senate, restated the case for execution and carried the day.[2] (The speeches of Caesar and Cato are preserved in a version by Sallust (*Cat.* 51–2), and Cicero's speech, which came after Caesar's but before Cato's, was published in 60 B.C. as the *Fourth Catilinarian*. Deliberative oratory, besides being employed in the senate, was also used in the popular assemblies, when legislation was put before the people, for example, or when a magistrate wished to address the people on some other topic of importance. In the late republic there were many 'popular' politicians (*populares*), such as C. Gracchus and P. Clodius, who made speeches in which they advocated policies with which the senate as a whole was not in sympathy, but which were likely to appeal to the people.

Forensic oratory too flourished under the republic. Whereas in Greece defendants pleaded their own cases, employing a speech-writer (*logographos*) if necessary, at Rome they turned for help to someone more eloquent than themselves to plead on their behalf. The *lex Cincia de donis et muneribus* (204 B.C.) forbade payment of fees to advocates, so advocates (*patroni*) tended to be repaid instead with political support: Cicero's activity in the courts, together with his speeches to the people, enabled him to attain each office in the *cursus honorum* (career ladder through the magistracies) at the earliest permitted age. As the speaker Maternus is made to say in Tacitus' *Dialogus* (a central text for the understanding of the relation between oratory and its political context),

The more able a man was at speaking, the greater the ease with which he attained to high office and the greater his pre-eminence among his colleagues in office; he obtained more influence with the powerful, carried more weight with the senate, possessed a higher reputation with the people.

(Tac. *Dial.* 36.4)[3]

Criminal prosecutions were always undertaken by private individuals, since there was no state prosecutor, and prominent senators were prosecuted not because they had committed a crime (although of course they often had), but because their accuser was an enemy who wanted them removed from political life. Enmities (*inimicitiae*) could be long-lasting: Tacitus talks of 'feuds handed down like family heirlooms' (*Dial.* 36.3). Trials were great public events, held in the open air in the forum (hence 'forensic' oratory). Large crowds turned out to see the spectacle: the praetor and the jury sitting up on the tribunal, the celebrated orators making their speeches, the aristocratic defendant dressed in mourning and the benches packed with his family, advisers (*advocati*) and supporters. 'What an orator needs is noise and applause', says Tacitus,

> a theatre for his performance: the old orators had all that every day. An audience large (and well-bred too) packed the forum; clients, fellow tribesmen, municipal delegations, a good proportion of the population of Italy came to support defendants – for in many cases the Roman people believed that what was decided mattered to *them*. It is well known that when Gaius Cornelius, Marcus Scaurus, Titus Milo, Lucius Bestia, and Publius Vatinius were prosecuted and defended the whole state came running to listen.
>
> (*Dial.* 39.4–5)

For the audience, a trial was a piece of theatre (Cic. *Brut.* 290), and the orators were well aware of this dimension: they played to the gallery with direct appeals to the ring of onlookers (*corona*) surrounding the court, and Cicero's *pro Caelio* (56 B.C.) consciously plays on characteristic elements of the comic stage.[4] Forensic oratory therefore had a cultural role as well as a political role. Successful speeches were written up and circulated after the trial not just (or even mainly) as vehicles for promoting the orator's political viewpoint, but as oratorical models for imitation and enjoyment.

Under the empire oratory lost most of its political importance, at least at the higher levels of politics. There was not much scope for deliberative oratory, except perhaps on the part of the emperor, who was required to recommend his decisions to the senate; Nero was said to have been the first emperor to make a speech which he had not composed himself (Tac. *Ann.* 13.3). Forensic oratory also suffered. With the emperor keeping a watchful eye over the conduct of magistrates, major criminal trials (now held before the senate or the emperor himself) became rare events. Advocates therefore had to content themselves with civil cases in the centumviral court, where restrictions had been placed on the length of speeches and the number of pleaders. The only criminal trials which were political were those for treason (*maiestas*), a charge which was now taken to mean conspiracy against the emperor: the law of *maiestas* provided opportunities for unscrupulous informers (*delatores*) to further their careers and enrich themselves at the expense of their high-ranking victims. For a time the *delatores* brought oratory into disrepute, by failing to satisfy at least the first half of Cato's definition (*Fil.* 14, = 80.1 Jordan *orator est ... vir bonus dicendi peritus*, 'an orator is an honest man skilled in speaking').[5] Except during the reigns of Tiberius and Domitian, however, trials for *maiestas* were on the whole relatively rare, and the situation otherwise was as Tacitus' Maternus describes it:

What need of long speeches in the senate? Our great men swiftly reach agreement. What need of constant harangues to the people? The deliberations of state are not left to the ignorant many – they are the duty of one man, the wisest. What need of prosecutions? Crime is rare and trivial. What need of long and unpopular defences? The clemency of the judge meets the defendants half way.
(*Dial.* 41.4)

Officially, great oratory and peace were incompatible, and the reduced scope for eloquence was a small price to pay for order and stable government (the view expressed by Maternus). Unofficially, however, there may have been people, very possibly including Tacitus, who would have concurred with the view of Cicero's Crassus: 'This [i.e. oratory] is the one art which among every free people, and most especially in states that are peaceful and settled, has always flourished more than others, and always reigned supreme' (*de Orat.* 1.30). At the local level, however, oratory did continue to be a valuable weapon: in courts and assemblies throughout the empire, fortunes and reputations were won and lost.

Epideictic oratory, meanwhile, came into its own under the empire. In republican times the Romans had seen it as a Greek practice for which they had little use. The Roman funeral *laudatio* (eulogy) technically belonged to the epideictic branch of oratory, but that was an ancient genre with its own conventions, which the conservative Romans were reluctant to discard. Once the republican system had given way to one-man rule, however, a suitable subject for panegyric was always to hand in the person of the emperor. The younger Pliny's *Panegyricus* (A.D 100, afterwards revised), a eulogy of the emperor Trajan, became the most famous example of the type, partly because Trajan was considered by posterity to have genuinely deserved his title *optimus princeps* ('best of emperors'). In epideictic oratory, persuasion is a much less important aim than it is in deliberative or forensic. The epideictic orator may sometimes wish to persuade his subject to live up to the praises heaped on him, or else he may hope to influence future holders of his subject's post. But otherwise his aim is not to persuade. Instead, he will seek to assure his subject of his loyalty, to place his subject in his debt and to display his eloquence before a distinguished audience.

As a cultural phenomenon, oratory continued to grow during this period. The crowds which under the republic had flocked to the forum now packed the declamation halls, where popular rhetoricians demonstrated the mastery of their art. The analogy with the theatre still applied: the subject matter of declamation, which was made up of tyrants, pirates, stepmothers and other stock characters, could have been taken straight from the comic poets. Rhetoric, the theoretical basis of oratory, was confirmed as the major element in post-elementary education: once Roman boys had learned the three R's, they hurried off to the rhetorical schools to be taught to speak and to argue. The influence of rhetoric duly extended not just to oratory but to poetry, history, philosophy and every literary genre. Already in the first century A.D. oratory had changed from being primarily a political weapon to being the principal ingredient in Roman education and cultural life, a position it held until the end of antiquity.

The topic which is the subject of this book is therefore one which is central to Roman politics, culture and society. The book opens with an account of the origin and development of rhetoric in Greece from the fifth to the first centuries B.C. (Ch. I): by the time it was adopted by the Romans in the mid-second century, rhetoric was already a discipline with a long history, and was firmly established as one of the main features of Hellenistic culture. Chapter II shows how rhetoric became established at Rome. The Romans seized on rhetoric (Cic. *de Orat.* 1.14), as on other Greek inventions, because they saw how it could be useful to them, and at the beginning of the first century B.C. Roman rhetoricians, teaching in Latin, found a ready market for their services. The third chapter gives a brief outline of the essential features of rhetorical theory: the three types of oratory (forensic or judicial, deliberative and epideictic), the five functions of the orator or 'parts of rhetoric' (invention, arrangement, style, memory[6] and delivery), the six parts of a speech (opening, statement of facts, partition or division, proof, refutation and conclusion or peroration), the four issues (conjecture, definition, quality and objection), the three styles (grand, middle and plain) and so on. Chapter IV attempts to assess how far this system influenced Roman oratorical practice in the century before Cicero. The lack of evidence makes certainty impossible, but it would seem that, while the Greek tradition did have an increasing influence on the early Roman orators, the native Roman tradition (to which, as we have seen, the funeral *laudatio* belonged) also remained strong, and it is this which is largely responsible for such characteristic elements of Roman oratory as pathos and humour.

The three following chapters are devoted to Cicero. Chapter V examines his views on rhetoric as expressed in his treatises: he was aware that the rules of rhetoric were only of limited value in real-life situations, and he insisted that the orator should have a broad general education including, for example, law and philosophy. The next two chapters compare his oratorical practice first with traditional rhetorical theory (Ch. VI), and then with his own views (Ch. VII).[7] Cicero did not adhere strictly to the rules of rhetoric, and he was increasingly prepared to depart from them as the situation required (*pro Milone* (52 B.C.) is the exception); the correspondence with the views expressed in his treatises is naturally closer, since the treatises were written in the light of his own experience. In recent years scholars have paid more attention to the aspects of Ciceronian oratory where there is little connection with traditional rhetorical theory than to the areas where the influence of rhetoric is strong: thus there have been studies of, for example, Cicero's argumentative strategies, his manipulation of ethos or character (his own, his opponent's and, in forensic speeches, his client's) and his exploitation of place or ambience.[8] Cicero knew and made use of rhetorical theory, but he also excelled in those aspects of oratory to which theory had made little contribution.

Chapters VIII and IX deal with, respectively, declamation in the early empire and the oratory of this period (most of which is lost). Declamation was, and is, easy to criticise, for the improbability of its themes, its remoteness from real life and its indifference to the procedures and customs of the law courts. Under a poor teacher (and there were probably many of these), declamation was no doubt a pointless activity. With a good teacher, however, it could be useful as an intellectual training for the forum or the senate-house, and it was in any case a highly popular cultural institution which attracted practitioners of all ages. It has been pointed out that the unreality of the declamation themes would in fact have been an advantage from an educational point of view, allowing students to develop general skills of argument without being hampered by the many particular points of detail inherent in actual laws; a more specific training in law, acquired at a law school or simply by attending at the courts, followed later.[9] Declamation is in some ways comparable to a modern university education in the arts: the subject studied is not usually closely related to the future occupation of the student, but precisely for that reason it constitutes a general training of considerable value, while also being intrinsically interesting and enjoyable on account of its cultural significance. Quintilian, who was concerned with rhetoric both as an academic discipline (Ch. X) and as an educational tool (Ch. XI), considered declamation a useful training, but wanted to make it more vocational, and nearer to the actual practice of the courts. He was not interested, as Cicero was, in promoting a wide general knowledge (at least at an advanced level) for aspiring orators. The *Minor* (or *Lesser*) *Declamations*, which show Quintilian's influence, give an idea of what he had in mind, by the practical way in which the themes are treated.

The survey is completed by chapters on the age of the Antonines (Ch. XII), the 'minor' rhetoricians of the later Roman empire (Ch. XIII) and the church fathers (Ch. XIV); the story ends with the death of Ennodius in 521. During these centuries rhetoric retained its usefulness (it provided a route into the civil service) and its popularity. Declamation held its place, and epideictic attained a new prominence. From the second century, however, intellectual culture was more exclusively Greek, the leading rhetoricians including men such as Hermogenes, who wrote treatises on style and on issue-theory, and Menander Rhetor, who wrote on epideictic.[10] It may seem strange to us that many of the church fathers, such as St Augustine, began their careers as rhetoricians; but, given the status of rhetoric in the Roman empire, one could hardly be counted an educated man unless one had acquired a knowledge of rhetoric.

The final chapter of the book (Ch. XV) gives Professor Clarke's personal view of the value of rhetoric. It is a view which will strike many readers as unduly harsh, and it would perhaps be more reasonable to put the emphasis not so much on the shortcomings of rhetoric as on its merits: for six centuries it delighted the masses and served to equip the educated élite with the power of thinking logically and speaking with clarity and elegance. One problem is that a great many rhetorical treatises have survived but very few speeches, besides those of Cicero. With more speeches, rhetoric and oratory would be set in their proper relation. It would be instructive, also, to have some specimens of the earliest Roman oratory. If we possessed, for example, the speech in which App. Claudius Caecus opposed peace with Pyrrhus in 280 B.C. (Cic. *Brut.* 61), we could not but be struck by the contrast with Cicero. To a large extent, the difference between the two would be accounted for by the arrival of rhetoric at Rome in the years which separated them.

The first edition of Professor Clarke's *Rhetoric at Rome* was published in 1953, and a second edition appeared in 1966. Since then, the book has held its place as the best short introduction to the subject,[11] and it remains a work which deserves to be read by every classical sixth-former and undergraduate. For this edition, the reviser, besides supplying this new introduction, has introduced the following changes: a bibliography has been provided for the first time; the sources of the quotations at the head of each chapter have been identified; misprints in the main text have been corrected; the notes have been corrected and rearranged to bring them into line with modern conventions, with quotations in Greek eliminated, the style of reference to ancient works updated and full bibliographical information provided for the first time (the substance of the notes, however, has not been altered); and the index has been corrected and harmonised with the present edition. In preparing this revision, it has been a privilege to assist in making Professor Clarke's classic study available to a new generation of readers.[12]

D.H.B.
1995

NOTES

¹ For the three types of oratory, see p. 24.

² On the course of the debate see E. D. Rawson, *Cicero: a Portrait* (London, 1975), 82–5; A. Drummond, *Law, Politics and Power: Sallust and the Execution of the Catilinarian Conspirators* (*Historia* Einzelschriften 93; Stuttgart, 1995), 23–7.

³ Professor Clarke's translation (p. 101). The other passages from Tacitus' *Dialogus* cited below are taken from the translation by M. Winterbottom in D. A. Russell and M. Winterbottom, *Ancient Literary Criticism* (Oxford, 1972), 432–59.

⁴ See K. A. Geffcken, *Comedy in the* pro Caelio (Leiden, 1973).

⁵ Cf. Herennius Senecio ap. Plin. *Ep.* 4.7.5 *orator est vir malus dicendi imperitus* ('the orator is a dishonest man unskilled in speaking'), referring to the *delator* M. Aquillius Regulus.

⁶ Professor Clarke passes over memory (p. 35). An orator who wished to memorise a speech would do so by associating each word or topic of it in his mind with some physical object. He would then visualise a route with which he was familiar, and mentally place the images (*imagines*) that he had formed of each object at strategic points (*loci*) in order along the route. Thus, when he came to give his speech, he would retrace the route in his mind, and the images, and hence the words or topics to be used, would present themselves to his mind in the correct order. After giving the speech, he would erase the images from his mind, but retain the memory of the route and its strategic points for use with his next speech. This system may seem incredible, but it is in fact the one used today by World Memory Champion Dominic O'Brien: 'My system is based on a series of mental landscapes or routes. When I remember 52 playing cards, I give each one an individual character – the two of diamonds, for example, is a very tall person – and then place the characters along a route I know well. They stay there for life or until I rub them off and put something else in their place.... When I memorised 35 packs of cards for my world record I had to have 35 individual routes in my head ... I am sure anyone can do what I have done. My brain is no different from anyone else's' (*Sunday Times Magazine* (29 November 1992), 78). See further H. Blum, *Die antike Mnemotechnik* (*Spudasmata* 15; Hildesheim, 1969); D. O'Brien, *How to Develop a Perfect Memory* (London, 1993). The ancient system of memorisation may be relevant to the debate about the publication of speeches: if an orator really did memorise his speech word-for-word, then he would have been able to write it down afterwards with total accuracy.

⁷ Professor Clarke's excellent summary of the Atticist controversy in Ch. VII (pp. 80–3) should, however, be qualified on one point. When Cicero claims that the Atticists model themselves on Lysias to the exclusion of more notable Attic orators such as Demosthenes he misrepresents their position: Demosthenes was regarded by all parties as the greatest of the Greek orators, but Cicero wished to characterise the Atticists as devotees of Lysias in order

that he himself, and not his Atticist opponents, might be considered Demosthenes' Roman counterpart.

On p. 83 Professor Clarke passes over the important topic of prose rhythm. Hellenistic Greek orators (whose speeches are lost) and the Roman orators who followed in this tradition (Hortensius and Cicero, for example, but not the Atticists) wrote prose in which careful attention was given to the rhythm of the words at the ends of the 'cola' (the shorter units which make up a sentence) and particularly those at the ends of entire periods. Scholars have counted and classified the rhythmical patterns ('clausulae') which Cicero used: the three most common have been shown to be the cretic-spondee (or cretic-trochee), cretic-double-trochee (or molossus-double-trochee) and double-cretic (or molossus-cretic), together with variations on those rhythms (the frequencies of these clausulae at the major sense-breaks have been calculated as 32.4 per cent, 30.1 per cent and 24.4 per cent respectively). The most common clausulae are essentially those which avoid the rhythms of dactylic verse (the 'hexameter ending' rhythm at 0.6 per cent is especially avoided). The end of a colon or period was a prominent point within the orator's flow of speech, and he wished to make it sound measured and distinctive. We know that audiences did notice and even applaud the effects which were created (Cic. *Orat.* 168, 213–14), and if modern readers are to attempt to appreciate Latin prose as the Romans did they too must seek to develop an ear for the various rhythms. For the basic facts on Cicero's prose rhythm see D. H. Berry, *Cicero: Pro P. Sulla Oratio* (Cambridge, 1996), 49–54, with bibliography at 49 n. 247; more generally, see W. H. Shewring and K. J. Dover in N. G. L. Hammond and H. H. Scullard (eds), *The Oxford Classical Dictionary*[2] (Oxford, 1970), s.v. 'Prose-rhythm'.

[8] See the items in the bibliography by Stroh and Classen (strategy), May (ethos) and Vasaly (place).

[9] See M. Winterbottom in B. Vickers (ed.), *Rhetoric Revalued* (Medieval & Renaissance Texts & Studies 19, New York, 1982), 59–70.

[10] These works have all been recently translated (the first of the two treatises attributed to Menander is unlikely to be his): see C. W. Wooten, *Hermogenes'* On Types of Style (Chapel Hill and London, 1987); M. Heath, *Hermogenes:* On Issues (Oxford, 1995); D. A. Russell and N. G. Wilson, *Menander Rhetor* (Oxford, 1981). Professor Clarke does not cover the Greek rhetoricians; for a brief account see G. A. Kennedy, *The Art of Rhetoric in the Roman World, 300* B.C.–A.D. *300* (Princeton, 1972), 614–41.

[11] The books of G. A. Kennedy (see bibliography) will also be found useful, but are of considerably greater length. On the important subject, beyond the scope of the present work, of the influence of rhetoric on Latin literature, see esp. Kennedy, *op. cit.* (n. 10), 378–427 (on Augustan literature); S. F. Bonner, *Roman Declamation in the Late Republic and Early Empire* (Liverpool, 1949), 149–67 (on Ovid, Velleius and Seneca's tragedies); id., *AJP* 87 (1966), 257–89 (on Lucan).

[12] I am grateful to my colleague Dr Malcolm Heath for commenting on a draft of this introduction, identifying three of the quotations at the start of the chapters and providing technological help.

I

THE GREEK BACKGROUND

Illae omnium doctrinarum inventrices Athenae, in quibus summa
dicendi vis et inventa est et perfecta.

Cicero, *de Oratore* 1.13

THE HISTORY of rhetoric begins in Sicily in the fifth century
B.C., with Corax and Tisias. The art of speech had of course
been cultivated before their time, for as long as Greek had been
spoken it had been spoken eloquently. But there is no reason
to doubt the truth of the ancient tradition, which goes back
to Aristotle, that the two Sicilians were the first to lay down
systematic principles of speaking.[1] They may justly therefore
be considered the founders of rhetoric.

The rhetoric of Corax and Tisias was born from the experience
of the law courts.[2] The tyrants had been driven out, and claims
for the restitution of private property were coming before the
courts. The man who could offer some useful hints on how to
present one's case would not want for pupils. This it seems is
what Corax and Tisias did. Their art was utilitarian and connected with the courts, and for all the accretions which rhetoric
underwent in the course of centuries, its originators set the tone.
Ancient rhetoric was always more concerned with forensic
oratory than with any other type.

The earliest rhetoric was, moreover, as befitted its practical
character, concerned mainly with argumentation. Its leading
idea was the argument from probability. A small man has
assaulted a large man and has to defend himself in the courts.
'Is it likely,' he may argue, 'that a man of my size would have
attacked one of his size?' The large man too can draw arguments
from the same source; was it likely that he would have assaulted
the small man, knowing that the argument from probability
would be all in his opponent's favour? It was Corax and Tisias
who first discovered the possibilities of this type of argument.[3]

Rhetoric soon passed from Sicily to the Greek world in general and Athens in particular. The age of the Sophists saw a variety of teachers professing the art of speaking. For to be able to argue effectively was an essential part of that πολιτικὴ ἀρετὴ which the Sophists taught. To make the best of yourself in a Greek city, which is roughly what πολιτικὴ ἀρετὴ means, involved being able to speak, to see the strong and the weak points in a case and to use them to your own advantage whether in the courts or in the assembly.

There was no single Sophistic rhetoric. Different men pursued different lines. Thrasymachus developed the appeal to the emotions; Theodorus of Byzantium classified the parts of a speech.[4] There were practitioners of rhetoric in the narrow sense, authors of textbooks, even of verse mnemonics.[5] There were also men of wider culture like Prodicus and Hippias, who studied words and their meanings, and Protagoras, whose activities touched on rhetoric at many points. He taught the art of speech as part of the art of politics, and claimed, in the famous phrase, to 'make the worse cause appear the better'; he was credited too with the handling of general questions as a mode of practice and with the writing of commonplaces.[6]

The most original of the Sophists in the rhetorical field was Gorgias. A native of Sicily, he may have had connections with Corax and Tisias,[7] but his interests went beyond theirs. For him speech was the instrument of persuasion, and so of power. It operated not only by argument, but by every method which could work on the hearer's personality. Above all Gorgias believed in the appeal to the ear. He invented a kind of prose poetry in which sense counted for little and sound for much, in which phrase balanced phrase and word jingled with word. While the extravagances of his style died with him, his influence lived on in all those who studied the writing of artistic prose. He had added a new department to rhetoric, that which the Greeks called λέξις and the Romans *elocutio*.

Words, Gorgias claimed, could make the lowly appear grand and the grand lowly; they could make old seem new and new old.[8] The claim is repeated by Isocrates, who carries on into the fourth century the Sophistic ideal with its delight in the exercise of the art of speech and its high-flown praise of its capacities. Isocrates was not a teacher of rhetoric in the formal sense, and he dissociates himself from the narrowly utilitarian rhetoricians. For him rhetoric is something higher; it is a part of that practical wisdom combined with general culture which he calls philosophy. Following where Gorgias had pointed the way, he devoted especial care to style. Instead of the tasteless jingles of Gorgias he cultivated an artistic balance and symmetry. Hiatus is avoided; sentences run their length smoothly and elegantly; all that is harsh and vigorous and interesting is eliminated from the style as from the matter.

While Isocrates maintained the optimistic belief of the Sophists in man and his powers, his greatest contemporary, Plato, regarded these powers as worthless and dangerous if not directed to the pursuit of justice and truth. Rhetoric, which Gorgias had praised as the finest of arts ($\tau\acute{\epsilon}\chi\nu\alpha\iota$), was to Plato no art at all, but only a knack. It was not based on knowledge; the orator needed only to make the ignorant think he knew more than the expert. It was to justice what cookery was to medical science; it gave people what they wanted, not what was good for them.[9] Rhetoric, said the Sophists, enabled man to influence his fellow men. A dangerous gift, in Plato's view, for the exaltation of the power of words led to the exaltation of power in itself. It was a short step from Gorgias to Callicles.

Such is Plato's attitude in the *Gorgias*. In the *Phaedrus* the tone is lighter and he is rather more sympathetic to rhetoric. He ends the dialogue with a compliment to Isocrates, a hint perhaps that he was prepared to come to terms with a rhetoric that recognised the primacy of philosophy. There was no mistaking the hostility of the *Gorgias*, and its echoes are heard in rhetorical literature throughout the centuries;[10] rhetoric could, however, and eventually did accept the view of the *Phaedrus* that the speaker must have a thorough knowledge of what he is speaking about and of the mind he is trying to influence.[11] This is not far from Cicero's view. But the resemblance between the *Phaedrus* and *De Oratore* is only superficial. Cicero, immersed as he was in the world of $\delta\acute{o}\xi\alpha$ and only fitfully interested in that of $\dot{\epsilon}\pi\iota\sigma\tau\acute{\eta}\mu\eta$, could, for all his professed admiration for the founder of the Academy, have little in common with him.

It was not to be expected that Plato's criticism would have much effect on the practising rhetorician of the fourth century.

It was an age of oratory, and rhetoric followed in the wake of oratory, observing, analysing and classifying. It claimed indeed not to follow but to lead, to show the orator how to speak. It is unlikely that in fact it exercised much influence on oratorical practice; none the less the intense activity of Athenian public life and of the law courts guaranteed a secure place to anyone who professed to teach the art of speech. Rhetoric was safe so long as the Athenian democracy lasted, and when the Athenian democracy declined it was too well established to fade with the society that nurtured its growth. So there was no lack of text-books even in the earlier days of rhetoric. One survives from the fourth century, that of Anaximenes, included in the Aristotelian corpus as the *Rhetorica ad Alexandrum*. In it we see the work of a practical rhetorician not insensitive to general ideas, belonging to a period when rhetoric was not yet stereotyped, and when the rage for systematisation had not yet reduced it to utter aridity. Some of Anaximenes's doctrine was accepted by later rhetoric; the classification into seven types of oratory, on which the treatise is based, did not survive. Noteworthy by comparison with later treatises is the space given to deliberative oratory and the meagre and unsystematic treatment of style.

Plato's attacks on rhetoric were no doubt known to Aristotle. But he wasted no time in arguing against his former master; as with poetry, so with rhetoric he was led by Plato's criticism to think for himself and to make a new approach to the subject. He was well aware of the limitations of rhetoric, but he saw in it a branch of human activity deserving serious study, and gave it a place in his comprehensive survey of the various branches of knowledge.

Plato had denied that rhetoric was an art. Aristotle meets this by claiming that it is an art, but one of a special character, not a science with its own subject matter, but a discipline similar to dialectic, and like dialectic unconcerned with the truth of its own conclusions.[12] As regards the moral aspect Aristotle shows his usual common sense. Rhetoric, he holds, is useful for bringing the truth to light, since some people cannot be convinced by facts; if it is right to be able to defend oneself by force, it is right to do the same by words. The power of words can be misused, but then so can all good things.[13]

The spirit of the *Rhetoric* is in the main objective and scientific, though Aristotle was not averse from giving practical hints, and was, according to the tradition, a teacher of rhetoric.[14] He includes not a little matter that was probably already traditional; the three types of oratory, the parts of a speech, the two kinds of proof (that devised by the orator himself and that given by the facts of the case), the orator's three aims (to instruct, to secure attention and to create good will) are there, either explicit or implicit. But there is much that is new and characteristic of Aristotle.

His individual point of view comes out clearly in his definition of the function of rhetoric as being not to persuade but to see the elements contributing to persuasion in any situation.[15] The definition makes rhetoric an intellectual study rather than a practical activity. Instead of moving on the surface as the ordinary rhetorician did, with his precepts for each part of the speech and each type of oration, Aristotle goes to the sources of persuasion. He investigates the characteristic form of rhetorical proof, the enthymeme or incomplete syllogism,[16] and the means of arousing emotion and of conveying a favourable impression of the speaker's character ($\pi\acute{a}\theta os$ and $\mathring{\eta}\theta os$),[17] which are to him elements equal in importance to demonstration. Rhetoric thus connects on the one hand with dialectic, on the other with ethics and psychology; the orator must be able to syllogise and must also have a knowledge of human character and emotions.[18]

Of ancient treatises on rhetoric Aristotle's was the most distinguished intellectually. But not all of it was well adapted to the needs of the schools, and its influence on the scholastic tradition was relatively small. Aristotle's treatment of *ethos* and *pathos* as on a level with argumentation found no favour with the writers of textbooks, while in the matter of argumentation they preferred particular applications to general principles.[19]

Aristotle's influence was naturally strongest in his own school. Theophrastus carried on his work with that objectivity and sober good sense which was always characteristic of the Peripatetics. His writings on rhetorical argumentation seem to have been very much in the Aristotelian tradition.[20] But his importance in the history of rhetoric lies in his development of the theory of style. Aristotle had treated the matter in some detail in the third book of his *Rhetoric*, his main theme being that style should be clear, appropriate and neither mean nor high-flown,

to which he adds a consideration of prose rhythm and some
remarks on metaphor and on vividness. Theophrastus developed
his master's ideas. His work on style is lost and cannot be recon-
structed with any certainty. But traces of Peripatetic criticism
can be found in many of the later writers, in particular in
Demetrius's work on style, which, so far as we can judge, is very
much in the tradition of Theophrastus. The Peripatetics sought
to analyse the constituents of good writing. They discussed the
choice of words and their arrangement, euphony and rhythm,
the characteristics of good and bad writing, and so on. Their
approach may be called rhetorical, since, thanks partly to their
influence, the formal study of style became a recognised part of
rhetoric, but they did not regard style merely as an element in
the art of persuasion. They drew their rules of what was good
and bad from existing works of literature, both prose and verse,
and these rules were applicable not only to oratory but to
writing in general. With them rhetoric merges into literary
criticism.

It was Theophrastus who first classified the four virtues of
style, correctness, clarity, propriety and ornament.[21] Whether
he originated the threefold classification of the grand, the plain
and the intermediate styles is not certain. According to Dionysius of Halicarnassus he made Thrasymachus an example of the
intermediate style,[22] which suggests that he recognised the
other two. But it has been argued that he had in mind rather
that mean which for a Peripatetic would be the best in style as
in other things, and that it was Dionysius who brought him
into line with the later doctrine of a third style between the
grand and the plain.[23] If Theophrastus did invent the doctrine
of the three styles it is not greatly to his credit. If the grand and
the plain styles correspond to recognisable types of writing, the
intermediate is manifestly nothing but a category designed to
include all that was neither one thing nor the other.

The decline of the Greek city state which followed the rise
of Macedon and the conquests of Alexander the Great had its
effect on rhetoric. In the days of great kingdoms ruled by
absolute monarchs the power of the orator was severely limited,
and the high claims made for rhetoric in the days of the Sophists
could hardly be maintained. Oratory tended to become
divorced from practical affairs, an elegant accomplishment

rather than a weapon for use in politics and the courts. The ancients ascribed the decay of oratory to Demetrius of Phalerum, the Athenian politician of the last years of the fourth century B.C.[24] He was also credited by some with having originated the practice of debating invented themes on the lines of those likely to arise in the courts and assemblies, a practice which under the name of declamation was to play so important a part in Roman education. That Demetrius himself was responsible for the innovation is by no means certain—Quintilian found the evidence unsatisfactory—but there was general agreement that the practice began in his time.[25]

In the Hellenistic age rhetoric falls into the hands of the schoolmasters. At some stage, we do not know when, an educational system took shape in which 'grammar', the study of language and literature, was followed by rhetoric, while in the rhetoric school the exercises were carefully graded. A series of preliminary exercises known as προγυμνάσματα, of an elementary and general character, led up to practice speeches.[26] Rhetorical theory was taught dogmatically from dry textbooks abounding in technical terms.

The rhetoricians of the Hellenistic age were men of small calibre, a narrow circle of professionals disputing among themselves on minor matters of classification and little concerned with the broader aspects of their art. The only one who showed any originality or intellectual power in this limited field was Hermagoras of Temnos, who flourished in the middle of the second century B.C. It was he who was responsible for giving the theory of *inventio* (εὕρεσις) that elaborate and systematic form that we find in the earliest Latin rhetorical treatises, and in particular for developing the doctrine of στάσις (*status* or *constitutio*) or the point at issue. He dealt in elaborate classifications and rules for argumentation to fit every occasion. His work was dry in the extreme,[27] but there was none the less something imposing about it. Perhaps because it was dry and difficult it found favour with the schools. Rhetoric as developed by Hermagoras had some claim to be considered a serious intellectual discipline.

But the rhetoricians were not the only persons to interest themselves in rhetoric; the philosophers, whether sympathetic or unsympathetic, did not ignore it. Of the Hellenistic philosophies one, the Epicurean, was consistently hostile. Epicurus cared nothing for the graces of style; he advised against political activity and had no use for literary culture. It was therefore natural that he should turn his back on a study as closely connected as rhetoric was with politics and culture. The Stoics on the other hand made a not unimportant contribution to rhetorical theory. Their approach was academic and remote from actual practice; Cleanthes and Chrysippus were said to have handled the subject in a manner calculated to reduce their readers to silence rather than inspire them to eloquence.[28] They claimed that eloquence like other virtues was possessed by the wise man only. They cultivated a keen dry dialectic very different from the orator's manner. They advised brevity and simplicity and the avoidance of all appeals to the emotions. These were hard sayings. Yet because Stoicism was the predominant philosophy of the Hellenistic world, it made itself felt even in rhetoric. A small amount of its logical and ethical theory found its way into the rhetorical textbooks; the Stoic virtue of brevity was added by some to the Theophrastian four virtues of style, and the Stoic dialectic was acknowledged to be not unprofitable to the orator.[29] There were even some high-minded Romans who carried Stoicism into practice to the extent of abandoning all the traditions of oratory and eschewing the appeal to the emotions.

Of the two older schools the Peripatetics, as we have seen, continued to work quietly on the lines laid down by Aristotle. The Academy for a while maintained their founder's hostility to rhetoric;[30] Cicero has recorded how in the latter part of the second century B.C. the pupils of Carneades took the lead among the philosophers of Athens in decrying the orator.[31] Yet even then the school had begun a practice which brought them near to their enemies. Arcesilaus, founder of the 'Middle Academy', first, we are told, debated both sides of a disputed question,[32] and Carneades followed the same practice. His brilliance in debate indeed attracted even rhetoricians, who shut up their schools and went to listen to him speaking.[33] The next step was taken when Philo, head of the Academy in Cicero's youth, actually taught rhetoric as well as philosophy.[34]

Philo was well known in Rome as well as in Athens, and this innovation of his no doubt resulted from the realisation that rhetoric had come to stay in Rome. Philosophers might, and did, continue to argue such nice questions as whether rhetoric was an art or not, but the average Roman cared nothing for such problems. Whether rhetoric was an art or not, it was, or appeared to be, useful, and this was sufficient to win pupils for its practitioners. The philosophers, who also hoped to find pupils in Rome, could not remain indifferent. They had to fight their rivals, the rhetoricians, or come to terms with them.

Generally speaking rhetorical teaching did not encroach on philosophical. But there was a debatable territory where the two disciplines might meet. What if the rhetoricians were to claim as their province those general questions which the philosophers regarded as their preserve? The claim was indeed made by Hermagoras. The subject matter of oratory, he laid down, was twofold; there was the θέσις or general question and the ὑπόθεσις or question involving particular persons and situations. Both were within the orator's province.[35] Whether Hermagoras was deliberately and provocatively claiming for rhetoric what had hitherto belonged to philosophy is doubtful. He seems to have done nothing to implement his claim, and the rhetoricians continued to ignore general questions.[36] Some of them, it seems, were by no means anxious to take them over even in theory, and willingly handed them back to the philosophers.[37] The philosophers for their part were naturally unwilling to lose general questions to the rhetoricians. Posidonius felt sufficiently strongly on the matter to make it the subject of his lecture to Pompey when the latter visited him at Rhodes.[38] Philo even made a counter-attack; not only did he teach rhetoric, but he handled particular themes, ὑποθέσεις, which had hitherto been the rhetorician's preserve.[39]

The time was ripe for a new synthesis, a healing of the breach between rhetoric and philosophy and a return to the ideal of the orator-statesman who was also a philosopher. It was on these lines, it seems, that Greek philosophers were thinking in Cicero's time. But such ideas belong more to Rome than to Greece. They were inspired by experience of Rome and intercourse with Roman statesmen, and they were given classic expression in the work of a Roman writer, Cicero's *De Oratore*. At this point therefore we end our survey of the Greek background and turn to the beginnings of rhetoric at Rome.

II

RHETORIC AT ROME UNDER THE REPUBLIC

Post autem auditis oratoribus Graecis cognitisque eorum litteris adhibitisque doctoribus incredibili quodam nostri homines dicendi studio flagraverunt.

Cicero, *de Oratore* 1.14

ACCORDING TO Suetonius, the introduction of rhetoric to Rome was similar to that of grammar, which after being un-honoured and indeed unknown at first, had made a humble start in the first half of the second century B.C.[1] At that period Rome's horizon was expanding. Her own undeveloped culture was coming into rapidly closer contact with the sophisticated civilisation of Greece. Romans were becoming familiar with the Greek-speaking lands of the Eastern Mediterranean, and Greek teachers were beginning to find their way to Rome. Among them were the rhetoricians.

They found a fruitful field for their activities. In the Roman republic great rewards were offered to the successful speaker, and useless though much of Greek learning might seem to the practical Roman, rhetoric at least could claim to open the way to success. The clever Greeks, who had reduced the art of speaking to a system, foresaw that in this active and powerful republic there would be a market for their wares. And they were right. As Cicero said: 'At first our countrymen knew nothing of art and did not realise that there was any value in practice or that there were any rules or system, but they achieved such success as could be attained by talent and reflection. Afterwards however, when they had listened to Greek orators, become acquainted with Greek literature and come into contact with Greek teachers, there was a remarkable burst of enthusiasm among our countrymen for the study of the art of speaking.'[2]

But the story was not quite as straightforward as Cicero suggests. The rhetoricians did not establish themselves at Rome without difficulty. In the year 161 B.C. the senate empowered the praetor Marcus Pomponius to expel both philosophers and rhetoricians.[3] This decree is clear evidence of opposition if not to rhetoric, at least to the Greeks who taught it. It falls within the lifetime of that vigorous opponent of Greek influences, Cato the Censor, and it is possible that his influence may have been in some degree responsible for it. For though he was an able orator himself, he may well have viewed with suspicion the subtle professionalism of the Greek rhetorician. His two recorded remarks on oratory, the definition of the orator as *vir bonus dicendi peritus* and the precept *rem tene, verba sequentur*, reveal a sturdy simplicity and a probably conscious opposition to all that was involved in the Greek τέχνη.[4]

Cato was the first Roman to write on oratory,[5] but he did not become the founder of a tradition. The Greeks were to conquer here as elsewhere, and Roman rhetoric was to become little more than an adaptation of Greek rhetoric. For the Greeks could not be kept out. They were expelled in 161 B.C., but must soon have returned, though perhaps at first only as tutors in private houses and not as public teachers. It is recorded that rhetoricians were among the numerous Greek teachers employed to train the sons of Aemilius Paulus, while Tiberius and Gaius Gracchus both had Greek masters of rhetoric, the former Diophanes of Mitylene, the most eloquent Greek of his day, and the latter Menelaus of Marathus.[6]

What we know of the oratory of the latter part of the second century suggests that rhetoric exercised an increasing influence, and it must have been firmly established in Rome by the end of the century.[7] But it was still mainly, perhaps even wholly, in the hands of Greeks. Early in the first century however there was a new development.[8] In the year 92 B.C. the censors Licinius Crassus and Domitius Ahenobarbus issued an edict to the following effect: 'It has been reported to us that there are men who have introduced a new kind of teaching, and that the youth are going to their schools; that these men have assumed the name of Latin rhetoricians; and that young men spend whole days in idleness with them. Our forefathers laid down what they wished their children to learn and what schools they were to frequent.

These innovations, which run counter to the customs and traditions of our forefathers, do not please us, nor do we think them right. Wherefore we deem it proper to make it clear to those who hold the schools and those who frequent them that we do not approve.'[9]

Who were these Latin rhetoricians and why did they incur the censors' displeasure? We know the name of at least one of them, for Cicero recorded in a letter that when he was a boy 'one Plotius' started to teach rhetoric in Latin. Crowds flocked to his classes, and Cicero wanted to go too, but he was prevented from doing so by some unnamed advisers, who considered that a better training could be provided in Greek.[10] The Plotius to whom Cicero refers was L. Plotius Gallus, a rhetorician of some note, who survived to provide Sempronius Atratinus with a speech in his action against Caelius in 56 B.C.[11]

Some further light on the affair of the Latin rhetoricians is provided by Cicero's *De Oratore*, for the Crassus who was jointly responsible for the edict of 92 B.C. was none other than the famous orator who takes the leading part in the dialogue,[12] and Cicero, who had made the dramatic date of the dialogue a year after the attempted suppression of the Latin rhetoricians, felt it necessary to make Crassus offer an apology for his action. 'It was not,' he is made to say, 'that I did not want the wits of the young to be sharpened; on the contrary, I did not want their wits to be blunted, while their impudence was strengthened.' The Greek teachers had some learning and culture, whereas these new Latin teachers were qualified to teach nothing but impudence. He hoped that the time would come when Latin teachers would be adequate, but it was not yet.[13]

So Crassus explains his action, on purely educational grounds. It may be that this is not the whole truth, and that political motives played some part in the affair. At that time Greek culture was the mark of the *optimates*, to whom Crassus adhered; Plotius Gallus was a supporter of Marius, and Marius was notoriously lacking in Greek culture.[14] He and the Latin rhetoricians were perhaps consciously opposed to the aristocratic circle who prided themselves on their knowledge of Greek; Crassus and Ahenobarbus sensed a dangerous atmosphere in the school and became alarmed at the prospect of the instrument of persuasion being put into the hands of demagogues through the medium of popular teaching in Latin. This reconstruction of the background of the censors' decree has found favour with a number of modern scholars.[15] It may be right; but Cicero gives no hint of political motives, and perhaps it is vain to try to be wiser than he.[16]

Whatever the cause of the attempted suppression of the new schools, it seems to have had little effect. Rhetorical teaching in Latin evidently continued in the years immediately following. The two earliest extant Latin treatises on rhetoric, that addressed to Herennius and Cicero's *De Inventione*, date from only a few years after the censors' edict, and it is evident that something of a tradition of Latin teaching lies behind them. Of the two writers Cicero was certainly, and the author of *Ad Herennium* possibly, young and inexperienced;[17] yet both move with ease in the complications of an elaborate technical terminology. This terminology appears to have been in the main already familiar when they wrote.[18] Moreover both use examples from Roman history and literature, examples which in many cases have all the appearance of being already established by school tradition. It seems highly probable that the teaching of rhetoric in Latin had continued in the years between 92 B.C. and the two treatises.

In the creation of the tradition of Latin rhetoric some part may have been played by one who would hardly have wished to be classed with the rhetoricians. Next after Cato, according to Quintilian, among Roman writers on rhetoric was the famous orator Antonius, a contemporary of Crassus and like him a protagonist in *De Oratore*.[19] His book on oratory, written at some time before 91 B.C., was incomplete, and in Cicero's opinion a meagre affair.[20] In *De Oratore* Antonius claims that it was based not on school learning but on experience,[21] but Quintilian records an extract which shows some acquaintance with the scholastic doctrine. All speeches, said Antonius, arose from one of three issues: whether a thing had been done or not done; whether it was lawful or unlawful; and whether it was good or bad.[22] Antonius is concerning himself with the *status* or *constitutio causae*. Evidently the influence of Hermagoras was beginning to make itself felt.[23]

Of the two works mentioned above, the treatise addressed to Herennius and *De Inventione*, neither can be dated exactly.

B

Internal evidence points to a date between 86 and 82 for *Ad Herennium*,[24] while *De Inventione* dates from when Cicero was a *puer* or *adulescentulus*.[25] This could not be later than 81, when he delivered his first speech at the age of twenty-five, and might be considerably earlier; 87 or 86, when he was nineteen or twenty, seems as likely a date as any. Scrutiny of the resemblances and differences between the two treatises has failed to produce any general agreement as to their relationship one to another.[26]

No more need here be said of *De Inventione* than that it shows the elaboration of the scholastic rhetoric by now established at Rome and the thoroughness with which a gifted and zealous student had mastered it. The treatise *Ad Herennium* is a more interesting production. Its author is unknown, for it has long since ceased to be regarded as the work of Cicero, and the plausible attribution to Cornificius based on references in Quintilian has not won general acceptance.[27] Whoever he was, the author has a high opinion of himself; at the outset he expresses a desire to devote himself to philosophy in preference to his present task,[28] but he has no doubts about his competence. In one place there is a rather naïve reference to *noster doctor* which almost suggests a schoolboy,[29] but whatever his age, it was no bungler who compiled this brisk handbook, which, after remaining unknown in the ancient world (unless it is the treatise by Cornificius known to Quintilian), survived to attain great popularity in the Middle Ages.

The recipient of the treatise, Gaius Herennius, cannot be identified, but we know that the *gens Herennia* was connected with Marius,[30] and from this we may assume Marian sympathies in both author and recipient. If therefore it is correct to associate the Latin rhetoricians with the Marian party, *Ad Herennium* may well derive from their school.[31] The character of the treatise itself bears out this surmise. It shows signs of sympathy with the *populares*,[32] and its author's confident tone and concentration on simplicity and clarity in preference to scholarly subtlety remind us of the charges of impudence and lack of culture brought by Crassus against the Latin rhetoricians. Though he is entirely dependent on Greek theory the writer does not acknowledge his debt, and in his opening paragraph allows himself a scornful reference to the *inanis arrogantia* of the Greeks, who thought up irrelevances through fear of seeming ignorant and in order to make the whole thing more difficult.[33]

If then the tradition of the Latin rhetoricians survives in *Ad Herennium*, we can get from this work some idea of what the innovation of Plotius Gallus was and what it was not. It was an attempt to popularise rhetoric and adapt it to Roman needs by teaching it in Latin, by dispensing with some of the complications of Greek theory and by using illustrations from Roman history and literature. It was not the invention of a new system. The Romans could never get away from the Greek τέχνη. They continued to abuse the Greek rhetoricians—and to use them.

Let us now attempt to reconstruct the rhetorical education of the earlier part of the first century B.C., the period when Cicero and his contemporaries were learning the art of oratory. It must be said at the outset that at this time there was nothing in the nature of a regular educational system, with an orderly progression from one stage to another, such as we find recommended by Quintilian. The professions of *grammaticus* and *rhetor* were not at first clearly distinguished at Rome, and the early *grammatici* also taught rhetoric. Moreover different teachers used different methods and each individual teacher varied his methods.[34] But at some stage in his career the student had to master the elaborate formal system of rhetoric developed by the Greeks, with its fivefold division into *inventio, dispositio, elocutio, memoria* and *actio*, and its numerous definitions, divisions and subdivisions. This was the indispensable foundation, the discipline that all had to undergo, much like Latin grammar in the old grammar school education of this country. The system was embodied in textbooks and was also the subject of oral exposition in lectures.[35] If we can generalise from the method followed by Cicero in teaching his son, the pupil was expected to memorise the system and might be subjected to a thorough catechism on it.[36]

In addition to learning formal rhetoric the student engaged in various exercises to promote fluency in self-expression. Suetonius, writing apparently of the Republican period, gives a list of exercises in use: *chriae*, fables, narrations, translations from Greek, praise and blame of famous men, *theses*, refutation and confirmation of legendary stories.[37] These, with the exception of translation, were the προγυμνάσματα already referred to. The general idea behind them was to teach one to say the same thing in a number of different ways. The most elementary exercise was the 'declension' of a *chria*. In this exercise a sentence recording some memorable saying was developed so as to illustrate the use of the various cases; for example, one would begin with *M. Porcius Cato dixit litterarum radices amaras esse fructus iucundiores*, go on to the genitive *M. Porci Catonis dictum fertur litterarum radices amaras esse fructus iucundiores*, and proceed through all the cases, singular and plural.[38] So too fables were recounted in a variety of forms, and narratives given first in précis form, then at length. In some of the exercises it was not forgotten that the pupil was training to be an orator, and he learned to argue for and against: to praise famous men and to blame them, to commend some common practice and to depreciate it (*thesis*), to confirm a legend and to refute it.[39]

An interesting glimpse of the methods of one Republican teacher is provided by a passage in *Ad Herennium*. The author is dealing with what he calls *expolitio*, that is, the developing of a theme in a number of different ways. His example is: 'The wise man will shun no danger on behalf of the state.'[40] This can be put in different words, thus: 'No danger is so great that the wise man thinks it should be shunned on behalf of the state. When it is a question of the perpetual safety of the state he who is inspired by sound reason will surely hold that no risks in life should be avoided on behalf of the prosperity of the state, and so firmly will he hold to that opinion that he will eagerly face the severest conflicts in life on behalf of his country.' Another way of varying is by the introduction of an imaginary conversation; 'The wise man will hold that every danger should be undertaken on behalf of the state. He will often say to himself: "I am not born for myself alone, but also, and even more, for my fatherland. My life is owed to fate, but let me pay the debt for the safety of my country. My country nourished me; it brought me in safety and honour to my present age; it nurtured me with good laws, excellent traditions and honourable upbringing. What adequate repayment can I make to the source of all these blessings?" The wise man will often speak thus to himself, and he will himself shun no danger on behalf of the state.' A further method of variation is by introducing an emotional heightening:

'Who is there whose thoughts are so lowly, whose mind is so hemmed in by the narrow bounds of envy, that he does not account that man as wisest and most worthy of praise, who on behalf of the safety of his fatherland, the security of his city and the prosperity of his state readily undertakes and willingly submits to dangers however great and terrible? For my part I cannot praise such a man as worthily as I would wish to; and I am sure that it is the same with all of you.'

There follows an example, too long to quote, of a more elaborate way of developing the same theme. First it is given in simple form, with a reason added; then two variants follow, either with or without reasons; next it is expressed in negative form ('It is wrong not to give your life for your country.'); then it is supported by a simile and an example. Finally we end with a peroration.[41]

The theory was that the pupil started with these preliminary exercises of a general character, and went on to those involving particular persons and circumstances, exercises, that is, more closely related to the speeches of the courts and deliberative assemblies. In Quintilian's day the tendency was for the general exercises to be squeezed out of the curriculum of the rhetorical schools by the demands of declamation.[42] According to Quintilian this had not always been so; indeed he tells us that exercises on general themes were for a long time the sole method of rhetorical teaching.[43] It is difficult to believe that this is true so far as the ordinary schools of Rome are concerned. We have already seen that fictitious cases on the lines of those likely to arise in the courts and assemblies were debated in Greece as early as the later fourth century B.C., and if this type of exercise was in use in contemporary Greek teaching it presumably came to Rome when rhetoric first arrived there.[44]

At any rate there is no doubt that it was established in the first half of the first century B.C. Crassus in *De Oratore* is made to approve the practice of debating cases similar to those of the courts, and elsewhere in the same work we are told that cases involving the letter versus the spirit of the law were a regular part of the school curriculum.[45] We are given an example of the sort of easy case that was set as an exercise to the young: 'The law forbids a foreigner to ascend the walls; he does so, and drives off the enemy. An action is brought against him.'[46] If

Cicero was consistent in avoiding anachronism in *De Oratore* these passages are evidence that the *controversia*, as it was later called, was established at the dramatic date of the dialogue, 91 B.C. If he was not, they are at least evidence that it was established at the date of composition, 55 B.C.

Ad Herennium and *De Inventione* both contain numerous examples of cases of different kinds, and we can legitimately assume that these, or at least some of them, were the subject of practice debates in the schools.[47] As declamation played so large a part in later Roman teaching, it is worth while to give some examples of the sort of themes that were debated in the Republican schools. 'A certain commander, being surrounded by the enemy and unable to escape, came to an agreement with them, by which he was to withdraw his men, leaving behind their arms and equipment. This was done, and so his men were saved from a hopeless situation with the loss of arms and equipment. The commander was accused of high treason.'[48] Then there is the case, familiar to us from Livy, of Horatius, who, returning from his victory over the three Curatii, met his sister, whom he found indifferent to the loss of her two brothers and lamenting the death of one of the Curatii to whom she was betrothed, whereupon he killed her, and was put on trial.[49] Another case given is that of some Rhodians deputed to go on an embassy to Athens. The authorities refused to give them the allowance to which they were entitled. They therefore refused to go and were indicted for their refusal.[50] Then there is the following case: 'The law forbids the sacrifice of a bull calf to Diana. Some sailors caught by a storm on the high seas vowed that if they reached a harbour which was in sight they would sacrifice a bull calf to the deity of the place. It so happened that at the harbour there was a temple of Diana, the very goddess to whom a bull calf might not be sacrificed. Ignorant of the law, they made their sacrifice on reaching shore and were brought to trial.'[51]

Of the cases quoted it will be seen that one is specifically drawn from Roman history, one from the history of Rhodes, while two are given no historical or geographical setting, though one of these, the first quoted, is known to be derived from an incident in Roman history.[52] The themes were chosen to illustrate certain types of case, and no objection was felt to fictitious examples,[53] or to those involving wild improbabilities:

The law ordains that those who leave their ship in a storm shall lose everything; the ship and its cargo become the property of those who remain on it.

Two men were sailing on the high seas, one the owner of the ship, the other of its cargo. They saw a shipwrecked man swimming and stretching out his hands to them; overcome by pity, they brought the ship alongside him and took him on board. Some time afterwards they too ran into a heavy storm, with the result that the owner of the ship, who was also the helmsman, betook himself to a boat, from which he guided the ship as best he could with the tow rope, while the owner of the cargo fell on his sword. The shipwrecked man went to the helm, and did his best to save the ship. When the waves subsided and the weather changed, the ship was brought into harbour. The man who had fallen on his sword was only slightly wounded and his wound quickly healed. Each of the three claimed the ship and its cargo.[54]

In Imperial times the *controversiae* were notorious for their remoteness from life, but the development in this direction had already begun in Cicero's youth. There is no doubt a difference; the ingenuities of the case just quoted sprang not so much from a love of the melodramatic and picturesque for its own sake as from a desire to exercise the young in all possible varieties of argument. But there is no doubt that even in Republican times the divorce between school teaching and the practice of the courts, which later became notorious, was already showing itself.[55]

Themes of the type later known as *suasoriae* are also referred to in the Republican treatises, and some of them too were no doubt the subject of practice speeches. Famous senatorial debates were recalled in such themes as Should Carthage be destroyed? or Should Scipio be allowed to hold the consulship under age?[56] Or an imaginary speech might be put into the mouth of a famous character like Hannibal.[57] We know from Juvenal that Hannibal was a stock subject for declamations under the Empire, and it seems that even in the Sullan period the schools were echoing with his deliberations.[58]

In addition to these school exercises the student read speeches and sometimes learned them by heart. Cicero as a boy memorised the peroration of C. Galba's speech in his own defence, while Crassus's speech against the law of Caepio was to him *quasi magistra*.[59] One method which dates back to the second century B.C. was that of Carbo, who memorised passages from existing speeches and then tried to paraphrase them. This however was not entirely satisfactory, for the paraphrase could hardly improve on or equal the original, and Crassus, who had followed Carbo's method, gave it up, and took to translating speeches from the Greek.[60]

The various exercises that we have described form a marked contrast to the practical training which Crassus in *De Oratore* claims to have received. 'My school', he says 'was the forum, my masters experience, the laws and institutions of Rome and the customs of our ancestors.'[61] An important part of the young orator's training in the old Republican tradition was the so-called *tirocinium fori*, a kind of apprenticeship served with a leading orator. 'In the days of our ancestors', writes Tacitus, 'a young man who was being prepared for the forum and oratory, after having been trained at home and thoroughly instructed in the liberal arts, was brought by his father or relations to the leading orator at Rome. By following him and frequenting his company he had the opportunity of listening to all his speeches in the law courts or at public meetings; he could hear him in argument and debate, and, so to speak, learn to fight by taking part in the battle.'[62] This practice dates from the days when the professional teacher was unknown and the father directed his son's early education, after which he learned the ways of public life by personal association. It still survived in the Ciceronian age alongside the new methods of Greek rhetoric. Cicero's father put him in the charge of Scaevola the augur, and Cicero himself in later life took the young Caelius under his wing.[63]

The best orators continued to engage in practice exercises long after they had ceased their formal training. It was Hortensius's failure to keep up his early assiduity in this respect that, according to Cicero, accounted for the decline of his oratory.[64] Cicero himself practised constantly throughout his life. No one, he claimed, went on declaiming for as long as he did.[65] He did so in Greek and Latin up to his praetorship and in

Latin even when he was quite old.[66] Declamation at that time meant a practice speech delivered in private; it was not yet a public performance aimed at display. One or two friends would join together for practice of this nature; in his youth Cicero declaimed with Marcus Piso or Quintus Pompeius or with Vibius Curius, in his old age with his 'big schoolboys', as he called them, Hirtius and Pansa.[67] Pompey is said to have resumed the practice of declaiming just before the Civil War, and Antonius and Augustus kept it up even during the war at Mutina.[68]

How serious a matter training for oratory was, and how it continued after schooldays were over, can be seen from Cicero's autobiography in the *Brutus*.[69] After assuming the *toga virilis* in 91 B.C., at the age of fifteen, he entered the forum, where he daily listened to the leading orators of the day, at the same time reading and writing and engaging in exercises oratorical and otherwise. He studied law under Quintus Scaevola and philosophy under Philo. In the year 88 the famous rhetorician Molo of Rhodes was in Rome and Cicero was studying under him. The following years were devoted to the study of dialectic and other branches of philosophy under Diodotus the Stoic, but in spite of these philosophical studies he did not let a day pass without practising speaking. This he did more often in Greek than in Latin, partly because there were more of the graces of style in the former language, and having once formed the habit one could apply it to Latin, and partly because the best teachers were Greek and they could not correct his exercises except in their own language.[70] In the year 81, at the age of twenty-five, Cicero began to practise at the bar, but it was not long before he discovered that his health was in danger. He was in the habit of speaking at the top of his voice with no change of tone, and his delivery involved a great and continuous physical effort; if he went on in this way, he was told, the results might be fatal. So he decided to go abroad, and in Greece and Asia Minor he continued his studies, rhetorical and philosophical. In Athens he attended the lectures of a rhetorician called Demetrius, and during his lengthy tour of Asia Minor he visited, or took about with him, all the leading rhetorical teachers. Finally he came to Rhodes, where he found Molo, and once more submitted to his instruction. When he returned to Rome his delivery was quieter and more varied, his style less exuberant and his lungs stronger. After his long education he was prepared for the exacting life of the Roman orator.

III

ARS RHETORICA

For all a rhetorician's rules
Teach nothing but to name his tools.
Samuel Butler, *Hudibras* 1.1.89–90

It is now time to give an account of the Art of Rhetoric as it was taught in the schools and expounded in the textbooks when rhetoric became established at Rome. It had grown up in the course of centuries and there were variations between the versions taught in the different schools. But the main outlines remained much the same, and many of the details were handed down unchanged from generation to generation. To most persons today this system is of little interest. It appears as an attempt by professional teachers to construct an obscure and difficult science out of the obvious. And so perhaps, in part at any rate, it is. Yet some of the best intellects of Rome did not think so. A study which engaged the attention of Cicero and Quintilian and which trained many Roman statesmen and men of letters cannot be entirely neglected, however repellent or frivolous it may seem to those brought up in different disciplines and systems of thought.

Complete systems of rhetoric are given in two works of the Republican period, *Ad Herennium* and *Partitiones Oratoriae*. In addition to these we have Cicero's *De Inventione*, covering one division of the whole, parts of *De Oratore*, which though deliberately unsystematic, is based on the main divisions of traditional rhetoric, and *Topica* which deals with an obscure province on the bor'ers of rhetoric and logic. From the Imperial period we have the massive work of Quintilian, which sums up with great thoroughness ancient rhetoric down to his day, and the lesser rhetoricians of the fourth and fifth centuries A.D. In the following outline the treatise *Ad Herennium* will be generally followed;

it is the most convenient guide, for it is relatively simple and it best represents the traditional rhetoric of the schools, the sort of thing that was taught by the ordinary rhetorician in Rome. *De Inventione* is a fuller and more careful, or one might say, more pedantic version, with considerable variations, of the most important part of the system of *Ad Herennium. Partitiones Oratoriae* follows a different method devised in the Academy.[1] Whatever its merits, it was not generally followed, and it had little influence on later rhetoric.[2]

The material of rhetoric was traditionally divided according to the different types of oratory, the different functions of the orator and the different parts of a speech. The three types of oratory are forensic or judicial, deliberative and epideictic (*genus iudiciale, genus deliberativum* and *genus demonstrativum*), the first concerned with accusation and defence in the courts, the second with the recommendation of a course of action in deliberative assemblies, the third with praise and blame.[3] In the Hellenistic rhetoric which Rome adopted the three types were given very unequal treatment; the rhetoricians had much to say about forensic oratory and little about deliberative, while epideictic was scarcely recognised as having an independent existence.

The functions of the orator (*officia oratoris*) or, as they were sometimes called, the parts of rhetoric,[4] are firstly *inventio*, invention, or, as the textbooks defined it, 'the devising of matter true or probable which will make a case appear more plausible';[5] secondly, *dispositio*, arrangement; thirdly, *elocutio*, style or presentation; fourthly, *memoria*, memory, and fifthly, *actio* or *pronuntiatio*, delivery. The last two stand apart as being matters more of nature than of art, and some authorities omitted one or both of them from the list.[6]

The parts of a speech (*partes orationis*) are the *exordium* or opening, the *narratio* or statement of facts, the *divisio* or *partitio*, that is, the statement of the point at issue and exposition of what the orator proposes to prove, the *confirmatio* or exposition of arguments, the *confutatio* or refutation of one's opponent's arguments, and finally the *conclusio* or peroration. This sixfold division is that given in *De Inventione* and *Ad Herennium*,[7] but Cicero tells us that some divided into four or five or even seven parts,[8] and Quintilian regards *partitio* as contained in the third part, which he calls *probatio*, proof, and thus is left with a total of five.[9]

Let us now see how the rhetoricians dealt with the different parts of the speech. Firstly, the *exordium*. The student was first informed that there were four types of case, honourable, base, doubtful and mean,[10] and that the exordium must suit the type; then that there were two types of *exordium*, the *principium* which performed its function without any beating about the bush, and *insinuatio*, the indirect approach, to be used when the speaker was for various reasons in an unfavourable position.[11] The orator's object in the *exordium*, and in particular in the first variety, was to make his listeners attentive, ready to learn and well disposed. Various precepts were given as to how this should be done;[12] for instance he was advised to secure attention by claiming that he was about to speak of important, new and unprecedented matters. At this point we have our first introduction to the doctrine of *loci*, the 'places' in which arguments can be discovered. The *loci* for making the audience well disposed are to be found in the speaker's character, in that of his opponent, in that of the audience and in the actual facts of the case.[13]

The precepts for *insinuatio* were of a more practical character.[14] When the case to be pleaded was discreditable, the audience was first to be reconciled to it by various means; the speaker would say that he shared his opponent's dislike of whatever the latter had objected to, but that it bore no relation to himself. He would disclaim the intention of saying anything about his opponent, but would do so indirectly. He would aim not at openly damaging a popular figure but at undermining his position. If his opponent appeared to have made a strong impression, he could say that he was going to demolish the other's strong points first, could express doubts as to where to begin, and so on. In cases where the audience was tired, he could begin with some amusing extemporary reference, say he would speak more briefly than usual, or adopt some other similar technique.

We now come to the *narratio*,[15] which, like so much in rhetoric, was divided into three classes. Firstly there was the straight-forward exposition of the facts of the case, the *narratio* in the usual sense of the term; then there were narrations which occurred incidentally in the course of the speech; thirdly there were those that had no connection with cases in the courts, this last category being divided, with typical pedantry, into those concerned with things and those concerned with persons.[16] Detailed precepts were given only for the first type, which, it was laid down, should be brief, clear and plausible.[17] The advice given under the last heading shows that the *narratio* was not necessarily an exact account of what actually happened.[18] The author of *Ad Herennium* tells us that if the facts are true one should none the less observe the rules for plausibility, for the truth does not always carry conviction; if they are false, they need to be observed all the more.[19] It was also suggested that when the events had to be explained away by the argument it would be best to dispense with a formal *narratio* and distribute the statement of facts throughout the speech.[20]

The third part of the speech is the *partitio* or *divisio*; here the speaker would first state what points were agreed between himself and the other side and what was in dispute, then would give an orderly exposition of what he was going to say.[21] There followed the *confirmatio*, which contained the most important part of the speech, the argument. This was treated with great elaboration by the rhetoricians; for it appealed to the logical interests of the Greeks, and lent itself to those elaborate analyses by which they made of rhetoric a serious intellectual discipline.

At this point[22] we are introduced to the doctrine of the *status* or *constitutio*,[23] that is, the question from which the case arises, a doctrine particularly associated with Hermagoras. The *status* (there is no English term which represents the Latin satisfactorily) was conventionally defined as the 'first conflict of the pleas arising from the answer to an accusation', though, as Quintilian points out, its essence lay not in the 'first conflict' between one side and the other, but in the kind of question that arose from the conflict.[24] The author of *Ad Herennium* tells us that some considered there were four sorts of *constitutio*, whereas his teacher recognised only three.[25] He is referring to the four στάσεις λογικαί of Hermagoras, στοχασμός (*coniectura*), ὅρος (*finis*), ποιότης (*qualitas*) and μετάληψις (*tralatio*), the last of which was commonly rejected as an independent *status*. This classification gave rise to much argument and discussion among the more theoretically minded rhetoricians, as can be seen from

Quintilian's painstaking survey of the many different existing views.[26] But for practical purposes the threefold classification that the author of *Ad Herennium* adopted from his master was sufficient.[27] The three *status* could be conveniently distinguished by the three different questions which were involved, *an sit, quid sit* and *quale sit*. In the terminology of *Ad Herennium* they are the *constitutio coniecturalis*, where the dispute is one of fact, whether an action took place or not; the *constitutio legitima*, where the dispute arises from the interpretation of law; and the *constitutio iuridicialis*, where the act is admitted but the question is whether it was justified or not.

Having decided on the *constitutio*, we must, the rhetorician tells us, decide on the *ratio*, the line of defence; then we must consider the *firmamentum*, the answer which the accusation makes to this defence. Thus we arrive at the *iudicatio*, the κρινόμενον, the question which arises from the defence and the counter argument of the accusation.[28] This piece of mystification appears to have originated with Hermagoras, who is rightly censured by Quintilian for his laborious and futile attempt at subtle definition.[29]

Let us now see how the doctrine of *inventio* was applied to the different *constitutiones* and their subdivisions.[30] In the case of the *constitutio coniecturalis*, where the question is whether the action took place or not, six types of argument are distinguished.[31] First there is that from probability. Under this head come possible motives and the man's previous life. The two should indeed be combined; if the accuser says the motive of the accused was avarice, he will attempt to show that he has always been avaricious; if he cannot do this, he will find some other vice to attribute to him; if no such attribution is at all plausible, he will say one should consider deeds, not reputation. Similarly the defendant will demonstrate the integrity of his past life, if he can; if he is notorious for evil living, he will first say that false rumours have been put about by his opponent. If all else fails, he will say that he is not defending his morals before the censors, but answering a charge in a court of law. The second argument is that from comparison; the accuser, for example, will say that the deed could not have helped anyone except the defendant. Then comes that from circumstantial evidence, divided into six parts: place, time (e.g. at what hour was the deed committed?)

duration (was there time for the deed to be completed?), opportunity, hope of fulfilment and hope of concealment. Fourthly there is the proof (*argumentum*) divided into past (e.g. where the accused was before the act, who his companions were, whether he said anything unusual), contemporary (e.g. whether he was seen at the time, whether any cries or other sounds were heard) and subsequent (e.g. whether anything was left behind to prove that the act was committed or to point to its author). Next comes consequence, *consecutio*, where one asks what are the usual consequences of crime and innocence. The accuser, for example, will say that his opponent showed all the signs of guilt, blushing, pallor, faltering, etc. If he did nothing of the sort the accuser will maintain that his demeanour was a proof not of innocence but of premeditation and brazenness. Finally there is *approbatio*, confirmation, which includes *loci proprii* and *communes*, topics peculiar to one side and those of general application.[32] As regards the latter, commonplaces, there were considered to be two types, disquisitions on the heinousness of certain notorious sins and sinners, and certain general questions which can be argued both ways, such as the credibility of witnesses and the desirability of believing rumours.[33] The author of *Ad Herennium* is here only concerned with the second type, for which he duly provides the arguments on both sides. Thus in favour of rumours it may be said that there must be some foundation for the report; there was no reason why anyone should invent the story; other rumours may be false, but this one is true. On the other side we can show by examples that many rumours are false; we can say that the story has been invented by our enemies or by malicious and slanderous persons; we can produce some rumour discreditable to our opponent, if necessary inventing one, then say that we do not ourselves believe it, but that it shows how easy it is to spread abroad such stories.[34]

We now come to the *constitutio legitima*, which, it will be remembered, is concerned with a dispute arising from the interpretation of law. Of this six varieties are distinguished: *scriptum et sententia* (the letter versus the meaning of the law), contradictory laws, ambiguity, definition, transference (e.g. where the competence of the court is disputed) and *ratiocinatio*, inference, where there is no law exactly covering the case.[35] In *De*

Inventione the first three and the last in this list are treated separately from the *constitutiones* as *controversiae quae in scripto versantur*,[36] while the fifth, transference, is, in deference to Hermagoras, made a separate *constitutio*,[37] and the second *constitutio* is called *definitiva*.[38]

Detailed suggestions were given for arguments on these different points. It will suffice to give by way of example those to be used for the intention as opposed to the letter of the law: The law-giver will be commended for only committing to writing as much as he thought necessary and leaving unwritten what he supposed could be understood; it will be said that it is the mark of a pettifogger to busy oneself with words and letters and neglect the intention; that what is written is impossible, or incompatible with law, custom, nature, or equity and right; that an opposite intention is either null or foolish or unjust or impossible or inconsistent with the intention of what has gone before or follows after, or disagrees with common law or with other common laws or with precedent. There should follow an enumeration of suitable examples to support the case.[39]

The third *constitutio, iuridicialis*, was divided into two, *absoluta* and *assumptiva*.[40] The first is where we claim that what we have done is right absolutely (here it was thought necessary to introduce a classification of the different sources of right, *ius*),[41] the second where the defence depends on extraneous considerations. Of this four varieties were distinguished; firstly there is *concessio*, where we admit the deed, but ask for pardon.[42] This is divided into *purgatio* and *deprecatio*. In the case of *purgatio* we claim that the deed was not done intentionally, and put the blame on chance or inadvertence or necessity. Precepts were given under these three headings, but it was observed that the three were closely related and the same arguments more or less could be applied to each of them.[43] *Deprecatio* was where no such pleas could be made, and it was necessary to appeal for mercy on the ground of past services, good character and the like. Such a defence, it was laid down, was not suitable to the courts; it could however be used in the senate and other deliberative bodies.[44] So much for *concessio*. Secondly there is *tralatio criminis*, when the deed is said to have been done as the result of someone else's misdeeds;[45] thirdly the closely related *remotio criminis*, when some other person or thing is said to have been responsible.[46]

C

Finally there is *comparatio*, where it is claimed that the course followed was better than its alternative.[47]

Having set out the arguments to be used in each *constitutio*, of which we have given only a small selection here, the author of *Ad Herennium* proceeds to give some general precepts regarding argumentation.[48] We should not, he states, linger too long on the same topic, nor return again and again to the same point, nor leave an argument incomplete, nor move on to another in a clumsy fashion. The most complete and perfect form of argument is said to be a fivefold one, consisting of *propositio*, a statement of what we are about to prove; *ratio*, a brief exposition of our argument; *confirmatio*, a confirmation of this by a number of proofs; *exornatio*, embellishment; and *complexio*, summing up.[49]

This section of *Ad Herennium* represents as much as the ordinary Latin teacher could assimilate of the general principles of argumentation as developed by the rhetoricians of Greece. For a general consideration of the topics of argument we turn to *De Inventione*.[50] Here we are told that arguments may be drawn either from the attributes of persons or from those of things. A list of eleven attributes of persons and four of things is given, in many cases with subdivisions. Thus the second class of attributes of things, those concerned with the actual performance of the deed, is divided into five—place, time, occasion, manner and facilities. Under the heading time we are told to consider not merely the past, the contemporary and the subsequent, but different types of past event, the fabulous past, recorded history and the recent past. Nor are we spared a definition of time,[51] which takes us far from the forum to the tranquil atmosphere of the lecture room. We need not follow the youthful Cicero further into the various divisions and subdivisions of the different types of argument, for it may be supposed that such theoretical niceties were the part of the system heard with least patience by the average Roman student.

The general consideration of the nature of argumentation led naturally on to logical fallacies and faulty arguments generally. A classification of these formed the substance of what the rhetoricians had to say on the penultimate part of the speech, the *reprehensio* or refutation of one's opponent's arguments. Even the practical author of *Ad Herennium* deals with this section from the theoretical point of view, giving a lengthy exposition of the various types of faulty argument, with illustrations, curiously enough, from the Roman poets.[52]

We have now reached the last part of the speech, the *conclusio* or peroration.[53] This the rhetoricians divided into three, *enumeratio*, recapitulation,[54] *amplificatio* and *commiseratio*. *Amplificatio*, a word generally used by rhetorical writers in a wider sense,[55] is the name given by *Ad Herennium* to what *De Inventione* calls *indignatio*, the arousing of indignation, and the ten topics of the former treatise are included in the fifteen of *De Inventione*. Similarly in the case of *commiseratio*, appeals for pity, Cicero is more elaborate than the author of *Ad Herennium*, and solemnly enumerates no fewer than sixteen different themes. Both authors however end with the advice not to linger too long on the appeal to pity, adding the apophthegm 'Nothing dries quicker than a tear.'[56]

So far we have been concerned only with the *genus iudiciale*, which, as has already been said, was treated with disproportionate elaboration. We now proceed to the *genus deliberativum*.[57] Deliberations were divided into two classes, according to whether the choice was limited to two alternatives or not; or into three, according to whether the desirability of the action discussed was absolute or relative or mixed.[58] The aim of the deliberative speaker is stated to be utility,[59] which is divided into two parts, that concerned with security and that concerned with honour. The former has two aspects, force and cunning,[60] the latter two also, the right and the praiseworthy.[61] The right (*rectum*) includes the four virtues, *prudentia*, *iustitia*, *fortitudo*, *modestia*. In the definition of these virtues and in the recommendations for treatment under these four headings we can see signs of Stoic influence.[62] But Stoic morality was not entirely suited to the forum, and we notice that precepts are given for speaking on the other side.[63] Virtue is not indeed to be openly depreciated, but it can be said that the facts of the case do not admit of the pursuit of the ideal, or that virtue is something other than what its advocates have claimed. What they call justice, for example, can be made out to be cowardice or perverse generosity, what they call courage to be the irrational daring of the gladiator.[64] The orator was advised to build up his speech on the same lines as in forensic speeches and to use the same methods of argumentation; and in the case of a conflict between safety and honour topics for argument were supplied to both sides.[65]

The third type of oratory is epideictic, the *genus demonstrativum*, which was conventionally defined by its subject matter, praise and blame, a definition hardly compatible with its claim to be a separate *genus*.[66] The topics of praise, which also serve, in reverse, as the topics of blame, are divided into mind, body and estate, to borrow the Prayer Book phrase. The author of *Ad Herennium*, among other precepts, lays down that in recounting the life of the person concerned the orator should begin with externals—family and education—go on to bodily characteristics, and then return to externals, considering what virtues were displayed in connection with them. His full and even pedantic treatment of this type of speech, beginning with the proem—to be drawn either from the speaker's character or from that of the person praised or from that of the audience or from the subject matter—shows that he had in mind a complete speech of praise or blame. Yet he tells us that the *genus demonstrativum* rarely occurs in real life, though occasions for praise and blame often occur in forensic or deliberative speeches.[67] Cicero, who in *De Inventione* gives this *genus* very meagre treatment, seems inclined in *De Oratore* to banish it altogether on the ground that it is unnecessary to treat every minor type of speech as if it needed special precepts peculiar to itself. In the end however he cannot bring himself to omit this section of rhetoric.[68]

So far we have dealt solely with one part of the rhetorical doctrine, that which concerns *inventio*. The second part, *dispositio*, can be briefly despatched.[69] The parts of the speech, as we have seen, were dealt with under *inventio*, which had thus encroached on the province of *dispositio*, so that little was left to be said under the latter head. We are however told that there are two types of arrangement, that according to the rules (the rules, that is, for the parts of the speech given under *inventio*) and that where the orator uses his judgment to vary the order.[70] Once you have admitted that the arrangement of the speech can be varied according to circumstances and that the orator should use his judgment, there is little that can be given in the way of instruction. It was however generally agreed that as regards arrangement of arguments it was best to put the strongest first and last, and the less strong in the middle, but, as

Quintilian observes, the position of the defence was different from that of the prosecution.[71] It was indeed impossible to lay down general rules to cover all cases. Quintilian justly observes that no one case is exactly like another, and that the pleader must rely on his own judgment. This did not prevent him from devoting a whole book to *dispositio*.[72]

On *elocutio* there is more to be said. When we come to this branch of rhetoric we are conscious of a change of emphasis. We are not here so much concerned with utilitarian ends or with logical subtleties as we are in the first branch, *inventio*. *Inventio* was drawn in part from the professional handbook, in part from philosophy; in *elocutio* a new source is discernible, that of literary criticism. The doctrine of style had been developed by those whose interest was less in the forging of weapons for victory in argument than in the analysis of existing works of oratory from the formal point of view. Such appears to have been the origin of two classifications which found a place in school rhetoric, that of the three styles (*genera dicendi*) and that of the four virtues of style (*virtutes dicendi*), the former possibly, the latter undoubtedly, of Peripatetic origin.[73] The three styles appear in Cicero as the *genus grande*, *medium* and *tenue*, whereas *Ad Herennium* uses the terms *grave*, *mediocre* and *attenuatum*.[74] They played a minor part in Roman rhetoric until Cicero in the *Orator* made adroit use of them to show that the best orators, such as himself, had all three at their command.[75] The four virtues of style appear in *De Oratore* much as Theophrastus enunciated them;[76] in *Ad Herennium* the first two, correctness and clarity, are regarded as subdivisions of *elegantia*, and appropriateness is replaced by *compositio*, euphony.[77] It thus appears that the four virtues had got somewhat confused in the school tradition, whereas Cicero restored them in their original simplicity and clarity.

The major part of what the rhetoricians had to say on *elocutio* was concerned with *ornatus*, and in particular with those departures from normal usage which served to embellish and enliven the orator's language, and which provided the rhetoricians with such a fruitful field for classification and definition. How much laborious thought they devoted to this branch of their subject we can see from Quintilian's lengthy discussion of the distinction between tropes, figures of speech and figures of thought.[78] On the whole they shed little light for all their labours, and wasted much effort on introducing confusing innovations of terminology and on discovering figures in modes of thought and speech which hardly deserved to be so called.[79] It is with a certain relief that we turn to the unpretentious treatment of the subject by the author of *Ad Herennium*, who knows only the division into *exornationes verborum* and *exornationes sententiarum*, and is content to give under these two heads a long list of technical terms followed by definitions and examples.[80] Unlike Quintilian, for example, he has nothing of the literary critic about him; his eye is on the oratorical effect of the various figures.[81]

It would be tedious and unprofitable to follow him through his list of figures,[82] but it may be of interest to select a few which he regards as particularly effective and to reproduce some of his comments.

The figure *repetitio*, the repetition of a word at the beginning of a series of clauses, better known by its Greek name *anaphora*, is described as full of charm, weighty and pungent, and is recommended as an embellishment and a means of rendering speech effective.[83] The allied figure *conduplicatio* (ἀναδίπλωσις) the doubling of a word or words, is said to have a great effect on the hearer, being compared to a wound inflicted more than once in the same place.[84] The collecting together of a number of points scattered throughout a speech, in particular of the various grounds for suspecting an accused person (*frequentatio*), is a *vehemens exornatio*, almost essential in the *constitutio coniecturalis*, and useful in other types of case.[85] *Permissio*, a figure by which the orator claims to be handing himself over to someone else's power—says in effect 'Do what you like to me'— is recommended as particularly good for arousing pity.[86] Pity and indignation alike may be aroused by a lively description of the consequences of an action (*descriptio*).[87] This figure was distinguished from *demonstratio* (ὑποτύπωσις), a vivid word picture of events, useful not only for *commiseratio* but also for *amplificatio*.[88] The same purposes were served by *conformatio*, more commonly known as prosopopoeia, the putting of a speech in the mouth of some character imagined as present or of some inanimate object or abstraction endowed with life, making the commonwealth speak, as Cicero puts it, and calling up the dead from the underworld.[89] This figure Cicero regarded as exceptionally effective.[90]

Two figures which the rhetoricians coupled together were simile (*similitudo*) and example (*exemplum*).[91] The lengthy treatment of the simile in *Ad Herennium* shows that its use was carefully taught in the rhetorical schools. The would-be orator is told that the discovery of similes will be easy if he conjures up before his eyes everything, animate or inanimate, dumb or possessed of speech, wild or tame, belonging to earth, sky or water, manufactured, accidental or natural, common or uncommon; from this wide field he can hunt out some simile which will serve one of the four purposes of the figure, embellishment, proof, clarity or vividness.[92] The *exemplum*, which serves the same four purposes as the simile, is the adducing of an action or saying ascribed to a particular person.[93] The two figures are described by Cicero as particularly moving.[94]

Some figures were recommended only with qualification. *Exclamatio* (apostrophe), the addressing of a person, city, place, etc., was to be used sparingly, and only when the importance of the matter justified it.[95] Very sparing use was advised in the case of *similiter cadens* (ὁμοιόπτωτον), the use of a series of words in the same case; of *similiter desinens* (ὁμοιοτέλευτον), the use of words with similar terminations;[96] and of *annominatio*, word play.[97] Such figures are witty and amusing rather than dignified and beautiful, and give the impression of having been laboriously thought up beforehand.[98] The *sententia*, the brief statement of a general truth, of which *Ad Herennium* distinguishes two types, the short and the longer, is to be used sparingly, *ut rei actores, non vivendi praeceptores videamur.*[99]

Finally we come to the last two parts of the rhetorical system, *actio* and *memoria*. There is no space here to describe the various aids to memory prescribed by the rhetoricians,[100] but something must be said of delivery, for this was a side of the art to which the ancients attached great importance.[101] If the author of *Ad Herennium* is to be believed, none of his predecessors had treated the subject in a systematic manner, on the ground that its nature was such that it could hardly be written about.[102] It may therefore be that he is not here representative, and that some students of rhetoric had the good fortune to escape the pedantic method of treating the subject which he followed.

There is little trace of the textbook in Cicero's treatment in *De Oratore*, nor indeed in Quintilian, in spite of his elaborate descriptions of the uses of the various facial expressions, bodily movements, gestures of hands and arms, and so on. His long and entertaining chapter on delivery[103] should be read by all who want to understand ancient oratory. But as our purpose here is to summarise what was laid down in the textbooks, we will continue to follow *Ad Herennium* as our guide.

The author divides the subject of *actio* into two parts, voice production and bodily action. As regards voice, the three qualities required were strength, durability and flexibility. The first was mainly a matter of nature, but the last two could be cultivated by exercise.[104] When we come to flexibility we are met with the inevitable tripartite division, into *sermo*, the conversational manner, *contentio*, the argumentative, and *amplificatio*, the emotional. The first has four subdivisions, the dignified, the instructive, the narrative and the humorous; the second has two, the rapid and the abrupt; the third also has two, the pathetic and the indignant.[105]

We will pass over the precepts for voice training, and proceed to the precise and curious directions on bodily action, which includes not only movement of the limbs, but also facial expression.[106] In using the colloquial manner, dignified or narrative, the orator will stand on the soles of his feet and adopt a gentle movement of his right hand, while his facial expression will be in accord with the mood of his language; in the instructive-colloquial he will bend forward a little; in the humorous he will express the mood by his face, not by gestures. In the continuous argumentative style the arm is moved rapidly, the facial expression is mobile, the look piercing; in the abrupt, the arm will be thrust forward rapidly, the orator will walk about, occasionally stamp his right foot,[107] and put on a piercing and intent look. When he is arousing indignation he will proceed as in the case of continuous argument, except that the gestures will be slower; in the pathetic style it will be appropriate to strike the thigh and beat the head,[108] and in many cases to use gestures subdued and firm and an expression sad and disquieted.

Such was the Art of Rhetoric. It bears all the marks of its Greek origin. It was the creation of the Greek intellect, with its intellectual subtlety and its love of logic and fine distinctions, but of the Greek intellect in its decline, no longer adventurous and creative, but confined within professional and pedagogic bounds. It was open to criticism, and it was sometimes criticised, for its pedantry and remoteness from life. But on the whole the Romans took to it with surprising readiness. From its first introduction to the end of Roman civilisation it was part of the intellectual background of the educated Roman.

ROMAN ORATORY BEFORE CICERO

Oratorem celeriter complexi sumus, nec eum primo eruditum,
aptum tamen ad dicendum, post autem eruditum.

Cicero, *Tusculan Disputations* 1.5

FROM THEORY we turn to practice. We have seen how rhetoric
came to Rome and how it was taught there. We will now survey
the oratorical practice of the Republican period and attempt to
discover how far it was influenced by rhetoric.

The question cannot be given a clear and simple answer.
Rhetoric, as Cicero said, springs from oratory. It formulates
rules which are derived ultimately from oratorical practice, and
if practice agrees with theory, this does not necessarily mean
that the theory has influenced the practice. It is possible to
speak effectively without having studied rhetoric.[1] Whenever
words are used with intent to persuade, the speaker will argue
as best he can and make use of turns of speech designed to
heighten the effect. Rhetoric only reduces to a system the
arguments and turns of speech which have proved to be effective.

None the less it would be surprising if rhetoric did not
exercise some influence on Roman practice. The Romans themselves evidently thought there was something to be learnt from
it; otherwise they would not have gone to school as they did to the
rhetoricians. Moreover what has been said above about rhetoric
springing from oratory needs some qualification as regards
Rome, for Roman rhetoric was taken over from the Greeks, and
so was derived from Greek rather than from Roman oratory.
There must have been an element in it that was alien to Roman
tradition. But when we attempt to estimate how far and in what
direction the native tradition was modified, we are baffled by
lack of evidence. Of oratory before Cicero's day we have only

fragments, and for the period which would be of special interest, the period before Greek influences began to make themselves felt, we are almost completely in the dark.

Roman oratory as a literary art begins with the elder Cato. Of written speeches before his Cicero knew only one of Appius Claudius Caecus, and some funeral orations, chiefly noted for their mendacity.[2] But though few speeches were written down before the second century B.C., there must have been a long tradition of public speaking in Rome. Cicero was justified in beginning his history of Roman oratory with a number of names of famous figures whose eloquence could only be inferred from the part they had played in events.[3] For Rome was a republic, accustomed to decide her affairs by debate and discussion, and the oratory of the senate and the *contio* no doubt had a long history dating back to the early days of the Republic.[4] Forensic oratory too must have been known long before it became part of literature. The *Lex Cincia* of 204 B.C., which forbade payment to advocates, shows that this characteristic Roman profession was well established in the third century.[5] Finally, the third branch of oratory, epideictic, was represented by the funeral oration, a Roman institution of long standing.[6]

Roman oratory then existed long before Cato. But we can only surmise what style of speaking was in use in those early days. It is sometimes assumed that before the advent of Greek rhetoric the Roman was a man of few words, blunt, simple, straightforward and dignified. It may be so. Yet this was surely not the natural manner of the people of Italy. Their ordinary speech, so far as we can judge, was lively, emphatic, exaggerated—in a sense rhetorical. For there is a rhetorical element in any spoken language, if by rhetoric we mean speech designed to create an effect on the hearer. This is the function of much of ordinary speech, not least among the unsophisticated; even peasants and uneducated persons, observed Quintilian, use hyperbole, 'for no one is content with the plain truth'.[7] Everyday speech does not consist in the main of plain, straightforward, unimpassioned speech.[8] There are certain modes of expression, rhetorical questions, exclamations, repetitions of words, which constantly recur in the emotional passages of Roman oratory. Such modes of expression are also found in those writers who reflect the style of conversation,[9] and were, we may assume, used in heated argument at the street corner no less than in pathetic perorations in the courts. Recognised and sanctioned as 'figures' by the rhetoricians, they were used with greater artistry by the professional orator, but they had their roots in popular speech, and were no doubt a part of excited oratory from the earliest times.

The Romans undoubtedly had a natural taste for the rhetorical, as the fragments of the early tragedians show. Compared with that of the Greek originals the Roman tragic style is heavy and over-emphatic; it expands and amplifies, makes use of alliteration and assonance. This emphatic manner was not learnt from the Greeks. The Romans always knew how to speak for effect. If anything they laid it on too thick, and the effect of conscious study was to remove something of the emphasis and exaggeration.

The fragments of the elder Cato are sufficiently numerous for us to be able to form some opinion of his oratory. It is an interesting study. He lived at a time when Greek influences were spreading; his attitude towards them was notoriously one of hostility, and it has been suggested earlier that this hostility extended to Greek rhetoric. Yet he himself was an effective speaker. Cicero noted the impressiveness of his eulogy, the pungency of his vituperation, the wit of his *sententiae*, the acuteness of his exposition.[10] The fragments of his speeches, notably different in style from his work on agriculture, show that there was little he did not know about how to present a case. Are we then to suppose that he was not so ignorant as he liked to make out of Greek theory and practice, or are his speeches an example of the untutored eloquence of the *vir bonus dicendi peritus*?[11]

That Cato's oratory was not a mere reproduction of textbook rules is obvious enough. Cicero's freedman Tiro, criticising Cato's speech for the Rhodians from his study desk, found a good deal wrong. The confident opening was contrary to all the rules about *exordia*; Cato's defence of the Rhodians was no defence at all, but an admission of their guilt; he was guilty of using a faulty enthymeme and dishonest sophistical arguments.[12] Cato certainly did not bother about the academic correctness of his arguments; as Gellius observed, this was not a mock fight, but a real one, in which every weapon had to be used.[13] But Cato's weapons were by no means blunt; he is capable of a subtlety which makes one think that, if it was the product of native ability and Roman oratorical tradition, he had little to learn from the Greeks in the art of argumentation.[14]

Among the fragments of Cato is a vivid passage from the speech *In Q. Minucium Thermum De Falsis Pugnis:*

Dixit a decemviris parum bene sibi cibaria curata esse. iussit vestimenta detrahi atque flagro caedi. decemviros Bruttiani verberavere, videre multi mortales. quis hanc contumeliam, quis hoc imperium, quis hanc servitutem ferre potest? nemo hoc rex ausus est facere; eane fieri bonis, bono genere gnatis, boni consultis? ubi societas? ubi fides maiorum? insignitas iniurias, plagas, verbera,vibices, eos dolores atque carnificinas per dedecus atque maximam contumeliam, inspectantibus popularibus suis atque multis mortalibus, te facere ausum esse! set quantum luctum, quantum gemitum, quid lacrimarum, quantum fletum factum audivi! servi iniurias nimias aegre ferunt: quid illos, bono genere gnatos, magna virtute praeditos, opinamini animi habuisse atque habituros dum vivent?[15]

This is no doubt the sort of passage Cicero had in mind when he remarked on Cato's mastery of the figures of speech and of thought.[16] But we should not necessarily assume that these embellishments were the result of a conscious following of rhetorical precept. Alliteration, which is much in evidence in the passage, and elsewhere in Cato's fragments,[17] is a feature of early Latin, and there is no need to look for a foreign source for it. Indeed it was if anything frowned on by the rhetoricians and literary critics.[18] The piling up of synonyms, to which Cato is particularly prone, was, to judge by its occurrence in Plautus, a feature of everyday Latin speech.[19] The rhetorical questions too, and the use of anaphora, as has already been observed, can be paralleled from the language of conversation. None the less the passage quoted is not mere indignant conversation; there is an artistry about it which raises it to the level of literature, and it is hard to believe that this artistry does not owe something, if only indirectly, to Greek influence. Perhaps we can accept Cicero's view of Cato as marking an intermediate stage between the eloquence of the untaught orator and that of the rhetorically educated.[20] The main element in his oratory was the Italian tradition; but he was sufficiently susceptible to the spirit of the age in which he lived to develop this tradition into something artistic. It is significant that he was the first Roman to publish his speeches and thus make oratory a part of Latin literature.

Whatever might be the merits of Cato, it was recognised that he lacked smoothness and rhythm.[21] These were the qualities cultivated by the Roman orators of the later second century who are known to have studied under Greek masters. Scipio Aemilianus evidently made some progress in this direction, for Cicero comparing him with his contemporary Laelius noted that the latter appeared uncouth and old-fashioned by his side.[22] When we look at his fragments after Cato's we are conscious of having moved some way towards Cicero's artistic sentence construction. But it was a younger contemporary of Scipio, Marcus Aemilius Lepidus Porcina, who, according to Cicero, was the first to display the smoothness, the periodic structure and the artistry of style that belonged to the Greeks.[23] The same conscious artistry must have been shown by T. Albucius, who flourished towards the end of the second century, and whose artful word mosaics incurred the mockery of Lucilius.[24]

Smoothness and verbal artistry were not qualities which in themselves led to success at Rome. The most famous orator of the age, Servius Galba, was noted for force and emotional power rather than for stylistic elegance. Cicero, looking back on the history of oratory and seeing in him no doubt a kindred spirit, proclaimed him as the first Roman to adopt the methods peculiar to the orator, digressions, exaggeration, pathos and commonplace.[25] But though Cicero describes his qualities in the terms of rhetoric, it would be a mistake to see in him a case of the conscious adoption of methods prescribed by the theorists. Galba was not a man of much learning.[26] He was a natural orator whose power failed him when he sat down in his study and took his pen in hand. His speeches as written were disappointing and curiously antiquated in effect.[27]

Galba provides the first recorded example in Roman oratory of a device which seems to have had unfailing effect, the production in court of weeping children. Having massacred in brutal fashion a number of Lusitanian envoys, he was obliged to defend himself against the octogenarian Cato. Seeing that his case was hopeless, he brought in his two sons and infant ward, and saved the situation by his own tears and those of the children.[28]

The age of the Gracchi, with its clash of ideals and personalities, was conducive to high and excited political oratory. The two brothers were famous for their eloquence; Cicero, in spite of his disapproval of the uses to which it was put, cannot forbear to praise.[29] They were alike in combining natural gifts with Greek learning; they differed however in their style of speaking. Tiberius had a quiet straightforward manner, Gaius was more vigorous and intense, energetic in his delivery, striding up and down and pulling his toga from his shoulders.[30] Tiberius's oratory is known to us only indirectly, though we can catch something of its tone from Plutarch. The speech justifying the deposition of the tribune Octavius gives the impression of a philosophical orator in the Ciceronian sense, able to argue from the general to the particular and to reinforce his arguments with the fruits of a wide reading, while the famous passage in which he commended his agrarian law to the Roman people has a power and directness which show that this pupil of the Greeks had learnt more than the graces of style.[31]

Of Gaius's speeches we have some fragments. We do not always catch the fire and passion for which he was celebrated. In one of the fragments he describes how a Roman consul arrived at an Italian town and had the men's baths cleared so that his wife could use them alone; she complained of delay and of the state of the baths, and the consul proceeded to administer a beating to the local magistrate responsible. The theme was a suitable one for the display of *indignatio*, yet compared with the similar passage in Cato's speech against Thermus, Gaius's description is curiously bald and flat.[32] Other fragments however show all the arts of rhetoric displayed in the service of pathos. Cicero recalls a passage of one of Gaius's speeches: 'Quo me miser conferam? quo vertam? in Capitoliumne? at fratris sanguine madet. an domum? matremne ut miseram lamentantem videam et abiectam?'[33] Cicero's theme is the importance of *actio*, and he tells us that Gaius's eyes, voice and gestures when uttering these words were such that even his enemies could not refrain from tears. But it was not only the delivery that gave the words their effect. Gaius was using a figure (*subiectio*) which the author of *Ad Herennium* recommends as particularly pungent and effective, and which was much cultivated by orators, Greek and Roman.[34] Figures such as this cannot be explained as deriving from popular speech; they must rather be the products of study and training. In places, too, Gaius shows a smoothness and elaboration of sentence construction which proves him the pupil of the Greeks. 'Quae vos cupide per hosce annos adpetistis atque voluistis, ea si temere repudiaritis, abesse non potest quin aut olim cupide adpetisse aut nunc temere repudiasse dicamini.' The sentence is quoted by Gellius as an example of a more careful and musical arrangement of words than was usual among the older orators.[35] On the other hand Cicero could give Gaius lessons in rhythm. Take that sentence, he says, from Gracchus: 'Abesse non potest quin eiusdem hominis sit probos improbare qui improbos probet.' How much better if he had written 'qui improbos probet probos improbare.'[36] Gaius, it appears, was ignorant of the magic of the double trochee.

The best forensic orator of the Gracchan age was C. Papirius Carbo.[37] It was an age when the oratory of the courts had become of increasing importance. In 149 the first of the *quaestiones perpetuae* was established under the Lex Calpurnia, which set up a special court to hear complaints against provincial governors, and after the introduction of the ballot in 137 the services of an advocate became more in demand in trials before the popular assemblies.[38] In these courts there was every opportunity for the superficial, unscrupulous type of orator. Such, it appears, was Carbo. He was ignorant of statute law, shaky on Roman traditions, and had only a superficial knowledge of private law. But he had a good voice, was fluent, acute and vigorous, and had an effective wit.[39] He was in his element when, himself an ex-Gracchan, he successfully defended Opimius, the murderer of Gaius Gracchus. He made no attempt to deny the murder, but claimed that it was justified by the interests of the state.[40] Two of his arguments have survived to show his plausibility and skilful use of verbal ingenuity: *Si consul est qui consulit patriae, quid aliud fecit Opimius?* and *Si Gracchus nefarie, praeclare Opimius.*[41]

Another famous advocate of the day was Scribonius Curio, whose defence of Servius Fulvius on a sexual charge was so much admired in Cicero's boyhood. The speech was full of commonplaces, on love, on evidence under torture, on rumours. Puerile as these seemed to the taste of a later age, they were comparatively new at the time and went down well.[42]

While Carbo's unscrupulous cleverness and Curio's trivialities won the applause of the courts and the rhetorical schools, there were still some who adopted a more dignified manner. Aemilius Scaurus preserved, at a time when it was in danger of dying out, a traditional style of speaking in which the character of the speaker and the impression he gave of reliability were of more weight than the actual speech, a style, says Cicero, more appropriate to the senate than to the courts.[43] Stoic precept too was not without its effect on oratory, for the school was now an important influence at Rome and several of the leading figures of the later second century are known to have fallen in greater or less degree under its influence. The Stoics believed in speaking the truth in plain words; they eschewed ornament and emotional appeal. Their style, says Cicero, was a meagre one, hardly calculated to win popular applause.[44] How true this was was shown by the experience of Rutilius Rufus. As a good Stoic he expressed the strongest condemnation of such theatrical tricks as had won Galba acquittal,[45] and when he was himself accused, quite unjustly, of maladministration, he disdained to use such arts. He made no appeals to the mercy of the jury and would not allow more than the simple truth to be said in his defence.[46] 'There were no groans or exclamations on the part of his advocates', says Cicero, 'no expression of grief or indignation, no appeals to the commonwealth, no supplication; why, no one stamped his foot, for fear, I suppose, that the Stoics might hear of it.'[47] Rutilius was condemned.

We now come to that period in which, according to Cicero, Roman oratory first equalled that of Greece, the period of Crassus and Antonius.[48] Crassus's oratorical career began in 119 B.C., Antonius's in 113, and their period of activity extended about ten years into the next century. There were other orators who flourished about the same time. There was Flavius Fimbria, fiery, outspoken, abusive; the learned lawyer Q. Scaevola; the elegant Catulus; M. Philippus, noted for his wit and skill in repartee and his powers of impromptu speaking.[49] There were also those representatives of the younger generation who appear in De Oratore, Julius Caesar Strabo, Cotta and Sulpicius. But all these, if we can believe Cicero, were outshone by Crassus and Antonius.

Of the two Crassus had the wider culture. He was a good

D

lawyer, had studied under Greek rhetoricians and philosophers and was familiar with Greek men of letters.[50] Antonius was not so learned, and what learning he had he did his best to conceal.[51] He was ignorant of law and not much of a Greek scholar.[52] But he was sufficiently interested in rhetorical theory to write a book about it, and Cicero, who often conversed with him in early years, found him by no means deficient in book learning.[53] Crassus published few speeches and Antonius none,[54] and if it were not for Cicero, we should know very little about them. As it is, our picture is not altogether a clear one, for Cicero tended to make the two orators of his boyhood, Crassus in particular, in his own image. None the less we can get some sort of a picture, blurred though it may be, of the oratory of these two masters.

Their activity was mainly forensic, but there was a strong political flavour about many of their cases,[55] and as in Cicero's day, personal considerations were often to the fore.[56] In cases like these it is unlikely that the careful, pedantic rules of the rhetoricians were of much help. Though in the absence of complete speeches we can say nothing for certain, it is most unlikely that the orators followed the textbook prescription. No doubt all speeches began with an exordium of some sort and ended with a peroration, but how many proceeded in orderly fashion from *narratio* to *divisio*, from *confirmatio* to *confutatio*? The rules for *inventio* were of little relevance to political charges such as that of *maiestas*. Even when they were relevant they might be of little assistance. In the case of Norbanus the whole question turned on what was meant by *maiestatem minuere*. The academic rhetorician laid down that a definition should be brief and exact. But, says Antonius in *De Oratore*, an exact definition lays itself open to attack; it smells of the schools; it makes no effect on the jury. So in defending Norbanus Antonius expatiated at length and with all his oratorical powers on the meaning of *maiestatem minuere*.[57] And even this part of his speech was of minor importance compared to the parts on which the textbooks had little or nothing to say.[58]

None the less the study of rhetorical *inventio* no doubt had some effect. It sharpened the wits of the Roman advocate and helped him to find arguments. Antonius, we are told, thought

of everything, and in the attack on Caepio which was one of
the main features of his defence of Norbanus he 'used every
available topic'.[59] Crassus specialised in expounding equity.
Scriptum versus *sententia*, the letter versus the spirit of the law,
was a favourite subject in the schools, and Crassus knew all the
arguments for *sententia*. He used them to good effect in defending
M'. Curius and completely overcame the prosecuting counsel
Scaevola by his wealth of arguments and examples.[60]

Both Crassus and Antonius seem to have had something of the
Ciceronian breadth of treatment. They could generalise, analyse
and appeal to history. Crassus had much to say on the right
and the good.[61] Antonius defending Norbanus, a *seditiosus
civis*, treated his audience to a disquisition on the different
types of *seditio*, with illustrations from Roman history, con-
cluding that in some cases they were justified and necessary.
Without civil strife, he argued, Rome would never have won her
liberties; popular movements were not therefore necessarily
criminal.[62]

Argument was reinforced by wit and pathos. Crassus was
famous for his wit.[63] In the case of Curius already referred to he
made effective use of this weapon against the lawyer Scaevola;
he produced many amusing examples of what would happen if
one followed the letter as opposed to the sense of the law, and
thus induced a general atmosphere of mirth and gaiety.[64] Wit
was not dealt with except very meagrely in the textbooks. It had
been discussed by Greek theorists, but there is no need to look
for foreign influences here. Wit as a weapon of oratory belongs
to the Roman tradition. So no doubt does pathos. 'Demosthenes',
wrote Swift, 'who had to deal with a people of much more
Politeness, Learning and Wit, laid the greater weight of his
oratory upon the Strength of his Arguments offered to their
Understanding and Reason. Whereas Tully considered the
Dispositions of a sincere, more ignorant and less mercurial
Nation by dwelling almost entirely on the Pathetick Part.'[65]
Whether this analysis of national character is correct or not, the
pathetic is a note which sounds stronger in Roman than in
Greek oratory. It sounded at full blast in Antonius's defence of
Aquilius, when he contrasted the former glories of the consul and
triumphant commander with his present piteous and precarious
condition, displayed his client in person, sorrowing and dressed

in mourning, tore open his shirt and showed his wounds.[66] In the speech for Norbanus Antonius relied not so much on argument as on the appeal to the emotions. 'I then completely changed my theme and proceeded to attack Caepio's flight and to lament the loss of the army. Thus my speech revived the grief of those who mourned the loss of friends and relations, and renewed a hatred of Caepio in the minds of the judges. When I was conscious that I had the case in my hands, because I had won over the goodwill of the populace and turned the judges in my favour, I began to introduce a milder manner.'[67]

As regards style much had no doubt been learnt from Greek precept and example. Cicero implies that there was book learning behind Antonius's selection and arrangement of words, his periodic structure and use of figures.[68] Crassus however was a more careful stylist than Antonius, and we have Cicero's testimony to his mastery of the *ornamenta dicendi*.[69] We have a few fragments by which we can judge his oratory for ourselves, notably the address to Brutus in the speech for Cn. Plancus.[70] Here we find the rhetorical questions and the use of anaphora which we have already observed in Cato, and with them that more sophisticated figure *subiectio*, which we noticed in C. Gracchus. There was another aspect of style which had been the subject of much study by the Greeks, though it did not bulk so large in the rhetorical textbooks as the figures of speech and of thought, that which concerned the arrangement of words and the structure of sentences. In the time of Crassus such matters were evidently attracting the attention of Roman orators. Crassus himself practised a euphonious arrangement of words.[71] As regards the structure of the sentence his preference was for short periods and for the brief phrase that Cicero called *membrum*.[72] In this he was following in the footsteps of the 'Asiatic' Hegesias, who had reacted against the Demosthenic period and adopted a jerky style which had become notorious. Unlike Hegesias however he did not deliberately avoid rhythm; his short clauses and sentences had a definitely rhythmical character.[73] He was not, it seems, excessively addicted to the double trochee so much beloved by the Asiatic school. It is a younger contemporary of his, Carbo, son of the Gracchan turncoat, who provides the classic example of this rhythm. In a speech which he made as tribune a sentence ending with a double trochee aroused a burst of applause which Cicero attributes solely to the effect of the rhythmical clausula.[74]

As regards delivery Crassus was relatively staid; he did not walk about and seldom stamped his foot.[75] Antonius on the other hand used every possible gesture and action to reinforce his utterances, and had even been known to kneel down in the course of a vehement speech in his own defence.[76] Whether such gestures are to be attributed to the study of *actio* as a part of rhetoric is open to question. Probably they came naturally to the Roman orator. One of Quintilian's objections to dictation is that the gestures which naturally accompany strong emotion become ridiculous when one is not alore.[77] However that may be, these gestures were an accepted part of oratory as it was generally practised at Rome, and our picture of the Roman orator must be of a melodramatic actor, strutting on his stage, thrilling his listeners by the carefully modulated tones of his voice and the expressive movements of his limbs, rather than of a model of *gravitas*.

And so we take leave of these shadowy figures who preceded Cicero. We have noted certain features in their oratory which can be attributed to their rhetorical studies, and on the whole no doubt Cicero was right in seeing a progressive development from the untaught oratory of early times to the more polished and sophisticated style which resulted from the conscious study of the art of speaking.[78] None the less it would be safe to assume that there was always a strong element in their oratory that owed nothing to theory, and that the long oratorical tradition which went back to the days when Rome knew nothing of rhetoric, remained unbroken.

V

CICERO'S RHETORICAL THEORY

Comment, dist Ponocrates, vos iurez, frere Jean? Ce n'est, dist le
moyne, que pour orner mon language. Ce sont couleurs de rhetor-
icque ciceroniane.

Rabelais, *Gargantua* ch. 39

OF CICERO'S extant works a considerable number are devoted
to rhetoric. There is *De Inventione*, dating from his youth, *De
Oratore* and *Partitiones Oratoriae* from the period of his maturity,
and the *Brutus*, the *Orator*, *De Optimo Genere Oratorum* and *Topica*
from his later years when his main activity, political and
oratorical, was over. These works may be divided into two
classes, technical and non-technical. In the first class come *De
Inventione*, *Partitiones Oratoriae*, a treatise written for the benefit of
Cicero's son, in the form of a catechism in reverse, with the
pupil asking questions and the master answering them, and
Topica, an exposition of the theory attributed to Aristotle,
written from memory during a sea voyage, to enlighten Cicero's
friend Trebatius, who had read a Greek work on the subject,
but was unable to understand it, and had applied in vain for
help to a professional rhetorician.[1]

In the second class come the rest of the rhetorical works.
Foremost among them is *De Oratore*, a discursive dialogue on
oratory in general, based on the scholastic doctrine, but treating
it in the elegant humane manner of a cultured and experienced
man of letters and man of affairs. The *Brutus* is a history of
Roman oratory in dialogue form, while the *Orator* attempts to
describe the characteristics of the complete and perfect orator.
The latter work is in effect a justification of Cicero's own
style of oratory and an answer to the critics who emerged in
his later years, and the same desire for self-justification inspires
the brief *De Optimo Genere Oratorum*, written as a preface to a

translation of the speeches of Demosthenes and Aeschines on the Crown. These works of Cicero's later life contain some new points which will be considered in a later chapter; here we will confine ourselves to *De Oratore* and those parts of the *Orator* which repeat the ideas of the earlier work.

How far can we consider these ideas as Cicero's own? He himself said of *De Oratore* that it embodied the principles of Aristotle and Isocrates and of the ancients generally.[2] Modern scholars have been inclined to look for the source of his ideas rather in the New Academy.[3] Cicero himself pointed the way to this view when he claimed to be an orator sprung from the groves of the Academy,[4] and there is a fairly clear indication in *De Oratore* that the main ideas of that work were associated with the Academic school.[5] But it would be a mistake to assume that Cicero was following at all closely an Academic source. We know what Academic rhetoric was like from *Partitiones Oratoriae*, and we have no certain evidence that any philosopher of the Academy treated the subject on the broad lines of *De Oratore*.[6] And even if Cicero owed not a little to the contemporary Academy, he also derived much from his reading in the whole field of rhetorical study.[7] The rhetoric of the schools, the theories of the philosophers, Roman traditions and Cicero's own experience are combined in a synthesis which has a sufficiently individual quality to allow us to recognise its author as an independent thinker on such matters. And even if none of the ideas or precepts in *De Oratore* is new—and it was difficult to be original in such a well worked field—the choice and combination remain Cicero's, as do the force and conviction and the elegance and charm with which they are presented.

Having said this, we must admit that for all his lively receptiveness, his competence and his charm of manner Cicero often disappoints us. He tends to fall between two stools. He does not throw to the winds the classifications of school rhetoric and the academic theories of the philosophers and give us the fruits of his experience as advocate and statesman. On the other hand he does not provide us with the intellectual delights of a profound theoretical analysis. He lacks the power or will to pursue an argument to its conclusions, and is too prone to compromise. In *De Oratore* he presents us with the contrast between Crassus the advocate of a universal culture and Antonius the representative of practical common sense, but he runs away from the problem he has posed, and at the beginning of the second book resorts to the lame device of making Antonius announce that his previous remarks did not represent his real opinion.[8] Again, the old quarrel between rhetoric and philosophy is laid to rest by the assertion that there is really no quarrel at all,[9] and the disturbing arguments of Plato are obscured by the comforting platitudes of his successors.

Let us first ask what was Cicero's attitude to the formal rhetoric of the schools. He had expounded this, or a part of it, in his earliest work, *De Inventione*. This he later regarded as immature, and in *De Oratore* he set out to produce something more worthy of his age and experience.[10] In this work he does his best to avoid the manner of the textbook; he shuns technical terms, substituting an elegant paraphrase, hurries over what is unimportant or too familiar, and digresses at length. He makes his characters several times give expression to that impatience with the Greek rhetoricians which had already been expressed by the author of *Ad Herennium*. These *Graeculi*, endlessly repeating their rules without ever having been near a law court, are compared to the philosopher Phormio, who treated Hannibal to a disquisition on the art of war.[11] They are like nurses feeding babies on little morsels of food.[12] Moreover it is claimed that the professors do not even know their job; in spite of their abundant leisure they do not succeed in classifying properly or expounding accurately.[13]

These expressions of impatience and contempt are no doubt dramatically appropriate in the mouth of the characters who are made to utter them.[14] Cicero himself perhaps would not have committed himself to them. For he had a certain respect for the rules of the *Graeculi*. At any rate he thought it necessary to bring up his son on the full rigour of the scholastic discipline, and the classifications of the schools can easily be detected in the flowing elegant prose of *De Oratore*. Indeed Cicero allowed himself the luxury of at once sneering at the Greeks and making use of them. He laughs at the idea of there being an Art of Humour; yet a little later we find him proceeding exactly in the manner of the textbook: *Duo genera sunt facetiarum* and *De risu quinque sunt quae quaerantur*.[15] He tells us, in connection with panegyric, that everything need not be referred to rules, and that everyone knows what to praise in a man, but he goes on to give a conventional list, derived from school rhetoric, of the sources from which panegyric can be drawn.[16] Even in the *Orator*, where Cicero is expressly avoiding an exposition of precepts,[17] and where he relies rather more than in *De Oratore* on his own experience, the traditional rules tend to intrude themselves.

Cicero knew that eloquence did not derive from rhetoric, but rather rhetoric from eloquence, and he makes Antonius remark that natural genius and diligence between them leave little room for the rules.[18] But he makes it clear that he thought there was some value in these rules. They do not create something new in our minds; they draw out what is already there. They serve to remind the orator to what each point should be referred and where he should look to prevent himself straying from the question at hand.[19] There are no doubt great men who can attain to eloquence without any knowledge of theory: but art is a more reliable guide than nature.[20]

Cicero, then, believed that one should know the school rules and that they were of some, though limited, use. But more was needed than a knowledge of the school theory. He himself was an orator sprung not from the rhetoricians' workshops but from the groves of the Academy,[21] and the oratory he describes in *De Oratore* and *Orator* was based on a broader and deeper culture than what was provided by the rhetorical schools.

In approaching his subject Cicero felt obliged first of all to justify oratory. Even the severely technical *De Inventione* begins with a preface on this theme. 'I have thought long and often', he begins, with all the solemnity of a man of twenty, 'over the problem whether the power of speaking and the study of eloquence have brought more good or harm to men and cities.'[22] He decides that eloquence should be combined with wisdom, and that the good and wise should not leave political life to the clever and bad, but should acquire enough eloquence to make themselves effective. His ideal is the man who possesses the highest virtue and authority, and eloquence to adorn these qualities and protect the state.[23] He supports his views by a piece of philosophising which must have formed part of the introductory lecture to many courses on rhetoric since the days of the sophists. The theme is that at one time men lived an uncivilised brutish existence, ignorant of right and wrong, of law and religion. It was oratory, in the hands of some wise leader, which led them to a civilised life.[24] The same idea reappears in *De Oratore*, as does the assertion that eloquence must be combined with wisdom.[25] Indeed that work adds little or nothing to the conventional justification of oratory given in *De Inventione*. Cicero is content with high-sounding assertions of the power of oratory to adorn virtue and dissuade from vice, to curb the violent and protect the oppressed.[26]

But these claims did not go unchallenged. Cicero makes one of his characters, the lawyer Scaevola, dispute the claim of oratory to have civilised mankind. Was it not rather men of practical good sense, without any special gifts for oratory, who performed this function? Eloquence had in fact been actually harmful at times, as in the case of the Gracchi.[27] Moreover it might be said that oratory was merely an instrument to serve certain purposes, 'to make the case you are pleading in the law courts appear to be the better and more plausible, and to make your speeches to the people and the senate as effective as possible, in fact to make the wise think your speech eloquent and fools even think it true'.[28] This cynical realistic view deserved to be considered and answered; but Cicero does not in fact answer it. In his practice he might use the arts and crafts of rhetoric to make the worse cause appear the better, and might boast of having thrown dust in the eyes of the jury,[29] but in his theory oratory was purely a power for good. Cicero did not think too much about the morality of rhetoric; the scruples of Quintilian were alien to the Republican period, when oratory was an all important weapon in the struggle for political power. Cicero would no doubt have been pained if any doubts had been raised as to the uses to which he put his own oratorical gifts. He never accused an innocent man, and if he sometimes defended a guilty man, was not this allowed by custom, by the principles of humanity and by the authority of Panaetius?[30]

Instead of answering the pertinent objections of the practical man Cicero involves himself in the theoretical dispute between the philosophers and the rhetoricians. This dispute, as we find it treated in Cicero's pages, does not go deep into the heart of the matter. Cicero knew Plato's *Gorgias*, but he is content to dismiss it with an epigram: 'In mocking the orators he showed that he was himself a supreme orator.'[31] Naturally enough he concerns himself less with Plato's criticisms than with the problem as it presented itself to his generation, and the controversies of the first century B.C., important though they no doubt seemed at the time, are of minor interest today. They arose, as we have seen, out of the mutually exclusive claims of the rhetoricians and the philosophers to be the educators of the young, and the point on which they centred was whether the general questions of a philosophical or quasi-philosophical nature which the orator might often have occasion to handle belonged to the province of rhetoric or were rather the property of philosophy.

Cicero claims such matters for the orator. In his view the orator possesses his philosophic lore in his own right and not as a loan from the philosophers. Or rather it had once been his possession, but been filched from him by the philosophers.[32] Oratory and philosophy had once been identical, and their divorce, for which Socrates is made responsible, was a regrettable development. Socrates had usurped the name of philosopher hitherto common to both sides, and since his time the philosophers had despised oratory and the orators philosophy.[33] So far as he takes sides Cicero is for oratory against philosophy. But he prefers to make up the quarrel. 'If anyone likes, he may, so far as I am concerned, give the name of orator to that philosopher who supplies us with a rich fund of matter and expression, or if he prefers to apply the name of philosopher to this orator of ours whom I declare to possess wisdom combined with eloquence, I have nothing against it; provided that it is agreed that no praise is due to the speechlessness of the man who has knowledge without being able to express it, or to the ignorance of him who has a supply of words without matter. If one must choose, I should prefer tongue-tied wisdom to loquacious folly; but if we are looking for the ideal, the palm must be given to the learned orator. And if the philosophers admit him to their number, there is an end of the controversy; if on the other hand they maintain the distinction, they must be judged inferior for this reason, that all their knowledge is to be found in the perfect orator, whereas philosophic knowledge does not necessarily imply eloquence, and eloquence, however much they may despise it, surely adds a sort of crowning grace to their science.'[34]

So then Cicero's ideal is the philosopher-statesman-orator. But it is in fact something less than this. For philosophy here means little more than having something to say, while oratory means being able to say it well. It will be noted that it is the learned orator (*doctus orator*) to whom Cicero gives the palm. We find in fact that what Cicero advocates is a wide general culture. The philosophy of his orator consists in knowing about philosophy, and philosophy is only one of the things he must know about.

That the orator should be master of a universal knowledge is indeed the main theme of *De Oratore*. As Cicero puts it in the preface to the first book, eloquence is comprised in the sciences of men of learning, and the theme is repeated in the dialogue itself. 'There is no subject which demands dignified and serious treatment that is not proper to the orator.'[35] 'No one can hope to be an orator in the true sense of the word unless he has acquired a knowledge of all the sciences and all the great problems of life.'[36] 'There is a vast field in which the orator can wander freely and everywhere find himself in his own domain.'[37]

Of this general learning philosophy was only a part, but a very important part. 'Let us first of all lay it down . . .', says Cicero in the *Orator*, 'that the perfect orator whom we are searching for cannot exist without philosophy . . . without philosophy no one can speak with breadth and fulness on great and varied themes. . . . Nor can one without philosophical training discern the genus and species of things, or define and analyse them, or judge between true and false, see logical contradictions and discern ambiguities. What shall I say of physics, which supplies much material to speeches, and of all the branches of moral philosophy, for the understanding and treatment of which a profound study of such matters is necessary?'[38] This ignores the fact that a certain amount of logical and ethical material had become embodied in the school rhetoric; it also ignores the cogent remarks of Antonius, who performs the function of *advocatus diaboli* in *De Oratore*. What need, he asks, for a theoretical knowledge of psychology? For an orator an empirical knowledge is enough. And as regards morals, he will follow common opinion; he will have no need to go into the philosophical problem of the *summum bonum*. What is wanted is that he should be 'an acute and clever man, his natural wit sharpened by experience, a keen observer of the thoughts, feelings, opinions and expecta-

CICERO'S RHETORICAL THEORY

tions of his fellow-citizens and of those whom he wishes to win over to a particular point of view'.[39]

The fact is that Cicero was interested in and attracted by philosophy and thought one ought to know about it, and so he introduced it into his educational programme. But this programme was designed for the training of the orator. He therefore persuaded himself that philosophy was of far greater use to the orator than in fact it was. In the *Orator* he demands a knowledge of logic, though the subject, naturally dull, needed the application of a little polish,[40] and of physics, the latter for the unconvincing reason that the contemplation of the heavenly bodies will result in his speaking in a more lofty and magnificent manner.[41] In *De Oratore* he is more realistic. Logic and physics he says, can be left on one side;[42] it is enough to have a thorough knowledge of moral philosophy. This branch too is justified on utilitarian grounds. It is required partly that the orator may know about the emotions of his audience which he wishes to play on, partly that he may be able to treat those themes which were always recurring, 'religion, piety, concord, friendship, the rights of citizens and of mankind, the law of nations, justice, temperance, greatness of soul and every kind of virtue'.[43]

The other main constituents of the orator's learning are law and history. An ignorance of law Cicero considers to be scandalous.[44] Obvious though this point may seem, it needed making, for the rhetorical schools did not include the study of law, and many pleaders must have approached their task well equipped to argue, let us say, for or against the letter of the law, but ill informed about the actual details of Roman law and judicial procedure.[45] After all, they could always follow Antonius's advice and apply to the professional where their knowledge was deficient.[46] So Cicero, indignant at the ignorance and impertinence of some of his fellow advocates and himself delighting in the study of Roman law and the revelation of old Roman manners it provided, permits himself the exaggerated claim that the Twelve Tables are of more value than all the libraries of the philosophers.[47]

History was chiefly of use in providing instances and examples to prove or emphasise a point. 'The recalling of past history and the production of instances from the past gives great pleasure and at the same time adds authority and credibility to a speech.'⁴⁸ But there is no doubt that Cicero had a real interest in history for its own sake apart from its oratorical application.⁴⁹ Here as elsewhere his educational programme includes more than can be justified on purely utilitarian grounds.

It is unnecessary here to go into details of Cicero's rhetorical precepts, for in most respects they are merely derived from the traditional doctrine of the schools. But there are one or two points which are peculiar to his theory or are given a particular emphasis by him, and these deserve special mention.

Firstly there is the treatment of general questions. We have seen how the rhetoricians and the philosophers had disputed over the *theses*, which Hermagoras had claimed as falling within the orator's province. In his *De Inventione* Cicero had taken Hermagoras to task for assigning to the orator questions that had nothing to do with him and which belonged rather to the philosopher.⁵⁰ He must later have regretted the confident tone with which he took sides on this matter, for he came to hold the view not only that these general questions were within the orator's sphere, but that all questions could and should be related to them. 'The perfect orator', he says, 'should always if he can remove the issue from particular persons and occasions; one can discuss the whole more freely than the part; and if something is proved in the general case, it must necessarily be proved in the particular.'⁵¹ For example in the case of the assassination of C. Gracchus by Opimius the orator need not consider the characters in the case; the question at issue is the general one, whether one who has killed a fellow citizen, contrary to the laws, but in accordance with a vote of the senate and in order to save his country, deserves punishment.⁵² But it was perhaps not so much the logical side of the matter that appealed to Cicero; it was rather the fact that general questions offered more scope for oratorical adornment than particular ones. Here the orator could really spread himself.⁵³

Cicero is indeed less interested in the appeal to the head than in that to the heart. 'Men's judgments', he tells us, 'are more often formed under the influence of hatred, love, desire, anger, grief, joy, hope, fear, misconception or some other emotion, than by truth or ordinance, the principles of justice, the procedure of the courts or the laws.'⁵⁴ Hence he gives special emphasis to the rhetorical appeal to the emotions, success in which, he holds, constitutes the chief excellence of the orator.[55]

The methods of playing on the feelings of the listener were enumerated in the textbooks, but only in connection with certain parts of the speech, the proem and, in particular, the peroration. This treatment, which Cicero had followed in *De Inventione*, did not satisfy him when he came to write *De Oratore*. In that work the subject is treated on its own, and not subordinated to particular parts of the speech.[56] Moreover his whole manner of discussing the subject is freer and less pedantic than that of the textbooks. He has got away from the fifteen methods of arousing indignation and the sixteen of arousing pity that he had faithfully copied out in *De Inventione*. His main emphasis now is on the necessity for the orator to feel the emotions he tries to arouse. 'It is impossible', he says, 'for the hearer to feel grief, hatred, prejudice, apprehension, to be reduced to tears and pity, unless all the emotions which the orator wishes to arouse in the juror are seen to be deeply impressed on the orator himself.'[57] If anyone wondered how the orator could be constantly moved to anger, grief or other emotions in matters which did not concern him personally, the answer was that the sentiments and topics he made use of had such power to move that there was no need for simulation. The very nature of the speech whose object was to move the audience would be such as to move the speaker more than anyone else. Like the actor, the orator would live his part.[58] Antonius, who in this part of *De Oratore* serves as Cicero's mouthpiece, records his defence of M'. Aquilius, and claims that his pathetic peroration came from the heart, and that when he displayed his client's wounds the action was not premeditated, but inspired by violent grief.[59] Speaking in his own person in the *Orator*, Cicero says much the same; in all his pathetic passages it was not so much his talent as his capacity for experiencing the feelings he expressed that accounted for his success.[60]

One of the methods of working on the audience to which Cicero devotes particular attention is the use of wit and humour.[61] Cicero prided himself on his mastery of this weapon and he gives in *De Oratore* a comprehensive account of its uses to the orator. Though the subject had been handled by Greek writers of the Peripatetic school,[62] Cicero was probably the first to incorporate a full treatment of it in a general treatise on rhetoric. As so often, he uses the theoretical classifications of the Greeks, but he illustrates with numerous anecdotes and examples from his own store. He is well aware, too, that wit is a thing which comes by nature rather than art.[63]

From the appeal to the heart we turn to the appeal to the ear. The consideration of style occupies most of the third book of *De Oratore*, and though in the main the matter is traditional, it is worth noting where Cicero lays the emphasis. Of the four *virtutes dicendi*, the first two, to speak *Latine* and *plane*, are, he says, easy; the remaining two, *ornate* and *apte congruenterque*, are the important qualities. It is these that make men thrill with terror, gaze open-mouthed at the speaker, cry aloud and think him a god among men.[64] Above all it is the ability to use *ornatus* that constitutes the crowning glory of eloquence.[65] How is this adornment to be come by? The answer is that it will come of its own accord to the learned orator.[66] 'Rerum enim copia verborum copiam gignit', says Cicero, giving a new turn to the old maxim of Cato, *Rem tene, verba sequentur*. If the matter is honourable, the words in which it is expressed will have a natural splendour. If the speaker is well educated, zealous to study and practised in arguing general questions, if he has chosen the most splendid models for imitation, he will not need any of the school precepts to teach him the graces of style. The abundance of his matter will lead him naturally and insensibly, with the aid of practice, to the adornments of style.[67] But Cicero, it seems, only half believes this theory. Crassus, who enunciates it, is told that he has been carried too far out to sea, and is forced to return wearily to the familiar paths of the textbooks.[68]

Our study of Cicero's rhetorical theory has perhaps emphasised its weakness rather than its strength. Yet when all that can be said in criticism has been said, we must acknowledge that he brought new life into a subject which had languished in the hands of pedants since the days of Aristotle. It was Cicero's achievement to lift rhetoric above academic pedantry and narrow professionalism to the higher level of a genuine humanism. To appreciate his contribution justly one must see it against the background of contemporary rhetorical teaching. One will then recognise the pertinence of the main theme of *De Oratore*.

In emphasising the importance of having something to say as well as knowing how to say it, and the desirability of combining the two main disciplines of the ancient world, rhetoric and philosophy, he was putting his finger on one of the weaknesses of ancient education. It was unfortunate that his message was so little heeded.

CICERONIAN ORATORY I

O flexanima atque omnium regina rerum oratio.
Pacuvius, *Tragoediae* 177 (111 Ribbeck)

OF ALL Roman orators none devoted so much thought and study to oratory as Cicero. He had a long period of education, was familiar with the literature of rhetoric and himself contributed to the theory of the subject. At the same time he was a practising orator, who pleaded numerous cases in the courts and took an active part in the debates of the senate. He is moreover the only Roman orator whose speeches have survived in bulk, so that in his case we have a unique opportunity of observing the interaction of rhetorical theory and oratorical practice.

Cicero's speeches were written out for publication after the event,[1] but there is little doubt that on the whole they give a faithful picture of the speeches as actually delivered. There is one well known exception, *Pro Milone*. In other cases additions were occasionally made.[2] More often the speech was shortened.[3] It may even be that in some cases several speeches were telescoped into one.[4] But the spirit of the spoken word is faithfully preserved, even where, as in the second *actio* against Verres and the Second Philippic, the speeches were never actually delivered. There is no attempt to get rid of repetitions and irregularities of arrangement. The fact that such features survive shows that when Cicero prepared his speeches for publication his aim was to preserve his actual words and not to tidy them up into a model oration.

Cicero's speeches then were real speeches, and any study of them which does not take into account the conditions under which they were delivered and the purposes which they were intended to serve will miss the mark. The rhetorical analyses found in older editions give the impression that Cicero constructed his speeches solely after the formulae of the rhetorical schools and without any reference to the practices of the Roman courts, the exigencies of debate and the immediate political situation. In fact Ciceronian oratory owed more to such factors as these than to the rules of the textbooks.

These rules were based on Greek practice, and when Greek rhetoric was taken over by the Romans little or no attempt was made to adapt it to different conditions. The practice of the Greek courts differed in more than one respect from that of the Roman courts. In Greece the witnesses were heard before the speeches were delivered, whereas in Rome in the normal criminal case they came after.[5] Thus in the Greek courts the speakers were in possession of all the facts of the case, and the rhetorical textbooks, being based on Greek practice, assumed that the substance of the speech would be argumentation, founded on the facts revealed in evidence. In Roman pleading much was left for the later stage when the witnesses were produced and interrogated, and it was perhaps inevitable that the preceding speeches should deal with generalities and personalities and matters not strictly relevant to the case.[6] One reason why *Pro Milone* conforms better than most of Cicero's speeches to the rhetorical model is that Pompey's laws had brought procedure into line with Greek practice by making the hearing of witnesses precede the speeches.[7]

Again, rhetorical textbooks presupposed a single speech on each side. At Rome in the period of Cicero not only were the speeches long,[8] but there might well be several of them. The practice had grown up of a defence being shared between a number of advocates.[9] In 54 B.C. Scaurus was defended by six speakers in addition to the defendant himself.[10] In defending Sestius Cicero was one of a large number of advocates,[11] and there were other cases in which he shared the defence with one colleague or with two.[12] In such circumstances it was natural that the defending counsel should share out the case between them, each concentrating on a particular aspect. Cicero himself usually spoke last because this was the point at which his emotional gifts would have greatest effect.[13] In such cases he would find most of the argumentation had already been done and would not consider it necessary to go over the ground again.[14] In these circumstances a speech constructed on the orthodox rhetorical model would be quite inappropriate.

In Greece it was usual for the accused to conduct his own case (often delivering a speech written for him by a professional); in Rome he usually had the services of one or more advocates. The advice in the rhetorical textbooks about securing a favourable hearing in the exordium and arousing pity in the peroration presupposed that the speaker was the accused person himself. These precepts could, however, be adapted without great difficulty to Roman conditions, as the advocate was often in close relation to his client. Cicero at any rate was able to identify himself with his clients' interests, so that there was no incongruity about his use of the traditional topics. It is curious to see how on occasion the peroration is made to conform to the Greek pattern by the device of prosopopoeia, by which an imaginary speech is put into the mouth of the defendant, who thus appears to be appealing for pity in his own person.[15]

It has often been observed that the forensic speeches of Cicero's mature period are largely irrelevant, that they deal hastily with the actual counts of the indictment and fully with extraneous matter. *Pro Archia*, short as it is, consists almost entirely of praise of Cicero's client and of the poetry which he practised. *Pro Sestio* is in the main an exposition of Cicero's political position. In *Pro Murena* the charge of bribery plays only a minor part;[16] about two thirds of *Pro Caelio* and four fifths of *Pro Plancio* have nothing to do with the actual charge. This habit of irrelevancy is due partly to the factors already referred to, the absence of full evidence on which to base the pleading and the practice of sharing the defence, but partly also to the traditions of the Roman courts and the political nature of many of the trials.

Roman custom allowed the advocate to indulge freely in personalities and irrelevant appeals, and it is clear enough from Cicero's references to his opponents that he was not peculiar in this respect. In *Pro Cluentio* the prosecution only touched on the charge of poisoning 'as a matter of form'.[17] In *Pro Murena* Cicero's handling of the defence was dictated by the prosecution.[18] In the case of Caelius it is evident that the defendant's private life bulked as large in the accusation as in the defence.[19] In defending Plancius Cicero found it necessary to defend himself as well, since the prosecution had said almost more about him than about the actual case and the defendant, and in the case of Publius Sulla, Torquatus the prosecuting counsel devoted the whole of his speech to an attack on Cicero, which of course demanded a reply.[20] Cicero was certainly far from reluctant to seize any opportunity for self-justification, but his claim that he never spoke about himself except under compulsion and in reply to the attacks of others was not entirely without justification.[21]

Unscrupulous personalities were indeed traditional in speeches of accusation. Cicero can refer to attacks on the defendant's private life as a *lex quaedam accusatoria*, and give a list of worthy men, including the blameless Rutilius Rufus and the upright Piso, who when on trial had had to listen to foul and unjust aspersions on their morals.[22] When Cicero himself conducted a prosecution, that of Verres, he prided himself, not without justice, on not following the usual unscrupulous methods of an accuser.[23]

Criminal trials were often intimately connected with the political struggles of the day, and the verdict was sometimes given on political rather than judicial grounds. We need only quote Cicero himself on this subject. 'During my recent consulship', he says, when defending Flaccus on a charge of extortion, 'I defended L. Murena the consul-designate. The prosecution was conducted by men of the highest distinction, and none of those who formed the jury thought that it was a question of listening to a charge of bribery; Catiline was waging open war, and guided by me, all realised that there must be two consuls on the first of January. Twice in this year I have secured the acquittal of an innocent and good man, a man of the highest distinction, Aulus Thermus. What delight throughout Rome, what congratulations followed, and all for reasons of public policy. In giving their verdict wise and responsible jurymen have always considered what is demanded by the interests of state, the safety of all and the immediate political situation.'[24]

The advocate was usually himself a politician and in many cases bound to his client by ties of friendship and common interest. Cicero often undertook a case in order to repay an obligation, and this was regarded as legitimate and praiseworthy. He gives as his reason for defending C. Rabirius not only interests of state, but also his old friendship with the accused.[25] In defending Murena he explains in answer to the bitter complaints of Sulpicius and Cato, who accused him of neglecting the ties that bound him to Sulpicius, that he had a close and long-standing friendship with Murena.[26] The speeches for Flaccus, Sestius and Plancius all open with references to the services of the accused to Cicero. In *Pro Archia* Cicero maintains with obvious exaggeration that he owes his interest in literary studies, and hence his oratorical ability, mainly to Archias, and is therefore under an obligation to help the man to whom he owes that ability.[27]

To these circumstances the academic rules of rhetoric were of little relevance. In his early speeches Cicero followed more or less the prescriptions of the textbooks, but as he grew older and more experienced and became more closely concerned with politics, he emancipated himself from them, and the speeches of his maturity are far away from the models of the schools. The exception is *Pro Milone*; this, as we have seen, was delivered under the exceptional conditions created by Pompey's laws of 52 B.C. It was also written up after the event and has something of the character of a rhetorical exercise.

Cicero's development can be observed fairly clearly in the matter of the arrangement of the speech. The textbooks ordained that the orator should open with a proem; should then expound the facts; define the point at issue and state what he proposed to prove; should prove his case by argument, then refute his opponent; and finally should end with a peroration. In one respect this scheme was clearly impracticable; refutation could not in practice be separated from argumentation. Cicero himself recognised this in theory, and his speeches bear out his opinion.[28] Apart from this Cicero's earliest speeches follow the model well enough. His first speech, *Pro Quinctio*, opens with a thoroughly orthodox exordium; a *narratio* follows; there is a clear *divisio*, followed by an orderly *confirmatio*, dealing in turn with the points outlined in the *divisio*. Finally there is a peroration with all the conventional pathos. *Pro Roscio Amerino* already marks an advance towards the freedom of the later speeches. Even in the exordium we notice the bold reference to Chrysogonus which shows that Cicero was beginning to speak from himself and not from the textbook. But in general the arrangement of the speech conforms pretty well to school teaching.[29] There is a proem, a *narratio* and a *divisio*, though not perhaps of an orthodox character; there is of course argumentation, and finally an unmistakable peroration.

In the later speeches the scholastic scheme is much obscured. In the accusation of Verres the facts spoke for themselves, and Cicero's speech might be said to consist almost entirely of *narratio*. On the other hand the defence in a case *de repetundis* would generally wish at all costs to avoid a *narratio*, and this part of the speech finds no place in Cicero's defences of Fonteius, Flaccus and Scaurus. In his civil cases we find the formal *narratio*,[30] but in his criminal cases there is seldom anything that really deserves the name until we come to *Pro Milone* and *Pro Ligario*, both the product of abnormal circumstances.[31] As Cicero himself said, 'when to use *narratio* and when not is a matter for the orator's discretion'.[32] The *divisio* too is sometimes missing, sometimes obscured and sometimes out of place.[33] In fact apart from the exordium and the peroration there is in many of the speeches little of the traditional arrangement.

We have seen that scholastic rhetoric devoted much attention to the doctrine of the *constitutio* or *status*, the question at issue, but it may be surmised that Cicero seldom had to think very hard about how to classify a case. 'In most of my criminal cases', says Antonius in *De Oratore*, 'the defence denies the charge',[34] and he speaks for Cicero too. There are one or two exceptions. *Pro Balbo* involves the interpretation of law. In *Pro Rabirio perduellionis reo* Cicero ventured on what Quintilian calls a *coniuncta defensio*, a mixture of *constitutio coniecturalis* and *iuridicialis*,[35] and in the other *Pro Rabirio*, as Quintilian observes, he begins by contending that the action cannot lie against a Roman knight, but later asserts that no money came into Rabirius's hands.[36] In the case of Milo it could not be denied that Milo killed Clodius. One line of defence was that recommended by some and adopted by Brutus in the speech he wrote as a rhetorical exercise, to admit the deed but claim that it was justified. Cicero preferred to use this as a secondary argument, and base his defence on the contention that Clodius had laid a trap for Milo,[37] thus making the question at issue, as far as it could be made, one of fact, which of the two laid a trap for the other.[38] Finally there is one case among Cicero's speeches of perhaps the rarest of all types, *deprecatio*, where guilt was admitted and an appeal made for mercy. This treatment, the textbooks said, was unsuited to the courts, and Cicero used it only when he pleaded for Ligarius before Caesar. 'I have pleaded many cases with you, Caesar', he says, '. . . but never one of this sort: "Pardon him, gentlemen of the jury; he made a mistake; he slipped up; he never thought . . .; if ever again. . . ." That is how one pleads before a father. In the courts it is: "He did not do it, did not consider it; the witnesses are false, the charge invented." '39

As regards the use of arguments Cicero had presumably, to judge by his expressed views on their utility, learnt something from the scholastic rules. The system provided the instrument for discovering all the topics of argument inherent in a particular situation, and no doubt the orator sometimes found it useful to run through in his mind the academic classification in case anything suitable had escaped him. But the experienced speaker could find the appropriate arguments without much difficulty,40 and if at times Cicero's practice agrees with the textbook precepts, it does not follow that he would not have argued in the same way if he had never read the textbooks.

Of the arguments prescribed by rhetoric for the *constitutio coniecturalis* the first was that from probability, including the man's previous life. Cicero dwells much on the life and character of his clients. In some speeches the theme falls into its place with other arguments, but in many cases the past life of the accused is dwelt on not so much as an argument contributing to the probability or improbability of the charge as a point in his favour irrespective of the crime of which he is accused. Cicero's praise of Archias is not designed to show the unlikelihood of his having assumed citizenship illegally, but simply to create a prejudice in his favour, and so it is in other cases where Cicero dwells on the merits of his clients.

Pro Milone is perhaps the speech where it is easiest to see the textbook arguments being deployed. There we find the argument from probability, including possible motives and previous life; the argument from comparison; circumstantial evidence (place, time and opportunity); arguments drawn from behaviour before the event and after.41 Generally however Cicero made little use of these familiar topics. 'Why', he asks in *Pro Caelio*, 'should I oppose the charge with the countless arguments that are available? I could say that Caelius's way of life is the very antithesis of such a terrible crime; that it is incredible that so gifted and sensible a man should have failed to see that a crime of such magnitude was not a business to be trusted to unknown slaves not his own. I could follow my own custom and that of other advocates and ask the prosecution where Caelius met Lucceius's slaves and how he got there; if in person, what incredible rashness! If through another's agency, through whose? I could enumerate every possible ground of suspicion; you will seek in vain for motive, place, opportunity, accomplices, hope of fulfilment and concealment, for any reason or subsequent trace of this dreadful crime. All such matters ... I pass over in the interests of brevity.'[42] Arguments of this sort were, it seems, too obvious, and only to be dealt with by 'passing over'.

Another argument that had become rather trite was that from the spirit as against the letter of the law. This was familiar both in the schools and in the courts. 'If their opponents appeal to wording and the letter and, as the saying goes, to the full rigour of the law, then they usually counter such unfairness with the honourable and weighty appeal to fairness and justice. Then they mock the formulas with their 'ifs' and 'if nots', and discredit verbal catches and the snares involved in a letter; they loudly exclaim that a case ought to be decided by fairness and justice not by cunning and astuteness; that a false accuser follows the letter of the law, whereas a good juryman adheres to the meaning and intention of the man who framed it.'[43] Cicero when he treats this theme in *Pro Caecina* is a little more subtle. He tries to show that both the letter and the spirit of the law are on his side.[44] He has it both ways. He argues for *sententia* against *scriptum* and convicts his opponent of a verbal quibble, but at the same time finds occasion to defend the lawyers and the law.[45]

Familiar themes from the schools can be recognised on occasion where Cicero resorts to commonplace. *Pro Roscio Amerino* offered an opportunity too good to be missed, and Cicero declaimed on the heinousness of parricide with all the exuberance of his youthful style and, as he recorded later, with great effect.[46] His later speeches often contain passages which might be classed as commonplace in the sense of *certae rei quaedam amplificatio*,[47] but these owe more to Cicero's general education and philosophical interests than to school rhetoric. The other kind of commonplace, for and against rumours, witnesses, etc, sometimes came in useful, as in cases *de repetundis*, when there was little the defence could do except impugn the prosecution's witnesses.[48]

While other parts of the speech often do not conform at all to the rhetorical model, the peroration seldom disappoints. Cicero did not often use the recapitulation which was recommended at this point, though there is an example in the Verrines, where the length of the pleading rendered it desirable;[49] as regards appeals to the emotions, however, a stock feature of the peroration, Cicero saw no reason to break away from tradition. His pathetic perorations were notorious.[50] His earliest speech, *Pro Quinctio*, ends with an elaborate appeal for pity. In *Pro Caecina*, the only other example of Cicero's pleading in a civil case that has come down to us complete, the pathetic note is absent from the peroration. But it is seldom missing in the criminal defences. Politicians scheming for office, hard-hearted provincial governors on trial for misgovernment, are depicted in the most piteous plight, weeping and appealing for mercy; their young children, their fathers, their mothers and sisters join in their tears and reinforce their appeals.[51] Even in the most inappropriate cases the pathetic note is dragged in. The gay young Caelius might be ill cast for the role of weeping suppliant, but his aged father could fill his place.[52] The tough Milo might have no use for tears and refuse to simulate them, but Cicero could not bring himself to dispense with a pathetic end to his speech; the client's eyes may be dry, but the advocate is dissolved in tears.[53]

If there is comparatively little of the school rhetoric in Cicero's forensic speeches, there is even less in his deliberative. Rhetoric had not much to say on this branch of oratory, and what it had to say was of an abstract and academic nature and of small relevance to either senatorial debate or speeches before the people.[54] Cicero's earliest political speech, that in support of the Manilian Law, though considerably later in date than his first forensic speech, is reminiscent of it in its regular plan and clear arrangement of argument. But when

Cicero was well established in public life, he did not compose his speeches with such care. His senatorial speeches bear little relation to the rules of arrangement; one has only to think of the first speech against Catiline, where Cicero ignores all the rules about exordia and opens with a series of indignant questions.[55] In the intimate atmosphere of the senate house and in the excitement of political debate the formalities of oratory went by the board.

According to Quintilian, the senate demanded a certain loftiness in those who addressed it, whereas a more impetuous style was suited to speeches to the people.[56] This no doubt is what should have been the case, but it is doubtful whether it was so in actual fact. A more dignified style seems to have prevailed in the *contio* than in the senate, if we can judge by Cicero's two speeches after his return from exile. That in the senate is in places rich in abuse and colloquial in style, whereas that to the people is formal and dignified.[57] Personal abuse is indeed a feature of Cicero's senatorial oratory; Quintilian mentions three speeches delivered in the senate which were full of vituperation. Of the three two are lost, but the violent tirade against Piso survives to illustrate Cicero's remarkable vocabulary of abuse.[58]

This chapter would not be complete without a brief consideration of Cicero's style in relation to rhetorical precept. As we have seen, the rhetorical textbooks under the heading of *elocutio* did little more than give a list of the figures of speech and of thought, and everyone who had been through the schools knew these and could and did use them. There is the story of Caespasius and his ruined peroration. 'Look gentlemen', he said, 'on the fortunes of mankind, look on the changes and chances of life, look on the aged Fabricius', and having said this he himself looked, and found that Fabricius had left the court. Everyone laughed, except Caespasius, who found himself unable to proceed with his peroration.[59] Cicero, who tells the story, sneers at the 'profound artistry' of the threefold repetition of the word 'look'. Such tricks were well known. Nosti illas ληκύθους.

But in spite of their hackneyed character the figures undoubtedly play an important part in Ciceronian oratory. The very figure of anaphora which Caespasius used with such disastrous

results occurs with unfailing regularity in Cicero's pathetic perorations. The characteristic feature of Cicero's oratory is the
appeal to the emotions; emotional appeal demanded *amplificatio*
and *amplificatio* demanded *ornatus*. The brilliant, fiery and
pathetic passages of Cicero, the passages where the audience
would be carried away by the power and beauty of the words,
depend for their effect partly on the rhythm and structure, but
partly also on the *lumina dicendi*. Rhetorical questions, exclamations, repetition of words, those old figures which, as we have
seen, had their roots in popular speech but had been refined by
art, and which had formed a part of excited oratory since the
earliest days, these we find again and again in Cicero, whenever
we are conscious of a heightening of the emotional effect, and
with them on occasion rarer and more sophisticated figures such
as prosopopoeia. Cicero has all the figures at his finger ends
and they are an essential part of his more elevated style. If
illustration is wanted we may turn to the first speech against
Catiline. We open with a series of rhetorical questions. 'Quo
usque tandem abutere, Catilina, patientia nostra?' How much
more effective, says Quintilian, than if he had merely said:
'Diu abuteris patientia nostra.'[60] There follows another rhetorical question combined with anaphora: 'Nihilne te nocturnum
praesidium Palati, nihil urbis vigiliae, nihil timor populi, etc.'[61]
Then we have the exclamation, 'O tempora, o mores,'[62]
followed by 'Senatus haec intelligit, consul videt; hic tamen
vivit. vivit? immo vero ... etc.' Here too is a figure; the first
word of one clause, Quintilian notes, is the same as the last
one of the preceding.[63] Shortly afterwards comes an *exemplum*,
which the rhetoricians regarded as a figure; then a case of
παράλειψις or *praeteritio* (nam illa nimis antiqua praetereo ...)[64]
then two examples of doubling (*conduplicatio*); 'Fuit, fuit ista
quondam in hac republica virtus ...' and 'Nos, nos, dico aperte,
consules desumus.'[65] Later on we have no fewer than two
examples of prosopopoeia; twice the fatherland is made to speak,
once to Catiline and once to Cicero himself.[66]

Whether these adornments were the natural product of the
orator's *copia rerum* and of the splendour of his subject matter,
as Crassus in *De Oratore* would have it, or were due to Cicero's
rhetorical studies, there is no doubt that they were an essential
part of the art of persuasion as practised by him.

CICERONIAN ORATORY II

Ieiunas igitur huius multiplicis et aequabiliter in omnia genera
fusae orationis aures civitatis accepimus easque nos primi, quicum-
que eramus et quantulumcumque dicebamus, ad huius generis
audiendi incredibilia studia convertimus.

Cicero, *Orator* 106

In the preceding chapter we have discussed Cicero's oratory
in relation to school rhetoric. But Cicero's own rhetorical
theory included much more than was contained in the scholastic
system, and it is pertinent to pursue our enquiry further and
ask how far his oratory corresponds with the characteristic
ideas expressed in his rhetorical works.

He himself considered his way of speaking novel and out of the
ordinary. 'I will say nothing of myself', he wrote in the *Brutus*,
'I will speak only of the other orators, none of whom gave the
impression of having studied literature more deeply than the
common run of men, literature which is the fountain head of
perfect eloquence; no one who had embraced philosophy, the
mother of all good deeds and good words; no one who had learnt
civil law, a subject most necessary for private cases and essential
to the orator's good judgment; no one who had at his command
the traditions of Rome, from which if occasion demanded he
could call up most trustworthy witnesses from the dead; no one
who by rapid and neat mockery of his opponent could unbend
the minds of the jurymen and turn them awhile from solemnity
to smiling and laughter; no one who could widen an issue and
bring his speech from a limited dispute referring to a particular
person or time to a general question of universal application; no
one who could delight by a temporary digression from the issue,
or could move the judge to violent anger or tears, or in fact—
and this is the special quality of the orator—could turn his
feelings whithersoever the occasion demanded.'[1]

It is evident that the qualities absent in others were those on which Cicero prided himself, and these qualities, literary culture, knowledge of philosophy, law and history, wit, ability to pass from the particular to the general, emotional power, play a large part in his own theory of oratory.[2] Thus he considered himself, naturally enough, to exemplify the ideal which he set out in *De Oratore*.

How far do the speeches bear out Cicero's conception of his own qualities? In the first place we may say that in them we find as good an example of the *doctus orator* as we can expect in the circumstances. Cicero does not of course display the full range of his learning before the audiences of the courts and public assemblies, but he contrives to introduce a number of literary and historical references and philosophical, or quasi-philosophical, disquisitions which showed that he was an orator of no ordinary education.

That literary allusions were something of a novelty in the courts is suggested by a passage of the early speech *Pro Roscio Amerino*. 'Do you think', says Cicero, '. . . that the old man in Caecilius had less regard for Eutychus his country-loving son than for the other—Chaerestratus, I think his name is—, that he kept one in the town as an honour and banished the other to the country as a punishment?' Here it seems there was an interruption from the other side: 'Why do you resort to such puerilities?'[3] and Cicero proceeds to explain the reason for the literary reference. The explanation is rather awkward, and in later years, when he was more sure of himself, Cicero managed things better. But there were still occasions when some apology was needed. In the speech against Piso he forbears to quote from the Greek poetry of Philodemus, fearing that even what he has already said on the subject may be out of keeping with the traditions of the senate where he is speaking, and in *Pro Sestio* he is careful to defend himself for describing a scene in the theatre: 'At this point, gentlemen, I ask you not to suppose that frivolous motives have induced me to resort to the unusual procedure of speaking in the courts about poets, actors and public festivals.'[4]

Cicero knows, too, how to make himself acceptable to an audience which may be a little suspicious of learning by means of adroit flattery. 'I am not speaking to an ignorant audience, but, as I suppose, in a highly educated and humane company.'[5]

So Cicero speaks to the senate. In the law courts, too, when defending Archias, he begins by paying a compliment to the learning and refinement of his hearers before coming forward as the champion of literature.[6]

On occasion Cicero even quotes poetry in his speeches. As Quintilian remarks, the practice pleased the hearers as well as showing the speaker's learning, since the charms of poetry provided a pleasant relief from the severity of the forum; moreover the sentiments of the poet could be used like witnesses to support the orator's statements.[7] There is a line from Ennius in *Pro Roscio Amerino*, but quotations are most frequent in the period following Cicero's return from exile, the period of *De Oratore*.[8] They are usually from the older Roman drama; they are introduced in an easy, allusive manner and often ingeniously woven into the argument, as in *Pro Caelio*, where Cicero purports to be in doubt as to what attitude he should adopt towards the young Caelius's misdeeds. Is he to play the part of the stern father in Caecilius or that of the lenient father in Terence? The quotations from comedy help to induce the right atmosphere of easy tolerance.[9]

Cicero does not of course go so far as to quote Greek in his speeches, but he does on occasion show his knowledge of Greek legend and literature. In *Pro Scauro* he refers to the story celebrated in one of Callimachus's epigrams, of Cleombrotus, who committed suicide after reading Plato's *Phaedo*.[10] Even in a speech before the people such allusions were not out of place; in *Pro Lege Manilia* he compares Mithridates to Medea scattering her brother's limbs in order to retard her father's pursuit.[11]

Towards the end of his life, when some people expressed surprise at his output of philosophical works, Cicero answered that he had always been interested in the subject, and pointed to the fact that his speeches were full of philosophic maxims.[12] It is true that even if Cicero had written no philosophical treatises, his speeches would reveal that he was at any rate familiar with the main tenets of the contemporary philosophies; he could criticise with knowledge the Stoicism of Cato, and the Epicureanism of Piso,[13] and allude briefly to the views of the philosophers on pleasure or on immortality.[14] But when he spoke of his speeches being full of philosophy he was using the term in a wide sense, to include maxims and disquisitions on such themes as gratitude, glory and piety,[15] or such a passage as that in *Pro Sestio*, where to assist in demonstrating the absurdity of accusing Sestius of *vis* he gives an account of the origin of society. 'At one time, when there was as yet no natural law or civil law, men wandered over the land scattered and dispersed, and owned only what they could obtain or keep by force of hand through killing and wounding. So those who first showed themselves to be of outstanding wisdom and strength of character, perceiving the nature of the human mind and its capacity for learning, brought men together into one place and transformed them from barbarity to justice and gentleness. Then grew up those institutions for the common benefit which we call constitutions and those unions of men that were afterwards called states, then those conjunctions of dwelling places which we call cities were fortified and divine and human law began to be recognised. And the great difference between this civilised and humane life and that old barbarous one lies in the contrast between law and violence.'[16] This is philosophy adapted to the courts; it is not definite enough to be unacceptable; it is vague, uplifting and almost wholly irrelevant, a mere adornment, but designed to give the impression that Cicero's case was based on a sure intellectual foundation.

Besides literature and philosophy the other two elements in the learning Cicero brought to oratory were law and history. As regards law Cicero had evidently taken considerable pains to equip himself adequately,[17] and in his early period did not refuse to undertake civil cases of considerable complexity, such as the defence of Caecina. After his consulship he gave up this type of pleading, and most of his criminal cases did not make any great demands on his legal knowledge. In one case, however, that of Balbus, although he had been preceded by other advocates, who, he said, had left him little to say,[18] he argued the legal point in detail and with a wealth of precedent.

Almost any speech will provide examples of Cicero's use of history. The great names of the past were constantly on his lips. Precedents are useful weapons to any advocate or political orator, but the Roman respect for tradition and belief in the virtues of past ages gave them perhaps a greater weight at Rome than they have had in other societies. 'Precedents', says Cicero, 'drawn from age-old tradition and from literary records, rich in grandeur, rich in antiquity . . . . . these afford the weightiest proof to the mind, the sweetest sound to the ear.'[19] 'No man', observed Charles James Fox of Cicero, 'appears to have had such a real respect for authority as he, and therefore when he speaks on that subject, he is always natural and in earnest and not like those among *us* who are so often declaiming about the wisdom of our ancestors, without knowing what they mean, or hardly citing any particulars of their conduct, or of their dicta.'[20] In fact Cicero does not always give particulars, and there are in his speeches many general appeals to the authority of *maiores nostri*. He could, however, produce details where necessary, and whenever he wanted precedents to prove his point he had them ready. Some are the stock examples from the rhetorical schools, but more come from Cicero himself, from the well stored mind of one who had a real interest in history for its own sake and whose equipment in this respect was at least as good as can be expected of a practising orator.

Examples have now been given of the way in which Cicero applied his learning in his speeches, and it remains to discuss those other features of his oratory, his wit and humour, his power of seeing the general question behind the particular case, his digressions and his pathos and emotional power.

Cicero was famous in antiquity for his wit, or perhaps one should say notorious, for he was thought by some to have used this weapon to excess and not always with taste.[21] After his death a collection of his witticisms was published in three books. It was too many; not all of the witticisms were up to standard.[22] Cicero's quickness in retort would be exercised not in the formal speech but in replies to interruptions and examinations of witnesses. In the actual speeches there was often occasion for other types of humour, ranging from the notorious puns on the name Verres[23] to the light urbanity of *Pro Caelio*. To classify and exemplify the various types of Ciceronian humour would not be a very profitable task;[24] it will suffice to mention one speech, *Pro Murena*, where the humour is integral to the conduct of the case. A large part of the speech is taken up with mockery of Cicero's opponents, Sulpicius and Cato, both unusually honest men. Though he respected Sulpicius's legal lore and Cato's Stoicism, his speech makes the former appear trivial and ridiculous, the latter inhuman and fantastic. Cicero's

F

in another source this is said to be criticis

humour was successful. He made all the judges laugh, and Cato himself smiled and observed: 'What a witty consul we have!'[25] Cicero won his case.

Cicero's claim that he could see the general question behind a particular case may seem impertinent in view of such speeches as *Pro Murena*, where he is more anxious to get away from than behind the issue. Indeed it must be admitted that in this respect Cicero does not live up to his theory. The theory was that in any case the particular persons and circumstances were of little importance in comparison with the general principle involved, and that in all questions with which he was confronted the orator could and should pass from the particular to the general. But more often than not such treatment would have been far from profitable. The particular person concerned mattered much, the general principle little. Cicero knew this well enough, and his theory, attractive and plausible as it sounds when expounded in his rhetorical works, was in fact of little relevance to his oratory. He does indeed discuss general questions on occasion, but only incidentally. In *Pro Murena* he treats of the relative merits of the military and the legal career, but this is of no relevance to the question of Murena's guilt.[26] In *Pro Caelio* he discourses on the upbringing of the young; but this is hardly the general question behind the charges against Caelius.[27] Cicero's θετικώτερον *genus* does not in fact amount to more than that predilection for general themes of a quasi-philosophical nature to which we have already alluded.[28]

A digression in Cicero's view might occur at any point in the speech if the occasion demanded it,[29] a convenient theory which allowed any amount of departure from the point. But theory had little to do with most of Cicero's irrelevancies, which sprang from the exigencies of debate and from the need to answer opponents, to divert the attention of the audience and to induce the right atmosphere. Cicero did, however, sometimes make use of the formal digression, designed to entertain and followed by a return to the point, as in the praise of Sicily and the story of the rape of Proserpine in the Verrines.[30] There was a famous example, too, in the lost *Pro Cornelio*, where, having mentioned the name of Pompey, Cicero broke off abruptly and digressed to sing the praises of the great commander.[31]

Finally we come to Cicero's emotional power. We have seen

how, following precept and precedent, he regularly introduced
the pathetic into his perorations. But his theory did not confine
emotional appeal to any particular part of the speech, and his
practice agrees with his theory. One has only to think of the
Verrine orations, where Cicero does not confine himself to a
bare narration of Verres's misdeeds, but repeatedly takes occasion to arouse the indignation of his imaginary audience.
Quintilian instances the account of the wrongs suffered by
Philodamus and the description of the scourging of a Roman
citizen,[32] and many other examples could be added. Even the
third speech, the most factual and least adorned, has its outbursts of indignation.[33]

Cicero tells us that there was no method by which the feelings
of an audience could be aroused or calmed that he had not
tried.[34] But what made his use of pathos so effective was his
power of feeling the emotions he wished to arouse. He would be
as much affected by his pathetic passages as his audiences; his
tears would flow and his voice falter. 'I have seen that little tear-
drop of yours', said Laterensis, referring to one of Cicero's
unsuccessful defences; to which Cicero replied unrepentantly
'You could have seen not only a little drop, but a flood of tears
and weeping and sobbing.'[35] After his description in *Pro Caelio*
of the death-bed scene of Metellus Celer he has to pause for a
while to recover himself before going on; the mention of Metellus
has made his voice falter with weeping, and sorrow has checked
the flow of his thoughts.[36] Cicero's sorrow in this and similar
cases was perhaps as genuine as an emotion so easily aroused can
be. At any rate it seemed convincing, and it generally had the
required effect. Even Caesar, when Cicero pleaded for Ligarius
before him, shook with emotion and dropped his papers from his
hand.[37] If such was the effect of Cicero's oratory in an uncon-
genial atmosphere, what must it have been in the familiar
surroundings of the courts? Under the spell the jurymen would
dissolve in tears, forget their reasoning powers and follow their
feelings. 'In my opinion', says Quintilian, 'the audience did
not know what they were doing, their applause sprang neither
from their judgment nor from their will; they were seized with a
kind of frenzy and, unconscious of the place in which they stood,
burst forth spontaneously into a perfect ecstasy of delight.'[38]

The qualities we have so far considered were not the only ones

that made Cicero's oratory what it was. He also had a style of
his own, and one which was not universally admired. Some of
his contemporaries, according to Quintilian, 'dared to attack
him as too turgid, as Asiatic and redundant, as too much given
to repetition and sometimes insipid in his witticisms, as feeble,
diffuse, and even, incredible as it may seem, effeminate in composition. . . . He was particularly attacked by those who wished
to appear imitators of the Attic orators.'[39]

What did Cicero's critics mean when they called his style
Asiatic? In origin Asiatic and Attic were not critical terms
at all, but merely referred to the place where the oratory was
composed. But critics observed a difference between the oratory
of Attica and that of Asia Minor, the former direct and un-
affected, the latter too often lacking these qualities. It would be
probably true to say that 'Asiatic' oratory was in essence the
oratory of the Hellenistic age rather than that of Asia. Its
faults were due to the temptation to idle display which sprang
from the divorce of oratory from practical affairs.[40] But
however that may be, the term 'Asiatic' came to be used of a
certain type of oratory, or rather of more than one type. Cicero
distinguished two, one pointed and epigrammatic, neat and
graceful rather than solemn and dignified, the other marked by
a rapid excited flow of words and an ornamental type of diction.[41]
It is not easy to grasp the essence of a prose style from descriptions of this sort, and the information that Hortensius combined
the two types only leaves us more in the dark.[42] But it would be
idle to find a precise critical meaning in what was not much
more than a catchword adopted by the would-be revivers of the
Attic style who came into prominence about the middle of the
first century B.C.[43] It was their aim to reproduce the straightforward simplicity of Lysias,[44] and they rejected as Asiatic the
opposite type of oratory, the bombastic, elaborate and over-
rhythmical.

The two leaders of this movement among Roman orators,
indeed the only two whom we can with certainty reckon as
Atticists, were Brutus and Calvus.[45] Their period of popularity was
brief,[46] but they were sufficiently formidable to provoke Cicero
to friendly controversy. There was an exchange of letters (now
no longer extant) between him and the two Atticists,[47] and
for the benefit of a wider public Cicero took up once more the

general theory of rhetoric in the *Orator*, where he repeated some of the principles enunciated earlier in *De Oratore* and added much more designed to convert his critics and justify his own style of oratory. The same purpose underlies *De Optimo Genere Oratorum*, and is faintly perceptible in the *Brutus*.

Cicero's method of self-defence is to accept his opponents' premise that Athens provides the best models, but to show that he had as much right as they had to be called Atticist. He does not defend the Asiatic manner; indeed he has many criticisms to make of it. He maintains that his critics' conception of Atticism is limited and inadequate. Lysias was the chief model of the neo-Attic school, though sometimes they tried to imitate Thucydides[48] or Xenophon, in spite of these writers not having been orators.[49] Cicero recognised Lysias's merits, but did not think him the best model. Calvus had learned from him a dull and arid style.[50] Cicero does not deny that the Lysianic qualities of clarity and good taste were truly Attic, but he maintains that they were only a part of Atticism. Demosthenes was as much an Attic orator as Lysias, and Cicero, who claimed to take Demosthenes as his model,[51] had a perfect right to be considered a true Atticist. Popular opinion, he maintains in the *Brutus*, is the final judge of oratory; the audience decides whether an orator is successful, though the expert may judge by what means he achieves his success. Demosthenes was a popular orator; so was Cicero. The Atticists on the other hand were too cold and stiff to hold their audiences.[52]

The model for oratory was admittedly to be found in Athens, but the virtues of the Attic style were not merely, as the neo-Atticists seemed to think, those of negative good taste. The Attic orators were not content with mere health; they had strength, muscle, blood. One should if possible imitate the power and variety of Demosthenes rather than the narrow range of Lysias. To speak in a full, rich and ornate style is perfectly compatible with Attic purity and faultlessness. A speech should not merely be unobjectionable; it should also arouse positive admiration. These qualities were present in Demosthenes, and the man who took him as a model would be not only a good Atticist, but also, what was more important, a good orator.[53]

In order to emphasise his point Cicero in the *Orator* makes play with the division of the three styles, *genus tenue, genus medium* and *genus grande.* He associates with it another tripartite division, that of the three aims of the orator, to instruct, to please and to win over. The plain style was suited for instruction, the middle style was that which gave pleasure, the grand style that which carried the audience away. The perfect orator should be master of all three styles, should be able to instruct, to please and to persuade.[54] Lysias, and his Roman imitators, excelled only in the plain style, whereas Demosthenes and Cicero had all three styles at their command.[55] Different types of speech would demand different styles, but in most speeches all three should be brought into play. The orator will know on what occasion and in what parts of his speech to use the different styles; he will be able to speak of ordinary things simply, great things magnificently and things in between in a middle way.[56] He must be guided by his good taste and sense of propriety: 'Always in every part of a speech as of life one must consider what is appropriate or befitting.' 'The foundation of eloquence as of everything else is *sapientia*', and *sapientia* is here not so much the wisdom of the philosophers as good taste, that quality which according to Horace is the *principium et fons* of good writing.[57]

With the same intention, that of justifying his own style, Cicero included in the *Orator* a careful and detailed study of prose rhythm and periodic structure, a subject which he had only briefly treated in *De Oratore*.[58] He was convinced that the use of rhythmical prose contributed in no small degree to the effect of the varied and vigorous style which he advocated. The Atticists had no use for the rounded period and preferred broken and abrupt sentences; Brutus favoured an iambic rhythm which suggested the language of ordinary speech.[59] In answer Cicero appeals to a number of Greek authorities and to the sensitive ear which expects and delights in harmonious rhythm. He compares the Atticists to those who would attempt to break up the shield of Phidias; the individual beauties would remain, the general effect be lost.[60] He suggests, too, that their rejection of the Ciceronian style was due to inability to use it rather than deliberate choice.[61] He was well aware that rhythmical prose without good matter and good vocabulary was an empty thing, that it must not approach too near to the rhythms of poetry and that it must only be used sparingly in forensic speeches.[62] But he insisted that it was a valuable element in good speaking, without which ideas and beauties of diction lost much of their effect. 'There is no thought', he says, 'which can help the orator unless it is expressed aptly and with finish, nor does any verbal beauty shine forth unless the words are carefully arranged, and in both of these cases the effect is due to rhythm.'[63]

While Cicero's claim to be a true Atticist was little more than clever argument designed to cut the ground from under the feet of Brutus and Calvus, his remarks on rhythm are founded on his own practice, and point to an important and recognised element in his oratory. There is no room here for the detailed study of his prose rhythm that would be necessary for an adequate treatment of this subject.[64] We must content ourselves with observing that the use of rhythm and periodic structure was certainly one of the most characteristic features of Cicero's style, and though he did not introduce it to Roman oratory, he developed it further than any of his predecessors. And he believed, no doubt rightly, that it contributed much to his success. 'My ears certainly delight in a completely rounded period, are conscious of abruptness and dislike redundancy. Mine, do I say? I have often observed a public meeting to break into cries at a rhythmical sentence ending.'[65] The appeal to the ear was as important as the appeal to the head and the heart.

It remains to add a brief note on Cicero's contemporaries. How far did they share his characteristics? There is not much evidence on which to go, but it seems that, whether owing to his influence or because of the intellectual atmosphere of the period, there were others who went some way towards realising the ideal of the *doctus orator*. Quotations from poetry were, we are told, common in the speeches of his contemporaries.[66] Others besides him displayed something of their philosophical education in their speeches; Cato succeeded in making his rigid Stoicism acceptable to Roman audiences, and Caesar, on that memorable occasion when the senate debated the fate of Catiline, argued much in the style of Cicero's philosophical oratory that death was no punishment but rather a release.[67] Pompey defending Balbus showed his accurate knowledge of law,[68] and there is evidence that others besides Cicero could produce precedents from history.[69] Nor was he the only Roman speaker who could sway his audience by emotional appeals. Hortensius was skilled in the use of pathos.[70] Scaurus, speaking in his own defence, made a deep impression on the court by his tears and by his references to his past popularity and his father's prestige.[71] In the debate in the senate on the return of Cicero from exile Publius Servilius Isauricus reduced Metellus to tears, according to Cicero, by his appeal to the family traditions of the Metelli.[72]

In the matter of style, as Cicero's controversy with the Atticists shows, there was something of a reaction from Ciceronianism among his younger contemporaries. But even the difference between Cicero on the one hand and Brutus and Calvus on the other may well have been less than it appeared at the time. Such at any rate was the impression of Tacitus. 'Cicero', he writes, 'admittedly surpassed the other orators of his day, but Calvus and Pollio and Caesar and Caelius and Brutus are rightly placed above their predecessors and their successors. The differences between them are irrelevant in comparison with their general similarity. Calvus is conciser, Pollio more rhythmical, Caesar grander, Caelius more biting, Brutus weightier, Cicero more vigorous, full and powerful; yet all are distinguished by the same healthy quality. If you looked at their works at the same time, you would recognise that for all the individual differences of talent there was a kind of family likeness as regards their taste and their aims.'[73]

VIII

DECLAMATION

Hoc habent scholasticorum studia: leviter tacta delectant, contrectata et propius admota fastidio sunt.

Seneca the elder, *Controversiae* 10 pr. 1

'WITH THE end of the Republic a new chapter opens in the history of Roman rhetoric. If one turns from Cicero's account of his early training in the *Brutus* to the *Controversiae* and *Suasoriae* of the elder Seneca, one is conscious of having moved into a different world. The forum and the senate house are forgotten and the centre of interest is now the school. And the school has thrown open its doors and become something like a theatre. The stage is held by the rhetorician, no longer a pedantic theorist and now rather a star performer. His performances are known as declamations.

The rise of this institution of declamation can be dated with some accuracy. The elder Seneca, who was born about 55 B.C., tells us that it was younger than himself and that he had watched it from its infancy.[1] Declamation then grew up with the end of the Republic, and there is an obvious connection between the political revolution and the change in rhetoric, for with the establishment of the principate the free life which had fostered the oratory of the Republic came to an end. In these circumstances one might have expected rhetoric to fade away, and give place to some new discipline adapted to the new shape of society. But rhetoric had survived the decay of the Greek city state, and it survived the decay of the Roman Republic. Instead of fading away it took on a new form. It lost touch with real life and became an independent self-centred activity, strangely out of touch with the movement of history, yet possessed of a remarkable and persistent vitality.

What exactly was the innovation that Seneca had watched

from its infancy? In the later Republic there were two forms of declamation, that of the student in the schools and that made by the adult after his school days were over. Both were designed as practice for the speeches of real life; the declamations of the schools were part of the rhetorical course, and those of the adult were made in private for the purpose of keeping himself in training. In the Augustan age both these institutions continued; declamation was still part of the school course and the old practice of private declamation by adults did not die out.[2] But alongside these established forms there grew up the public declamation, aimed not at practice but at display, given by a professional rhetorician.[3] It was here that the innovation lay.

The rhetorician now became something more than a mere teacher. Juvenal may depict him as a poor hard-worked schoolmaster, doomed to hear the same theme treated over and over again by his pupils, but this gives only one side of the picture.[4] The schoolmaster was also a public performer. It was not every rhetorician who, like Porcius Latro,[5] could refuse to listen to his pupils' efforts and describe himself as not a teacher but a model, but even the lesser men would have their moments of glory, when their halls would be thrown open to the public and the great men of the day, perhaps even the Emperor himself, would attend.[6] The declamation in fact became a social occasion. It remained what it had always been, an exercise for the young, but the professors, in addition to demonstrating to their pupils, entertained the general public with their performances.[7] Sometimes the pupil was to be heard declaiming with his masters, imitating and outdoing them; we hear, for instance, of an infant prodigy, Alfius Flavus, who used to draw large crowds while still a mere boy.[8] Sometimes, too, adults who were not professional teachers would revisit the schools and join in the declamations.[9] But in the main declamation was an activity for the professional, the rhetorician who spent his life in the schools and devoted himself to this art.

Not only was the public character of the declamations a novel feature; the themes were new too. 'The older *controversiae*', writes Suetonius, 'were based either on history, as is sometimes the case even now, or upon some event of recent occurrence in real life;[10] and so they were usually presented with the names of the places concerned added.' He proceeds to give two ex-

amples drawn from published collections, the first of which is
as follows:

'Some young men from the city went to Ostia in the summer
season and arriving at the shore found some fishermen drawing
in their nets. They made a bargain to give a certain sum for
the haul. The money was paid, and they waited for some time
until the nets were drawn ashore. When they were at last
hauled out, no fish was found in them, but a closed basket
of gold. Then the purchasers said that the catch belonged to
them; the fishermen that it was theirs.'[11]

In this example the scene is certainly laid in a real place,
but the story itself is hardly historical. If it is a fair specimen,
the old and the new *controversiae* were not after all so very
different. Probably there was no sharp dividing line; we have
already seen that the themes of the Republican schools were
not always drawn from history or real life or given a definite
geographical setting. There was also no doubt some overlapping.
The new type of theme seems to have been well established at
the time when the elder Seneca was studying under Marullus,
which would presumably be soon after Philippi,[12] and they
were probably used in some schools even before then. The
Greek rhetorician Aeschines is described by Seneca as one of
the new declaimers, and he was a contemporary of Cicero.[13]
Cicero himself is said to have declaimed a *controversia* of a
thoroughly 'new' type.[14] But we can no doubt accept Suetonius's
account of the matter as generally true. There was a difference
between the old and the new *controversiae;* there was a change
in the subject matter from the real to the unreal, the specific
to the vague, the sober to the romantic and melodramatic.

The elder Seneca mentions more than one hundred declaimers. They came from various parts of the empire; Asia
Minor still produced rhetoricians, as of old, but there were also
men from Gaul and Spain, those 'new men from the munici-
palities and colonies and even the provinces' with their thrifty
hard-working habits of whom Tacitus speaks.[15] The Latin
declaimers are now in the majority;[16] the Greeks might still
be the masters of rhetorical theory, but they were no longer,
as they had been in Cicero's youth, the leaders in declamation.
There were even Greeks like Cestius Pius and Argentarius who
made a point of declaiming in Latin.[17]

Four of the declaimers, according to Seneca, were in a class by themselves: Porcius Latro, Arellius Fuscus, Albucius Silo and Junius Gallio.[18] Of these Fuscus was probably a Greek by origin,[19] Albucius came from Novaria in Cisalpine Gaul, while Latro and (probably) Gallio were Spaniards. We have an entertaining portrait of Latro by Seneca, his close friend and contemporary.[20] He was a man who did nothing by halves; when writing he would work for days and nights on end; when on holiday he would be transformed into a complete countryman. When he returned from holiday he spoke with all the more vigour and vehemence, exulting in his freshness and getting as much as possible out of himself. 'His body was naturally well knit and hardened by frequent exercise and so never failed to support the vigorous motions of his burning intellect. His voice was strong, but indistinct and husky not by nature, but as a result of late hours and neglect. But thanks to his lungs it could be raised, and however little strength it might seem to have at the beginning, it grew in power as he went on. He took no trouble to exercise his voice; he could never unlearn the manly country ways of his native Spain; he took things as they came, did nothing to train his voice, did not raise it gradually from the lowest pitch to the highest and down again in equal intervals, did not rub off his sweat or refresh his lungs by taking walks. Often he worked throughout the night and then went straight from breakfast to declaim. And nothing could stop him from doing something which is very harmful to the health; he generally worked after dinner and did not allow his food to be digested evenly while he rested in sleep, but drove it to his head disturbed and unsettled. And so his eyes lost their brightness and his skin its colour. He was gifted with a naturally good memory which he improved by training. He never had to re-read what he had written in order to learn it by heart. He had learnt it as he wrote; and this might be thought all the more surprising in that he did not write slowly and carefully but almost as quickly as he spoke.'

Of Seneca's four great declaimers two, Latro and Albucius, committed suicide. Of the lesser men who appear in his pages one went mad,[21] and several others, to judge by Seneca's comments, behaved as if they were mad. In the unreal atmosphere of the schools, with their mutual admiration and false values, it was hard to preserve one's balance, and a man who seemed sane within their walls would appear hardly normal outside.[22] When it came to speaking in the courts the great declaimers were often quite helpless. Latro was ill at ease outside the schools;[23] Cestius, the idol of the *scholastici*, took fright at the prospect of having to defend himself.[24] Albucius gave up appearing in the courts after an unfortunate experience. 'Are you willing', he asked, 'to settle the matter by oath? Swear then, but I will dictate the oath: Swear by your father's bones which lie unburied, swear by your father's memory . . .' and so on, until he had exhausted the topic. When he had finished, his opponent rose and accepted the proposal. Albucius protested: 'I did not make a proposal; I only used a figure.' His protests were in vain. 'If this is allowed', he cried, 'there will be an end of figures.' 'We can live without them', was the answer.[25] Truly, as Cassius Severus said, the declaimers were all but an entirely different species.[26]

Of the two forms of declamation, the *suasoria* and the *controversia*, the former was accounted the easier and more elementary exercise.[27] In it the speaker gave advice to an historical character, or a group of persons, as to what his or their action should be in some crisis.[28] Subjects were taken from Greek or Roman history,[29] but scant respect was shown for historical facts. The most flagrant example is the *suasoria* in which Cicero is faced with the possibility of buying his life from Antony by burning his books.[30] This is pure fiction.

The treatment too was generally as unrealistic as the theme. Occasionally a rhetorician showed a gleam of realism and historical sense. In the *suasoria* about Cicero Pompeius Silo took the line that Antony was not to be taken seriously; he would kill Cicero whether he burnt his books or not. After all there were plenty of copies of the books; Antony was not such a fool as to suppose it mattered in the least whether Cicero burnt them.[31] More typical was Cestius Pius's treatment. 'This was a worse punishment than death and that was why Antony had chosen it; life was short in any case and especially for an old man; one must think of the future which held out the prospect of immortality to the great; life was not to be bought at any price . . .' and so on.[32]

Suasoriae in fact were not used as an exercise in historical imagination; they seem to have been primarily regarded as offering an opportunity for picturesque descriptions of scenes, rivers, cities and customs.[33] The style seems to have been generally violent, impetuous and high flown.[34] A product of the schools, if ever in after life he was called upon to give a real speech of advice, would, Quintilian suggests, have to acquire a very different style from what he had used in the *suasoriae*.[35]

Far more popular with most declaimers than the *suasoria* was the *controversia*, the imaginary case on some disputable point of law. To illustrate the character of the themes in use in the Augustan age and later we cannot do better than quote some examples from the first book of Seneca's collection.

'The law requires that children support their parents or be imprisoned. Two brothers disagreed. One had a son. His uncle fell on evil days, and, in spite of his father's veto, the boy supported him. For this reason he was disinherited, but did not protest. He was then adopted by his uncle, who inherited a fortune. The father then fell on evil days, and, in spite of the uncle's veto, the young man supported him. He was disinherited.'[36]

'The law requires that a priestess must be chaste and undefiled, and born of chaste and undefiled parents. A certain virgin was captured by pirates and sold. Bought by a brothel-keeper, she was forced to prostitution. When men came to her she persuaded them to leave her untouched while giving the usual fee. A soldier came to her whom she was unable to persuade. He took her in his arms and tried to force her, and as he did so she killed him. She was accused and acquitted, then returned to her own, whereupon she tried to obtain a priesthood. Her claim was contested.'[37]

'The law ordains that if a man catches an adulterer in the act and kills both parties he is free from blame. Another law permits a son to punish adultery on the part of his mother. A brave man lost his hands in battle; he caught his wife, who had borne him a son, in the act of adultery. He ordered the young man to kill them; he refused and the paramour escaped. The father disinherited his son.'[38]

'The law ordains that in the case of rape the woman may demand either the death of her seducer or marriage without dowry. A certain man raped two women in one night; one demanded his death, the other marriage.'[39]

'A man was captured by pirates and wrote to his father asking to be ransomed. The father refused. The daughter of the pirate chief made the young man swear to marry her if he was set free. He did so. She left her father and followed the young man. He returned home and married her. An heiress appeared on the scene. The father ordered him to leave the pirate chief's daughter and marry the heiress. He refused, and was disinherited.'[40]

'The law requires that children support their parents or be imprisoned. A certain man killed one of his brothers as a tyrant. The other he caught in adultery and, in spite of his father's entreaties, killed him. He was captured by pirates and wrote to his father to be ransomed. The father wrote to the pirates promising to pay double if they cut off his son's hands. The pirates let him go. He refused to support his father when the latter was in need.'[41]

The above examples introduce us to some of the favourite themes of the schools, disinheritance, rape and adultery, capture by pirates, tyrannicide and loss of limb. The world of the declamations was a fantastic and melodramatic one, and for that reason perhaps popular in a humdrum age. Augustus had brought peace and security to the world; the declaimers revelled in violence, in fire and shipwreck, poison and hanging.

Melodrama is of course not unknown in real life, and strange stories come out in the courts; but there is no doubt that these controversial themes were for the most part far removed from ordinary experience. Such was the opinion of Messala in Tacitus's *Dialogue*, and for all the parallels which have been discovered between the themes of declamation and recorded incidents of Roman life,[42] the pages of Seneca bear out his words, *quales per fidem et quam incredibiliter compositae*.[43] Even in the few cases concerned with historical characters[44] the lively imagination of the rhetorician often embroidered the situation with apocryphal details. Cicero is killed by Popillius whom he had previously defended on a charge of parricide. 'Few historians', remarks Seneca, 'have recorded that it was Popillius who killed Cicero and these say that it was not on a charge of parricide that Cicero defended him, but in a private case. The declaimers decided that it was a case of parricide.'[45] Tyranny and tyrannicide were subjects not without contemporary reference, and it is natural to suppose that the freedom with

which they were discussed in the schools was not unconnected
with the discretion necessary outside. But after reading Seneca's
reports of the declamations on these subjects one is inclined to
acquit the declaimers of seditious thoughts, so unreal and remote is the atmosphere.[46] Latro's tactless remarks about
adoption made in the presence of Augustus suggest that the
men of the schools were characterised by a certain innocence.[47]
'Schola', says Pliny, 'et auditorium et ficta causa res inermis
innoxia est.'[48] Moreover words came to mean little to the
trained rhetorician. Haterius could commend Cato and liberty
in the schools, but in his dealings with Tiberius he was abject
enough.[49]

The laws on which the *controversiae* were based were, it seems,
in general fairly closely related to contemporary Roman law,[50]
but there was no particular interest in legal accuracy, and no
objection to the use of distorted or fictitious laws, or those
derived from Greek sources. For example the notorious option
of the victim of rape to choose either the death of her seducer
or marriage with him never existed anywhere in law, and the
law requiring children to support their parents under penalty
of imprisonment is Greek rather than Roman.[51] Moreover, even
where the legal situations envisaged were closely parallel to
Roman practice, no effort was made to make them identical.
Quintilian points to close parallels between various scholastic
themes and questions that actually occurred in the Roman
courts.[52] Though his evidence indicates that *controversiae* were
not always remote from real life, the very fact that he stresses
the correspondence between the practice of the schools and that
of the courts shows that it was generally accepted that the
former might have their own code.

Little attempt was made in declamation to reproduce the procedure of the courts. One could speak for as long as one liked
and take whichever side one liked.[53] There was no debating,
and each speech stood on its own. Thus when the declaimer
spoke for the prosecution he included a refutation, as if he
was answering another speech, as well as the *narratio* appropriate to an opening speech; the objections he answered were
purely imaginary.[54] So far as it was based on court practice at
all declamation was based on that of Greece, and this presumably explains the fact that, contrary to Roman practice,

the plaintiff or defendant was usually made to speak in his own person and not through an advocate.[55]

Seneca has preserved under a separate heading the *divisio*, or analysis of the points at issue, used by the rhetoricians when treating scholastic themes. The standard division was that into *ius* and *aequitas*, law and equity.[56] This had presumably developed from the more limited problem, long familiar in the rhetorical schools, of the letter versus the spirit of the law, but the emphasis it is now given to the exclusion of everything else is new. The division into *ius* and *aequitas* was regularly followed by Latro, who began with a careful analysis of the legal aspect. This does not necessarily mean that he was expert in the actual laws of his day; indeed he was by no means strong on such matters.[57] However, within its limits his method provided a serious exercise in legal interpretation and argument. But the flashier type of declaimer did not, it seems, bind himself to the scholastic type of division; here, as elsewhere, he went in for the striking and ingenious.[58] For instance in the case of the would-be priestess with dubious antecedents Albucius said: 'Let us suppose that there were three candidates for the priesthood: one who had been a captive, one who had been a prostitute and one who had killed a man. I reject all three.'—and proceeded to treat the case under these three headings. Arellius Fuscus said: 'I will show that she is unworthy of the priesthood, firstly even if she is chaste, secondly because we do not know whether she is chaste, and thirdly because she is not chaste.'[59]

But the analysis was less important for the treatment than what was called the *color*, which can best be defined as 'the particular aspect given to a case by the skilful manipulation of the facts'.[60] It is a vague term (the Augustan rhetoricians cared little for the old scholastic precision in terminology) which came into fashion with the rise of declamation and described something which formed an important part of that art. The themes, imprecise and often inconsequential, needed filling out; the motives of the characters needed explanation. In a real case one naturally seized on anything which represented one's client in the most, and one's opponent in the least, favourable light. In a *controversia* one used one's imagination to the same end. And as the same subjects were treated again and again, there was a tendency to avoid the simple and natural

G

and resort to the far-fetched and unnatural. The colour was often make-up.

Let us take the *controversia* already quoted about the young man who married the pirate chief's daughter and was disinherited for refusing to marry the heiress. The father would obviously be an unpopular character, and some colour had to be found to make his action sympathetic. So Latro depicts the pirate chief's daughter as inspired not by pity but by lust; Romanius Hispo makes her motive not love but dislike of her father. Arellius Fuscus has the ingenious idea that the heiress had nothing to do with the father's desire to get rid of his daughter-in-law; he simply disliked the girl and thought that her piratical upbringing disqualified her for civilised society. Gallio made a point that no one else had thought of: the father was afraid the girl might be a spy on behalf of the pirates.[61]

In another *controversia* a son, three times disinherited, was found by his father secretly mixing a potion, which he claimed was poison to be taken by himself. The father naturally did not believe this, and accused the son of parricide. Albucius defending the son made out that it was not poison at all; he was only testing his father's feelings by pretending he was going to kill himself. According to another declaimer, Murredius, the potion was a sleeping draught.[62] The prize for inept invention goes to Gargonius for the *color* he used in defence of the father who promised to pay the pirates a double ransom if they cut off his son's hands. 'I dictated', says the father, 'the words "I will pay double if you do not cut off his hands"; the copyist left out the word "not" by mistake.[63]

Certain rhetoricians had their favourite 'colours'. Latro was apt to make his characters victims of strong emotion. Arellius Fuscus made frequent use of religion. Junius Otho specialised in dreams, a colour which in Quintilian's day was considered altogether too easy and had gone out of fashion.[64]

Of serious argument there was little in the declamations. How could there be, when the declaimer could give his own colour, and the only objections he had to answer were those he put forward himself? Besides, argumentation was difficult, and provided few opportunities for embellishment.[65] What won applause was the vivid description or the striking epigram. If the *suasoria* offered more opportunities for description, there were openings in the *controversia* also; there were examples of men labouring under violent emotion and reduced to piteous circumstances, and such scenes the declaimer liked to bring before the listener's eye in a few vivid touches.[66] The *sententia*, however, was the characteristic feature of the declamatory style. The term was originally applied to the aphorism, the expression in short and memorable form of some truth of general application, but it came to be applied to any striking remark, particularly one made at the end of a period.[67] Quintilian bears witness to the rage for *sententiae* among the imperial rhetoricians. Nowadays, he says, they want every passage and every sentence to strike the ear by an impressive close; they think it a disgrace, even a crime, to take breath except at a point designed to produce applause.[68] The fashion had started in the time of Augustus. It was encouraged by the conditions of the declamation schools. The speaker having no other purpose than to entertain and impress would seek for applause as a comedian for laughs; the themes were so empty in themselves that only adventitious sparkle could enliven them, and so hackneyed that only novelties could amuse. Roman ears were no longer hungry, as they had been in Cicero's youth, for the rhythmical period; they required a new stimulant and they got it in the ingenuities of the *sententia*. The manner became a habit; the rhetorician 'could not ope his mouth, but out there flew'—not a trope but a *sententia*.

Sententiae abound in the pages of the elder Seneca. Here are some examples from the *controversia* about the man who seduced two victims in one night;[69] 'Iam se parabat in tertiam, nisi nox defecisset.' (Latro) 'Perieras, raptor, nisi bis perire meruisses.' (Triarius) 'Toto die pereat qui tota nocte peccavit.' (Gallio)[70] 'Gratulor vobis, virgines, quod citius illuxit.' (Triarius) 'Quaeritis quid isti finem rapiendi fecit? dies.' (Argentarius)[71] This brief selection of *sententiae*, with their superficial neatness and fundamental emptiness, will serve as specimens of what passed for wit in the rhetorical schools. There were not enough good epigrams to go round; to satisfy the demand the rhetoricians sometimes resorted to what was so far fetched and allusive as to be hardly intelligible. It mattered little. Even the meaningless could win applause.[72] Sometimes the rhetorician was reduced to filching the *sententiae* of others.[73] Or he would imitate and go one better. Cestius Pius says of the seducer of two victims, 'non est una contentus'; Argentarius follows him with 'non est una contentus, ne una quidem nocte'.[74] Fabianus makes a poor man's son who refused to be adopted by a rich man say: 'Nolo dives esse.' Vibius Rufus improves this to 'Nescio dives esse.'[75]

History and philosophy, those two branches of the orator's learning on which Cicero laid such stress, had their place in the declamations, but the history is reduced to stock examples and the philosophy to commonplaces. The rhetoricians had their store of examples to illustrate such themes as the inconstancy of fortune and the contempt of riches, and these they readily drew on, sometimes when the example was far from relevant.[76] Porcius Latro was famous for his knowledge of history, but though his range may have been wider, he seems to have used history much as the others did and with no greater regard for relevance.[77] Philosophic commonplaces were freely introduced. A genuine moral sentiment sometimes comes out in the fervent denunciations of war, avarice and luxury, and the commendations of pity and humanity, but often enough the *locus philosophumenus*, as it was called, was little more than an irrelevant adornment. Latro used to compose *sententiae* on such themes as fortune, cruelty, the evils of the age and riches, which could be used equally well in any *controversia*. These and similar adornments he called *supellex*, furniture, and employed them to enliven the arid declamations of his master Marullus.[78] Fabianus, who in view of his subsequent conversion to philosophy may be credited with some sincerity in his moral disquisitions, was indifferent to their relevance. Advising Alexander not to cross the ocean, he dilated on the fickleness of fortune; speaking for the poor man's son who refused to be adopted by the rich man, he launched into a lengthy tirade against wars and luxury.[79]

Tedious as the declamations seem to us today in the abbreviated versions preserved by Seneca, they must have been remarkable performances. A good declaimer was a virtuoso, with much of the actor about him. For, as Quintilian says, when he spoke he impersonated the various characters who were protagonists in the set themes, sons, parents, rich men, old men, etc., and thus had to be almost as versatile as a professional actor.[80] The vivid delivery, combined with the melodramatic themes and the epigrammatic sparkle, was irresistible. Applause was frequent and unrestrained. Latro might try to cure his pupils of the habit of applauding every *sententia*,[81] but the habit persisted. Indiscriminate applause was the rule in the schools. The listeners would jump from their seats at the end of each period and rush forward with excited cries.[82] *Sententiae* of the master rhetoricians would be passed round, learnt by heart and repeated, while those of the lesser men would be the subject of lively discussion and criticism.[83]

The work of the elder Seneca shows that one could be a devotee of declamation without losing one's critical sense, but the *scholastici* tended to live in a world of their own, sheltered from the blasts of criticism. Plato's θεατροκρατία prevailed; the audience was master. Cestius Pius admitted frankly that he gave his listeners not what he liked but what they liked.[84] If he did not pander to the tastes of the young, says Petronius's Agamemnon, the rhetorician would soon lose his pupils.[85] So within the schools mutual admiration prevailed.

Seen from outside they bore a different aspect. The young men, according to Encolpius in Petronius, learn nothing but folly in the rhetorical schools.[86] 'It is hard to say', says Messala in Tacitus's *Dialogue*, 'whether the actual place or the fellow pupils or the character of the exercises does more harm to the young mind.'[87] In school exercises, according to Cassius Severus, the question of superfluity did not arise, for the whole thing was superfluous.[88]

Under the Empire there appear to have been two schools of thought about declamation.[89] Some regarded it as having nothing to do with pleading in the courts and being designed solely for display; others saw it as a preparation for practice in the courts. If the former view was accepted, declamation was presumably justified by the pleasure it evidently gave to both performers and listeners. But if it was to be judged by its utility as practical training it was a failure. Critics had no difficulty in showing how poor a preparation it provided for speaking in the courts. We need only quote the remarks of an orator of the Augustan age, Votienus Montanus. 'He who composes a declamation writes not to convince, but to please; he seeks out every trick of style, avoiding argumentation, because it is tiresome and lacking in charm; he is content to delight his audience with epigrams and descriptions. He wishes to commend himself, not his case. This fault of avoiding the essential while aiming at brilliance follows the declaimers even into the courts. Then again they imagine their opponents as stupid as they like; they reply as and when they like. Their mistakes cannot be punished; their follies cost them nothing. Their stupidity grows in security and cannot be shaken off even in the courts where it may be dangerous. They are helped along by frequent applause and they can rest their memory at regular intervals. But in the courts, where they are no longer greeted by applause at every gesture, they either break down or get into difficulties. Further, there is no interruption to arouse their annoyance; no one laughs or indulges in deliberate insult; there are friendly faces all round. So in the forum they are put out first of all by the very setting.... In the school declamations everything is soft and easy. In the courts one is given a case, in the schools one chooses it. In the courts one flatters the judge, in the schools one orders him about; in the courts one must concentrate while the noise of the crowd sounds around one and one's voice must carry to the judge's ears; in the schools all eyes hang on the speaker. And so just as people coming out of dark and shady places are blinded by the glare of a bright light, so they coming from school to forum find everything new and unfamiliar and disturbing, and do not develop the strength of an orator until they have been trained by frequent humiliations and had their boyish minds, softened by the luxury of the schools, hardened by genuine work.'[90]

When such criticisms were passed on the schools of declamation by the Romans themselves, it is unnecessary to underline them or add to the indictment. It should however be observed that declamation can hardly have been wholly useless or wholly bad in its influence. Quintilian, in spite of his many severe criticisms, made use of it himself and was convinced of its value. It is probably true that the extravagances found in the pages of Seneca were of comparatively short duration; after a time some of the froth settled down. Certain undoubted weaknesses remained, but the sensible teacher could make use of declamation to give a serious training in thought and expression. In any case in spite of all criticism declamation continued; the old themes were debated until the end of Roman civilisation. 'We all value one another so much upon this beautiful deceit; and labour so long after it in the years of our education, that we cannot but ever after think kindlier of it than it deserves.'[91] The Roman who had been through the schools came to forget their follies, looked back to them with a kindly sentiment and accounted even their unreality a virtue. The aged rhetorician Isaeus was to Pliny one of the happiest of men, innocent and straightforward, exempt from the corruptions of the world, privileged to carry on into old age one of the pleasantest of the occupations of youth.[92]

ORATORY UNDER THE EMPIRE

Novis et exquisitis eloquentiae itineribus opus est, per quae orator
fastidium aurium effugiat.

Tacitus, *Dialogus* 19.5

WITH THE death of Cicero the great tradition of Roman
oratory came to an end. 'Conticuit Latiae tristis facundia
linguae.'[1] To some this was no matter for regret. The greatest
poet of the Augustan age exhorted his countrymen to leave to
others the arts, including that of oratory,[2] and made the only
wholly unsympathetic character in his epic an orator. Whether
or no Drances was meant to suggest Cicero,[3] it is hard to resist
the impression of something like a parting kick at the old
Republican régime and its characteristic figure, the political
orator. In the new world of Augustus there was no room for such
a figure. The Emperor himself set the tone in cultivating a
direct matter-of-fact way of speaking, in which the graces of
style were sacrificed to intelligibility.[4]

But the ancient world could not so easily turn its back on the
past. Cicero was not forgotten; the ideal of eloquence continued to
haunt men's imagination; the rhetoricians had a secure hold over
the educational system. Moreover there was still some place for
the orator in society. His art still opened the way to success, enabled him to help his friends and protect himself. He was still
courted and admired and pointed to in the streets.[5] Eloquence,
as a speaker in Tacitus's *Dialogue* points out, brought Eprius
Marcellus and Vibius Crispus, both men with no advantages of
wealth or character, to their position of influence and importance.[6]
Even the teacher of rhetoric could rise to a position of dignity,[7]
and, if the worst came to the worst, he could go back to teaching.

Si Fortuna volet, fies de rhetore consul;
si volet haec eadem, fies de consule rhetor.[8]

Or, as Valerius the ex-praetor who taught rhetoric in exile put it: Fortune makes senators of professors and professors of senators.[9]

There is no doubt that there was still plenty of scope for the advocate and high rewards to be won.[10] But there had none the less been a change from Republican days. The old courts continued to flourish, but the great political trials of the Republic were a thing of the past. The Emperor and the senate encroached on the province of the old *quaestiones*. Augustus set the fashion of personally administering justice; Tiberius followed suit, and Claudius was notorious for the zeal with which he exercised judicial functions.[11] The senate acquired a new importance as a criminal court; here cases of treason were tried and accusations heard against members of the senatorial body. It was hardly to be expected that the advocate would enjoy full freedom either before the Emperor himself or before a senate that had lost much of its independence. When Piso was tried before the senate for alleged responsibility for the death of the Emperor's adopted son Germanicus, he found some difficulty in obtaining advocates, and Tiberius had to urge those he obtained to do their best in his defence.[12] It can easily be imagined that in trials of a political complexion such as now came before the senate a certain constraint would be felt. As Quintilian puts it, 'The courts have never required such silence' (he is referring to the convention of the rhetorical schools, where by judicious ambiguity you could say what you liked against the tyrant) 'but they do require something else not unlike it, and much more difficult for the speaker, when he is hampered by the existence of powerful persons whom he must blame if he is to prove his case.'[13]

Not only was the orator hampered by this necessity for discretion; his role in society also was limited by the imperial system. 'The more able a man was at speaking', says a character in Tacitus's *Dialogue*, looking back to Republican days, 'the greater the ease with which he attained to high office and the greater his preeminence among his colleagues in office; he obtained more influence with the powerful, carried more weight with the senate, possessed a higher reputation with the people. Able speakers had numerous clients even from abroad, were respected by magistrates about to leave for the provinces and courted by them on return, seemed marked out for praetorship and consulship and were far from powerless even out of office, when they guided senate and people by their advice and influence.'[14] 'In addition there was the high rank of the defendants and the greatness of the cases tried, factors which in themselves contribute much to eloquence. For it makes a great difference whether you have to speak about a theft, a rule of procedure, a praetor's interdict, or about electoral bribery, the plunder of a province, the murder of fellow-citizens.'[15] Now things were different, and the part played by the orator was more modest. Even the conditions of oratory were less favourable than they had once been. The length of speeches was restricted, as was the duration of trials and the number of pleaders. The surroundings, the meagre audiences, the casual informal manner, even the dress worn by the advocates, were inimical to high oratory.[16]

That oratory had declined from the high level it had reached in the time of Cicero was generally agreed, and the decline was widely discussed. It is the theme of the preface to the first book of Seneca's *Controversiae*, of the opening paragraphs of Petronius and of Tacitus's *Dialogue on Orators*. Quintilian too, turned his attention to the subject; his work on the causes of the decline of oratory is lost, but his views on the subject can be discovered from scattered passages in the *Institutio Oratoria*.

Seneca, the earliest of these writers, suggests three possible reasons for the decline. The first is the luxury of the age, the second the lack of rewards, the third a kind of law of nature by which decline follows high achievement. The first reason, which seems to appeal most to Seneca,[17] and leads him to a despondent diatribe against the decadence of the younger generation, was one which came easily to those brought up on contemporary Graeco-Roman moralising; it is less convincing to moderns who note that the same laments about moral decay were heard in the age of Cicero. But there is a sense in which moral decline affected oratory. There was always a strong element of the unscrupulous about the Roman orator, but under the Republic he was not subjected to the corrupting influences of despotism. The unscrupulous accuser was matched by the unscrupulous defender, and if justice was not always done, at least both sides could have their say. Under the Empire there was not even this rough justice. There were all too many *viri mali dicendi periti* who put their talents at the service of power. Tacitus has branded one of them, the rhetorician Romanius Hispo: 'Needy, obscure, restless, he wormed his way into the confidence of a vindictive prince by secret delations and soon became a source of peril to all the most distinguished citizens; influential with one man, he was hated by everyone else, and left an example which others followed to become wealthy and formidable when they had been poor and insignificant, and to bring ruin first on others, then on themselves.'[18] It is Tacitus, too, who describes the great orator Domitius Afer, so often honourably mentioned by Quintilian, as 'quick to use any crime as a means to his own advancement'.[19]

Seneca's second reason for the decline of oratory, the lack of rewards, is elaborated by Tacitus, who more than any other writer on oratory has the historic sense, and is conscious of the revolution brought about by the establishment of the imperial system. He derives the decline of oratory not only from the loss of the old incentives and the other changes in external circumstances, but from the very character of society. 'It is with eloquence', (I borrow the younger Pitt's famous extempore translation[20]) 'as with a flame. It requires fuel to feed it, motion to excite it, and it brightens as it burns.'[21] The disorderly state of society under the Republic provided the conditions for the growth of great oratory, conditions which were absent in a quiet well-ordered society. It is better that the state should not produce bad citizens like Catiline, Milo, Verres and Antonius, but it was such men that gave Cicero the material for oratory. Peace is better than war, but it is war that produces great soldiers. So it is with eloquence.[22]

Whether this explanation commends itself or not, there is no doubt that to relate the change in oratory to political changes was more to the point than to blame the growth of luxury. Seneca was also to the point when he referred to the inevitable cycle by which decline follows a climax.[23] For whether such a cycle is inevitable or not, it is certain that there was a general feeling that the summit of achievement had been reached, and this feeling contributed to the sterility of imperial oratory. Cicero became accepted as the classic orator of Rome. In the time of Quintilian he dominated rhetorical teaching and theory.

He influenced, by way of reaction, even those who rejected him as a model. Aper, the self-conscious modernist in Tacitus's *Dialogue*, glories in having got away from the long-winded boring manner of the Ciceronian age and evolved a new style suited to an age of hustle.[24] On the other side were the traditionalists who could only look back to Cicero, and to whom it was the highest praise to say that an orator was worthy to be numbered among the ancients.[25] There is a revealing passage in Pliny's letters where one Satrius Rufus is said to make no attempt at rivalling Cicero, but to be content with the eloquence of his own age; Pliny, on the other hand, is not content with the eloquence of his age but tries to rival Cicero. For it is sheer folly, he adds, not to imitate the best examples.[26] Thus we have a sterile division between the traditionalists looking back to the past, attempting to imitate and rival Cicero, and the modernists consciously rejecting the great tradition and contenting themselves with lowered standards.[27]

To Seneca's three reasons for the decline of oratory other writers add a fourth, the bad system of education. Something has already been said of the criticisms which the rhetorical schools aroused. They deserve to be considered in greater detail here, for they throw some light on the character of imperial oratory and in particular on the interactions of rhetoric and oratory. In considering the oratory of the Republic we attempted to assess the influence of theory on practice. In the imperial age theory, it seems, did not count for much;[28] it was rather the practice of the schools that influenced that of the courts. There is plenty of evidence to show that there was such an influence; so far from forgetting school habits when he went out into the world, the young orator carried them with him, and did his best to reproduce the manner of the declamation hall in the court of law. A man's manner of pleading, says Quintilian, depends on his manner in declamation.[29]

The product of the schools brought with him to the courts a distaste for serious argument and a preference for what was easy and attractive.[30] He indulged in ornamental digressions, and aimed at giving pleasure and showing off his powers rather than at helping his client.[31] Needless to say, he revelled in *sententiae*.[32] His style in general was mannered and affected, lacking in strength and masculinity.[33] Tastelessness of matter as well as of manner was encouraged by the schools. Seneca's account of a case involving a lady found by her husband with a handsome slave in her bedroom reads strangely like the report of a declamation, with the counsel using the most outrageous 'colours' without regard to probability or decency.[34]

Even in details school practice was reproduced. We have seen how in declamation it was customary to include in one speech both *narratio* and refutation; the reason for the custom—to train the pupil at the same time both to speak first and to speak second—was forgotten, and the products of the schools would follow the custom they were used to, inappropriate though it might be, in the courts.[35] Having become accustomed to speaking without an opponent, they would answer imaginary objections such as only a fool would make.[36] Used to an atmosphere in which they could invent as they pleased, they would utter prepared phrases such as 'He stretches out suppliant hands to embrace your knees', or 'The wretched man is locked in the embrace of his children', or 'See he summons me back', even though nothing of the sort was taking place.[37]

There is little doubt that the influence of the declamations was not a good one. But there was decadence even apart from such influence. Cassius Severus was not a man of the schools, was indeed a severe critic of them,[38] but it was with him, men said, that the decline began.[39] He deliberately adopted a new style suited to the new age. He had a good voice and delivery, a vigorous manner and a biting wit. His oratory was powerful and to the point, and no one was better able to sway his listeners as he wished.[40] But judged by the standards of the great tradition of Roman oratory he could not be wholeheartedly approved. Quintilian recommends him as a model only with reservations. He lacked dignity of style.[41] He allowed his bile to prevail over his judgment. He was the first, says a critic in Tacitus's *Dialogue*, to despise the orderly development of his subject matter, to take no account of modesty or restraint in his words, to brawl rather than to fight.[42]

But all was not bad taste and triviality or malignant abuse in imperial oratory. Mamercus Scaurus, who died in A.D. 34, had, we are told, a dignified, serious, old-fashioned manner.[43] Domitius Afer, for all his villainies, must have been a good speaker to justify Quintilian's eulogies, and the fact that he could be classed with the ancients suggests that he was exempt from the corrupt manner of the day.[44] Crispus Passienus, Nero's stepfather, won a similar commendation from an anonymous poet, and, in view of Quintilian's admiration for him, may have deserved it.[45] In the time of Quintilian, largely no doubt as a result of his own efforts as guide to errant youth, good sense and Ciceronianism had to some extent returned. Looking round him in his retirement, Quintilian saw no cause for anything but optimism. Today, he writes, there is a wealth of talent in the law courts. There are consummate advocates who can rival the ancients, and there are young men, hard-working and with the highest ambitions, who imitate and follow them.[46]

We have no body of oratory extant by which we can judge how far this optimism was justified, but Pliny's letters provide us with a certain amount of information about the oratorical activities of this period. In one of them he describes the pleading in the centumviral court, which tried civil lawsuits.[47] He expresses his dissatisfaction with the trivial nature of the cases and the poor calibre of the advocates with whom he had to appear, most of them pert young men fresh from the schools, with hired applauders to help them along. This practice of hiring an audience to applaud had begun before Pliny's time with one Larcius Licinus in the first half of the first century A.D., and had prompted Domitius Afer to exclaim: 'This is the end of the art of oratory.' The decline, says Pliny, was in fact only beginning then; things were now much worse.[48]

But this letter, it seems, was prompted by a passing mood of depression. In general Pliny was well satisfied with his profession. 'Oratory is still held in honour', he exclaims, after finding the centumviral court crowded when he was due to speak.[49] His speeches were read as well as listened to, and there were young men who looked to him as a model.[50] There were, too, opportunities for pleading more important cases than those of the centumviral court,[51] cases which recalled the great trials of Republican days. Indeed, when we read Pliny's letters we may at first be inclined to feel that little has changed from the days of Cicero. There are still duels of invective in the senate house; provincial governors are still tried for extortion; pathos is still a weapon for the defence. There are long and exciting trials, with the accused greeted by cheering crowds after acquittal.[52] But the resemblance is superficial. Pliny's anxious looking back to the great models of the past shows him a man of the Empire. 'I have tried to imitate Demosthenes, who has always been your model', he writes to a friend, 'and Calvus who has recently become mine, at least so far as the figures of speech go, for only the favoured few could attain to the power of those great men. . . . But I have not entirely avoided the adornments of Cicero.'[53] He admits that one of his speeches was composed with Demosthenes's *Meidias* in hand, not, he hastens to add, in the hope of vying with it, but so far as is possible and appropriate, of imitating and following.[54]

He is of course an admirer of Cicero, but when we read his remarks on oratory we can see how he differs from his great predecessor. He recommends the old methods, familiar from *De Oratore*, of translation and paraphrase, but he adds, what Cicero never recommended, the rewriting of one's own old speeches.[55] This, like the practice of reciting speeches, suggests a more dilettante attitude than that of the Republican orator. Pliny also recommends the practice of other types of literature, such as history and letter writing;[56] in Cicero the emphasis is rather on knowing history, and letter writing to him was still letter writing and not part of the *institutio oratoria*. To Pliny it is style that counts most. 'Good invention and grand delivery are found sometimes even in barbarians; but an appropriate arrangement and a varied style are denied to all but the well educated.'[57] This is not exactly new; Cicero had said much the same.[58] But in Cicero there is an emphasis on the substance as well as the style of oratory which we miss in Pliny.

Of Pliny's oratory only one specimen survives, the Panegyric of Trajan. Its survival is an indication of the tastes of later ages when panegyric became the main function of the orator. Pliny's speech however has something of the spirit of earlier oratory about it. It was not in origin a formal panegyric, but a speech of thanks made to the Emperor by Pliny in his capacity of consul; it was revised and expanded after delivery, and in the course of expansion the panegyric element was developed.[59] How far, we may ask, does Pliny follow rhetorical precept? If we turn to Quintilian as the best evidence for contemporary teaching,[60] we find that on the whole Pliny pays little attention to the precepts of the schools. He does not begin with the time before his subject's birth, treating his country, parents and ancestors.[61] He does not observe the threefold division of goods of mind, body and estate.[62] Of the two methods suggested by Quintilian of celebrating a man's character, tracing his career in chronological order and dealing separately with his various virtues,[63] neither is followed at all closely. Pliny's method is nearer to the first than to the second alternative, but he does not, as Quintilian recommends, begin with childhood and proceed through education to maturity.[64]

This independence of rhetoric is what we should expect. Apart from the fact that school rules were seldom followed exactly by a mature orator, the Panegyric does not strictly qualify as epideictic oratory, as it was not composed solely for display. Pliny for all his flowery elaboration is still a Roman, and even the additions he made to his speech in his study were made in part with a practical purpose, that of showing by example to future Emperors the way in which they should go.[65] Epideictic had not yet, as it was later to do, completely prevailed over the older Roman traditions of oratory.

X

QUINTILIAN AND RHETORICAL THEORY

In grave Quintilian's copious works we find
The justest rules and clearest method join'd.
Pope, *An Essay on Criticism* 669–70

RHETORIC IN the time of Quintilian had three aspects, the theoretical, the educational and the practical. It was an intellectual system, the object of much laborious thought, and, like the academic subjects of today, burdened with a voluminous 'literature'; it was also an educational discipline, and finally it was still to some extent what it had been in origin, the weapon of the statesman and the advocate, the means of winning power and influencing one's fellow-men. Quintilian was well qualified to deal with all these aspects. He was a thoroughly competent academic rhetorician, a worthy occupant of the professorial chair, and he was an eminent teacher and educationalist; he was not, and could hardly have been in his age, a political orator, but he was a highly successful pleader in the courts and fully alive to the factors that made for professional success. The three aspects of rhetoric are combined in the *Institutio Oratoria*, though the last is not very prominent, and in the main it is Quintilian the rhetorical theorist and Quintilian the teacher rather than Quintilian the barrister that is seen in this great work. His rhetorical theory will form the subject of this chapter and his educational theory of the chapter which follows.

In the preface to the first book Quintilian tells us that he had been urged by friends to write on rhetoric, but for a long time had declined on the ground that there existed numerous works on the subject already. To which they replied that it was difficult to choose between the various views expressed by previous writers, and there was still room for a new work which, without being original, would help them to make their choice.[1] This is roughly speaking the view that Quintilian himself took of his work. 'I am not a superstitious adherent of any school, and have thought it right to give my readers every opportunity of making their own choice. I have myself collected together the opinions of numerous authorities and shall be content if I am praised for industry where there is no scope for originality.'[2] Quintilian does not then invent a new system of his own, nor does he follow any one authority. He works on the basis of existing doctrine. On disputed points he gives the views of others and decides between them. He is generally conservative, and where there are various views prefers to follow the commonly accepted doctrine rather than the theories of ingenious but perverse innovators.[3]

Though he says truthfully that he belongs to no school, there is one authority for whom he has an unbounded respect, namely Cicero. It was Cicero, he says, who shed the greatest light on both the practice and the theory of oratory.[4] 'I hardly venture', he says elsewhere, 'to differ from Cicero.'[5] Cicero's speeches are of course quoted again and again by way of illustration, his characteristic ideas on oratory are reproduced, and even his obscurer technical works like *De Inventione* and *Topica* are treated with a respect that would perhaps have surprised their author.

With Cicero as guide Quintilian steers his way skilfully if somewhat laboriously through the maze of technicalities constructed by generations of rhetoricians, rhetoricians who, as Quintilian says, had often begun by adding some improvement where there was scope for improvement, and had then gone on to alter where there was none, just to show their originality.[6] His method is not the genial discursive method of *De Oratore*, nor the dry dogmatic one of *Ad Herennium*. If he is less readable than Cicero, it is because he is more conscientious in handling his complicated material; if he is less clear than *Ad Herennium* it is because he has read more and thought more than its author.

His attitude to traditional rhetoric can best be given in his own words. 'Let no one demand of me a set of rules of the type given by the average textbook, or expect me to offer students of rhetoric a set of rigid immutable laws. . . . Rhetoric would indeed be a small affair and easy of attainment if it could be embodied in one short code; in fact most rules are liable to be changed by the nature of the case, by circumstances of time and place and by the dictates of necessity. Thus the most important quality for the orator is judgment, because he has to adapt himself in various ways to the needs of the situation. . . . I do not deny that it is generally expedient to follow these rules, otherwise I should not be writing now; but expediency may also suggest some other course to us, in which case we shall disregard the authority of the professors and follow that course. . . . I do not want young men to think themselves sufficiently educated if they have learned by heart one of the short textbooks in circulation, or to think nothing can harm them if they obediently follow the decrees of the specialists. The art of speaking demands much hard work, continual study, a variety of exercise, long experience, the highest prudence and an ever-ready judgment.'[7]

But Quintilian could not and did not wish to break away from the past history of rhetoric. Indeed he shows an almost excessive respect for his predecessors. He sometimes allows himself to censure with more or less severity the pedantries of some of the authorities,[8] but he always gives fair and patient consideration to their views. Quintilian was, it should be remembered, a professor, and he has much of the character of the modern academic writer. He is learned, honest and fair-minded; at the same time he is excessively anxious to include all that has ever been said on his subject and unable at times to see the wood for the trees.

The framework of Quintilian's treatise is provided by the traditional divisions of school rhetoric. He accepts the five-fold division into *Inventio, Dispositio, Elocutio, Memoria* and *Actio*,[9] and handles his material under these heads, though when he surveys his work as a whole, *Inventio* and *Elocutio* stand out as the main branches, and *Dispositio* appears as a branch of the former, while *Memoria* and *Actio* belong to the latter.[10] He also accepts the traditional three types of oratory, forensic, deliberative and epideictic, and, like other ancient rhetoricians, devotes far more attention to the first than to the other two. Epideictic and deliberative are briefly despatched in the course of Book III, before Quintilian comes to the main part of his task, forensic oratory.[11]

Quintilian's learning and common sense give even his technical chapters a quality which raises them above the level of the
textbook. But a greater interest attaches to those additions and
insertions which were due either to Ciceronian influence or to
Quintilian's own thought and experience. The influence of
Cicero is responsible for the special section which, in addition
to occasional remarks elsewhere, he devotes to the appeal to the
emotions.[12] Here the sober Quintilian catches some of the fire of
Cicero. 'Arguments generally arise out of the case and there are
always more of them to support the better cause, so that the
party who wins by their means merely knows that his advocate
has not failed him. But when the minds of the judges require
force to move them and their thoughts have to be drawn away
from the contemplation of the truth, there we see the peculiar
task of the orator.' As soon as the judges begin to feel emotion
they begin to take a personal interest in the case, and 'the judge
overcome by his emotions abandons all attempt to discover the
truth'.[13] To the reader familiar with Cicero it comes as no surprise when he reads on to be told that in order to stir the
emotions of others it is necessary first to feel them oneself.
Quintilian here, strangely enough, seems unaware that Cicero
had said this before him, and claims to be giving the result not
of teaching but of nature and experience.[14] If he was not as
original as he claimed,[15] it seems that he had at any rate tested
the theory by experience. His power to feel emotion he regarded
as an important factor in his oratorical success; he himself had
frequently been so moved when speaking as to be overcome by
tears, to turn pale and to show all the symptoms of genuine grief.[16]

There is not the same feeling of personal conviction in the
long section on wit and humour which follows, and which no
doubt owed its position in the *Institutio* to Ciceronian example.
Quintilian, one feels, was a bit too scrupulous and high-minded
to use this weapon with the zest of Cicero. 'One of the greatest
difficulties of the orator in this connection', he says, 'is that
humorous remarks are generally untrue, and there is always
something mean about untruthfulness.'[17] 'In the battles of
the courts I prefer it when I can use gentle humour.'[18] 'The
good man will preserve his dignity and respectability in everything he says.'[19] The grave Quintilian, one feels, was not
a great humorist.

In one respect there is a striking difference between Cicero and Quintilian. The Ciceronian demand for a broad general education met, as we shall see in the next chapter, with only a limited response from Quintilian, and Cicero's enthusiasm for philosophy is by no means shared by his admirer. 'There will be no need', he writes, 'for the orator to swear allegiance to any philosophic school.'[20] More important than philosophy as an inspiration to the orator is the great Roman tradition. 'Who will teach courage, justice, loyalty, self-control, simplicity, contempt of pain and death, better than men like Fabricius, Curius, Regulus, Decius, Mucius and many others? If the Greeks excel in precepts, the Romans—which is much more important—excel in models of good living.'[21]

Quintilian follows Cicero to the extent of adopting his theory that rhetoric and philosophy had once been united and had subsequently parted company, that the material of philosophy belongs by right to the orator and that the latter is forced to borrow from the philosopher only because he has regrettably lost what should be his own.[22] But it cannot be said that Quintilian shows any desire to heal the breach. There is an unusual tone of bitterness in his references to philosophers, whom he describes not only as remote from practical affairs but as arrogant, vicious and hypocritical.[23] In fact the old quarrel between rhetoric and philosophy seems to have broken out again. Philosophy had changed its character. In the days of *De Oratore* the philosopher had been half professor, half preacher; now he was wholly a preacher. And he demanded a wholehearted allegiance, and was apt to dismiss literature and culture as frivolous distractions. He might appear to the rhetorician as an unwelcome rival who took pupils away to his own school. Quintilian has a scornful reference to those who, finding the rhetorical course too difficult, grew beards, underwent a brief course in the philosophical schools and then assumed a puritanical air of superiority which was merely a cloak for private vice.[24] There is a hint of jealousy about this passage.[25] Moreover the philosophers were either uninterested in public affairs or in active opposition. Thrasea had boycotted the senate; Domitian expelled the philosophers.[26] Quintilian, the tutor of Domitian's adopted sons, the man whose ideal was the *Romanus sapiens*,[27] the good citizen capable of playing his part in public affairs,[28] would not be likely to feel much sympathy with those whose outlook was so remote from his own.

In the section on *elocutio* we see the approach of the experienced teacher who is conscious of a mission to recall the young from the current debased style to sounder standards. After he has covered the conventional ground of the figures, Quintilian adds in his tenth book a consideration of the means of acquiring facility, by reading, writing and practice. This was outside the scope of traditional school rhetoric, and though Quintilian owes something to earlier writers such as Dionysius of Halicarnassus, the book is to a large extent the fruit of his own study and experience.

Although he claims that *elocutio* is the most difficult part of rhetoric and that it should be the chief object of study,[29] Quintilian is careful not to encourage an excessive attention to words independent of matter.[30] One should, he says, devote care to words, but even more to matter.[31] Beauty of style is best when it comes naturally and is not deliberately sought after.[32] Attention to style may defeat its own ends if carried to excess.[33] He attacks the excessive self-criticism of over-conscientious stylists who 'even when the best words have been discovered, try to find something more archaic, far fetched and unexpected, not understanding that where the words of a speech are praised it implies some inadequacy in its meaning'.[34] The best words are the obvious and natural ones, and those which are most closely connected with the matter.[35] Quintilian's prescription for composition is to know the theory of rhetoric, to read widely and so acquire a good vocabulary, to apply arrangement and to practise; if one is used to doing this, matter and words will come to one spontaneously and simultaneously, and there will be no need to make any special search for words.[36]

This is sound advice, which might well have been pondered by later rhetoricians such as Fronto. One misses, however, in Quintilian the Ciceronian belief in the wide learning which is to supply the *copia rerum*. For Quintilian the theory of rhetoric is sufficient to provide one with one's material, 'if one approaches the business of composition in a natural manner, considering what the theme demands, what suits the character concerned, what is the occasion and what the temper of the judge'. 'In this way', he adds, 'nature herself prescribes one's opening and what follows.'[37] But nature for Quintilian is, to use Pope's phrase, 'nature methodis'd', methodised in the rules of rhetoric. The matter is to be drawn from the theme and from the circumstances of the case and developed on the lines laid down in the text-books. It did not occur to Quintilian that the barrenness and loss of confidence which seems to have afflicted so many of his contemporaries might be due in part to the narrow bounds to which invention was confined by his theory.

We have yet to deal with the fundamental idea which informs the *Institutio*, the idea that the orator must be a good man. This idea finds expression in the preface to the first book, is alluded to elsewhere in the work and is elaborated in the final book.[38] The definition of the orator as a good man goes back to the elder Cato, whose *vir bonus dicendi peritus* Quintilian quotes.[39] But a 'good man' meant more to Quintilian than it did to Cato. Since the days of the censor Rome had developed a greater sensitivity in moral matters, thanks mainly to the teaching of the Stoa, and though Quintilian was no Stoic, he could not wholly escape the pervasive influence of the school.[40] But his view of rhetoric, if it is in part a revival of the old view of Cato and in part the ultimate offspring of Zeno's zeal for virtue, is also essentially Quintilian's own,[41] the result of his upright, serious character and also no doubt of his experiences as a teacher. The view that the orator must be a good man was, of course, implicit in the age-old disputes about the uses and abuses of oratory, but it is doubtful whether any professional rhetorician before Quintilian had expressed himself as he does. 'My subject is the education of the perfect orator, and the first essential for such a one is that he should be a good man. There-fore I demand of him not only outstanding gifts of speech, but all the excellences of character as well.'[42] It is safe to say that no previous treatise on rhetoric had begun like that. The tradi-tional emphasis in rhetorical literature was on oratory rather than on the orator, on the art rather than the man; thus Aristotle, though he emphasises the importance of conveying an impression of the speaker's character, regards this as only one of the elements in persuasion, parallel to argumentation. Even Cicero, in spite of his titles *De Oratore* and *Orator*, does not get away from the tradition. Quintilian, while absorbing the whole tradition of rhetorical theory, adds a new emphasis on the orator as a man as well as a practitioner of the art of speaking.

The principle that the orator must be a good man guides Quintilian throughout his discussion of the old academic problems, What is rhetoric? Is it useful? and Is it an art?[43] He divides rhetoricians into those who think bad men can be orators and those who confine the name to the good. In the first category he would include all those who, whatever their exact definition, made rhetoric essentially the art of persuasion.[44] The definition which Quintilian accepts is *bene dicendi scientia*, a formula for which he claims no originality, though he does not attribute it to any specific authority.[45] Taking advantage of the convenient ambiguity of the word *bene* he claims that the science of speaking well includes the orator's character as well as all the oratorical virtues, for 'only the good man can speak well'.[46] Fortified by this rather dubious piece of reasoning Quintilian attacks the question whether rhetoric is useful. He admits that it can be misused, like other good things, but this is no reason for thinking it an evil thing.[47] There is, however, no real problem for those who accept Quintilian's definition; if the orator is a good man, there can be no doubt about the usefulness of oratory.[48] There is no need to follow Quintilian through his discussion of the trite question whether rhetoric is an art. It is enough to remark that here again his identification of the orator with the good man is brought into play. It had been argued by some that orators spoke indifferently on either side; therefore rhetoric could not be an art. But this implied a rhetoric divorced from morality; it was highly unlikely that the *vir bonus* would speak on either side indifferently.[49]

In his last book Quintilian returns to the theme of the orator as good man and discusses it without reference to the theoretical controversies that had been handed down from past ages. Let our orator, he says, be Cato's *vir bonus dicendi peritus*, the essential part of the definition being the first two words.[50] The orator must be a good man, not only because of the harm which would otherwise be done to society, but also because one can hardly attribute either intelligence or common sense to the bad man. Again, only the man free from all vices will be free to concentrate on so exacting and glorious a study as oratory.[51] If it is maintained that, granted equal natural gifts and training, the bad man may be no worse an orator than the good, the answer is that the purpose of a speech is to convince the judge that the case put forward is true and honourable, and this the good man will do more easily than the bad.[52]

Though Quintilian holds that goodness is the essential thing and skill in speaking only of secondary importance, he would hardly have written twelve books on the education of an orator if he had thought that goodness was enough. In fact not only did he believe in an elaborate education, but he fully accepted the fact that the orator might have to say some things which at first sight might seem inconsistent with his demand for perfection of character. Quintilian did not, as some of the Stoics did, hold that it was enough to say the truth in plain words. He knew all the tricks of the trade and would not forbid their use to the perfect orator. He even in one place goes so far as to claim in support of his definition of the orator that the good man lies more plausibly than the bad.[53]

Why, some might ask, all these rules and precepts? The good man would surely accept only good cases, and these would defend themselves by their truth. To this Quintilian answers that one must know how to defend the false and unjust if only to recognise these arts in others.[54] Again, audiences being as they are human and truth being as it is exposed to so many dangers, it is necessary to call in art to assist truth.[55] At times the general good even demands that the orator should defend what is untrue.[56] He may wish to secure the acquittal of a guilty man if he knows that he can be reformed or that he will be useful to the state.[57] In fact the good man does not always speak the truth or even defend the better cause. But what matters is not so much the act as the motive. 'We must not merely consider the nature of the case which the good man defends but his reason and purpose.'[58]

One has the impression that Quintilian has not faced all the difficulties raised by his definition of the orator. Rhetoric was in part a purely utilitarian training of the barrister in the tricks of his trade, but it had become the main element in higher education, and rhetoricians like Quintilian with a high moral sense were hard put to it to reconcile the morality demanded by the educational side of rhetoric with those non-moral elements which came from its function as a practical training.

For all the admiration that the *Institutio* arouses in the reader, he is inevitably conscious of certain limitations in its author's outlook, limitations which arise from Quintilian's professional outlook, from the fact that he fully accepted the tradition in which he had been brought up. Archbishop Whately spoke of him as possessed of much good sense, but a good sense which was 'tinctured with pedantry—with that ἀλαζονεία, as Aristotle calls it, which extends to an extravagant degree the province of the art which he professes.'[59] He had not the ability to see his subject from the outside; brought up on rhetoric and long engaged in teaching it, he had no doubts about its value. Nothing could be more admirable than his work—until one begins to question the foundations on which it was built. For even apart from the general question of the intellectual value of the formidable system that we find expounded with such scholarly and loving care in his work, there was a certain unreality about the whole process of the education of an orator as conceived by Quintilian. To what end, we are prompted to ask, is this elaborate training directed? We have the answer in Book XII. The perfect orator, we read there, has never yet existed—for though Cicero might be called perfect in the ordinary way of speaking, he still did not quite satisfy the highest standards—but may exist in the future.[60] He will be as perfect in character as in powers of speaking. He will be unlike any figure who has appeared in the past, unique, perfect, a man of the noblest feelings and noblest powers of expression. He is not only advocate but statesman; he will direct the counsels of the senate and guide the people from error to better things.[61] It is the old ideal of the orator-statesman. But what place was there for such a figure in the time of Domitian? It is well after reading the *Institutio* to turn to the *Dialogus de Oratoribus*, and when we read the latter work we begin to see Quintilian's weakness. For the *Dialogue* has what Quintilian's work lacks, a sense of history and of the realities of contemporary life. Quintilian is singularly unconscious of the changes that have taken place in the world since the days of Cicero. Tacitus knew better. He knew that the days of great oratory were over.

Quintilian's perfect orator remained a dream. If he was ever to exist, he could only be the Emperor, and the one Emperor whose character might have satisfied Quintilian's demands turned away from rhetoric, congratulating himself on his escape, and chose as his masters those philosophers whom Quintilian had scorned.[62]

QUINTILIAN AND RHETORICAL TEACHING

Quintilianus doctor egregius.
Cassiodorus, *de Rhetorica* 10 (498 Halm)

THOUGH RHETORICAL theory occupies the greater part of the *Institutio Oratoria*, most modern readers find more interest in the educational side of the work. Quintilian's originality lay largely in the fact that he was the first to interpret the art of oratory as including all that was necessary for the training of an orator from his earliest years. Others before him had ignored the preliminary stages; he first brought them within the sphere of rhetoric.[1] In this he was reflecting the spirit of the age. Under the Empire the schoolmaster came into his own. Vespasian founded chairs of rhetoric supported by public funds.[2] Pliny took a delight in finding tutors for his friends' sons and founding a school in his native town, and looked back wistfully to schooldays as the happiest period of one's life.[3] The bad-tempered or scandalously immoral type of teacher, Orbilius or Remmius Palaemon, gave way to the conscientious educationalist.

The early part of Quintilian's work contains much sound educational precept which has a value independent of his professed aim of producing the complete orator, but it hardly concerns us here. We must pass over the orator's early training and confine ourselves to rhetorical education in the generally accepted sense.

Quintilian was essentially conservative in educational as in rhetorical theory. He accepted the existing system, under which the rhetorician's main work was lecturing on the theory of rhetoric and teaching declamation. We shall see later how he used declamation; as regards theory it may be assumed that Quintilian's lectures in his school were on the same lines as his treatment in the *Institutio*, and no one who has read that work through can doubt that his teaching was thorough and scholarly.

Another traditional function of the rhetorician was the teaching of composition through the elementary exercises known as *progymnasmata*. In Quintilian's day, however, these had passed to the *grammaticus*, who had encroached on the province of the rhetorician, and was even handling certain types of declamation. The rhetoricians were quite content to be rid of the *progymnasmata* and to concentrate on what they regarded as higher work.[4] Quintilian did not approve of this development; *grammatice*, he holds, should stick to its own business, and rhetoric should not shirk what is an important part of its task.[5] He does not, however, restore the *progymnasmata* completely to the rhetorician, but divides them between the two schools, the more elementary type of exercise being assigned to the *grammaticus*.[6] The more advanced ones, which were more closely connected with oratorical practice, are reserved for the school of rhetoric. Under the rhetorician, according to Quintilian's scheme, the pupil begins with exercises in historical narrative and proceeds to defending or impugning the credibility of stories, fictitious or historical. He then goes on to the praise or blame of famous men, comparison between two historical characters, commonplaces and theses and the commendation or denunciation of laws.[7]

In this connection Quintilian makes one of his cautious suggestions for reform. These exercises were written, but it was the common practice also to learn them by heart and recite them on an appointed day. This practice Quintilian disapproves of; it would be better in his view to learn by heart the works of others rather than the pupils' own compositions. But the existing practice was popular with parents,[8] and there is no evidence that Quintilian himself succeeded in getting it abandoned.

One of the problems for the Roman educationalist was how to combine the specialised teaching of the rhetorical schools with the broad general education which was generally considered desirable. Cicero had given eloquent expression to the view that the orator should be learned in history, law and philosophy and well read in literature, and there were also certain other subjects which the educated man was expected to know something of. The Hellenistic ἐγκύκλιος παιδεία, or general education, included music and mathematics, two subjects which would appear to have little connection with the literary and rhetorical studies of the Roman schools. Quintilian, however, gives them a place among the studies preliminary to entry to the rhetorical school,[9] and by ingenious special pleading tries to show that they have their value in oratorical training.

Music, he argues, was originally united with philosophy; therefore, since philosophy had usurped the functions of oratory it really belonged to the latter. It was useful too for the orator to know about gestures, arrangement of words and inflexions of the voice, and it was music that handled such matter. Again, the future orator must read poetry, and poetry cannot be understood without music. Finally, there was a *controversia* about a piper who had driven someone mad by playing in the Phrygian mode; how could one declaim on this theme without a knowledge of music?[10] As for mathematics (*geometria*), there were lawsuits about boundaries and measurements. Logical deduction and syllogistic method were used in mathematics—and in oratory. Astronomy—a branch of mathematics—taught that nothing was irregular and fortuitous, and this piece of knowledge would be found useful by the orator.[11]

The lengthy treatment which Quintilian gives to music and mathematics, and the enthusiasm which breaks out after all the dubious utilitarian arguments are done with, are surprising. But Quintilian is conscious that he has to contend against the objections of those who regarded these subjects as useless to the orator, and it was easy for him to expatiate on their value since he expected them to be finished with before the boy entered on his rhetorical training. Learning to speak and to write was in his opinion too exacting a study to allow of any other simultaneous study.[12]

By contrast the studies on which Cicero laid such emphasis are given comparatively meagre treatment by Quintilian. History he regards more as a branch of literature than as the study of the past. He would have liked historians to be read as part of the curriculum of the rhetorical schools, no doubt because of the speeches included in their works,[13] and he includes historical writers in his summary of Greek and Latin literature in Book X, not without preliminary warning that their style is not altogether suited to the orator.[14] Style is his primary interest in this part of his work, but he notes also an important advantage to be derived from history, the knowledge of facts and precedents, which will provide the orator with valuable arguments.[15] To this theme, familiar to us already from Cicero, Quintilian returns in a brief and rather perfunctory paragraph in Book XII.[16]

The study of law has no place in Quintilian's educational scheme. It is only after he has finished with school days and is depicting the mature orator that he gives us a chapter on this subject.[17] Here, following as so often in Cicero's footsteps, he insists that the orator should be well acquainted with the law and should not have to go for help to professional advisers. The latter are after all often unsuccessful orators who have given up pleading because it is too difficult. Legal science is only a mixture of knowledge and common sense; the knowledge can be easily acquired and the common sense belongs to the orator already.[18]

Knowing Quintilian's admiration for Cicero we might expect to find him urging the study of philosophy on his pupils. But, as we have already seen, he did not care for philosophers, and though he admits the oratorical uses of philosophy, he does so somewhat grudgingly. He does however make it clear that he expects his orator to have a thorough knowledge of philosophical, or at least of ethical, theory, and reviewing the various branches of philosophy, dialectic, ethics and natural philosophy, he finds that each of them has its oratorical uses. His attitude is indeed rather ambiguous; at times we may get the impression that his ideal of the *vir bonus* can be attained without the aid of philosophy, but he was not in fact prepared to go as far as that. The orator must still depend on the philosopher.[19]

If Quintilian shows no great enthusiasm for the study of law and philosophy it should be remembered that, unlike Cicero, he had been a practising teacher and was primarily concerned with the discipline which he himself had taught. Music and mathematics might find a place in the stage before the rhetorician took over, but philosophy and law had no place there or in the rhetoric course proper.[20] Philosophy belonged to the philosophers and law to the lawyers.

Literature was to some extent catered for by the *grammaticus*, one of whose traditional functions was the interpretation of the poets, but lectures on literature were considered below the dignity of the rhetorician,[21] and the prose writers, who were not touched by the *grammaticus*, would thus be left out. Quintilian himself introduced for some of his pupils the reading of the historians and orators, but the experiment was not a success. Though Quintilian remained convinced of its value and recommended it to posterity, tradition proved too strong for him.[22] The method he suggests is that the pupil should be made to read a speech aloud, and that this should be accompanied by comments on the argument, the style and so on. The master should not only comment himself, but should ask questions. 'I will venture to say', writes Quintilian, 'that this form of exercise will be of more use to learners than all the textbooks of the authorities. . . . There are few cases in which precept is not less valuable than practice. If the teacher is to declaim to provide his hearers with a model, will not the reading of Cicero and Demosthenes be more profitable?'[23] After thus recommending the innovation he adds revealingly, 'I wish that the reluctance to do this did not equal the pleasure it would cause.'[24] Quintilian himself did not abandon rhetorical theory and declamation for the reading of texts, and it is safe to say that his followers, too, adhered to the traditional methods.

But though Quintilian's attempt to introduce the reading of texts into the curriculum was not successful, he believed that the orator should be well read. His best known chapter is a critical reading list for would-be orators, a list that comprises most of Greek and Latin literature.[25] The course is not part of the formal instruction of the rhetorical school; it is rather to enable those who have learnt what can be learnt from their teacher to put their lessons into practice as well and as easily as possible.[26] It is important, too, to note where the chapter comes in the economy of the whole work. It follows the rules for style, and is connected with them. Rules do not by themselves produce facility of speech; reading is required.[27] 'It is from these and other works worth reading', writes Quintilian after his survey is completed, 'that we must draw our supply of words, the variety of our figures and our methods of arrangement.'[28] Reading is to make a ready man rather than a full man.

We pass on to the most important part of the rhetorical education, the declamation. Quintilian, as we have seen in an earlier chapter, was a severe critic of declamation as it was practised in his day, but this does not mean that he rejected the practice altogether. So far from doing this, he regarded it as by far the most valuable method of education, if properly used, and he certainly employed it himself in teaching.[29] The subjects chosen should in his view be as true to life as possible. *Controversiae* ought to be what they were originally intended to be, a preparation for the courts, and the incredible themes, with their 'magicians, plagues, oracles and stepmothers', should be banished, or at any rate, if this is impossible, the foolish and ridiculous should be avoided.[30] It is clear, however, that the conventions of the schools were too strong for any radical reform. Quintilian is prepared to concede that students should occasionally let off steam on the wilder themes, and though he suggests certain improvements, the addition of names, the use of longer and more complicated themes and a more familiar and less solemn style, there is no evidence that even he, with all his influence and authority, had introduced any of these improvements.[31] His common-sense view of declamation as preparation for real practice was not shared by all, and some maintained that its object was simply display.[32] Quintilian is prepared to admit that it involved an element of display, and it followed from this that certain inconveniences from the practical point of view had to be put up with.[33]

The extent to which Quintilian accepted declamation is evident throughout his work. The attentive reader will notice that often his advice is concerned with declamation rather than with the speeches of real life. Seneca's *non vitae sed scholae discimus* applies in part even to Quintilian's school.[34] Particularly is this the case with his treatment of deliberative oratory. His examples are drawn from past history or legend as treated in the *suasoriae*. Thus 'When we advise the arming of slaves in the Punic War' is his example of an occasion where expediency is preferred to honour; and advice is given as to how to treat the well-known *suasoriae* about Cicero and Antony, and what arguments to use in urging Julius Caesar to accept the crown, evidently a familiar theme of the schools.[35] His remarks on style in the *genus deliberativum* are wholly concerned with school

I

declamation,[36] and it is only at the end of the section that we come to a brief allusion to the world outside the schools.[37]

In his treatment of the *genus iudiciale* Quintilian, having himself been a practising advocate, is nearer to reality, but here, too, his advice is often explicitly or implicity concerned with school declamation.[38] He thinks it worth while, for instance, to include advice on matters such as the rewards due to tyrannicides, which belonged solely to the world of the *controversiae*.[39]

Quintilian then was to some extent, as most teachers no doubt are, the victim of educational tradition. He could not get away from declamation, and he accepted it as he found it. But no doubt in his case even unrealistic themes were treated in a thorough and sensible manner which made them a useful training in thought and expression. He had no use for the showy and superficial, or for the tortuous obscurities popular with some declaimers. He subjected his themes to a careful analysis, and developed them on the lines of common sense. In a sphere where the unnatural had long reigned supreme, he followed the guidance of nature.[40]

There survive two collections of declamations ascribed by manuscript tradition to Quintilian and known as *Declamationes Maiores* and *Declamationes Minores*. The first, a collection of nineteen fully worked out declamations, passed as Quintilian's work in the fourth century, but it is hard to believe that any of the declamations included in it are from his hand. Most of them are quite out of keeping with all that we know of his attitude to declamation, and even the more sober of them seem to have little Quintilianic about them. The Lesser Declamations, though they have no external evidence in their favour,[41] have a greater claim to be considered Quintilianic. They are evidently the notes of a pupil taken down in the classroom and not originally intended for publication.[42] The declamations, the master's 'fair copy', are given in outline, sometimes very briefly, in other cases in greater detail, though never in the complete form in which they would have appeared if the master had published them. Prefixed to and interspersed with the declamations there are in many cases notes of the master's oral expositions, to which the manuscripts give the title 'sermo'.

Was this master Quintilian himself? In the *Institutio Oratoria* there is a reference to two unauthorised publications of Quintilian's lecture notes made during his lifetime,[43] and it has been suggested that one of these was what has come down to us as the Lesser Declamations.[44] This is clearly not the case; the lectures in question were evidently not on declamation but on rhetorical theory.[45] But the Lesser Declamations may none the less be notes from Quintilian's teaching, published after the appearance of the *Institutio*. There is much that is Quintilianic about them. The method of handling declamation, the rhetorical doctrine, the tone and the manner all remind one of Quintilian.[46] On the other hand so much of what appears in Quintilian was common property that too much stress should not be laid on these similarities, and in one respect there is not quite so close a correspondence as we should expect if Quintilian and the master of the Declamations were one and the same person. In the course of the *Institutio* something like fifty declamation themes are quoted or referred to. It is probable that a considerable proportion of these themes were those that Quintilian was accustomed to use in teaching, and we should therefore expect to find them reappearing in the Declamations. In fact of the 145 themes in the extant part of the collection only one is identical with a theme referred to in the *Institutio*,[47] though three more are closely similar.[48] Even allowing for the fact that nearly two-thirds of the original collection is lost, we should expect to find a greater degree of correspondence. To the cautious scholar therefore the master of the Declamations will be not Quintilian but rather 'school of Quintilian'.

We may take the Lesser Declamations, then, as evidence of the existence after Quintilian's death of a school of rhetorical teaching inspired by him and preserving his methods of handling declamation. The subjects are on the old lines. We are still in an artificial world, where pirates roam the seas, sons are disinherited, tyrants are slain, stepmothers play their traditional role and victims of rape exercise their traditional option of either marrying their seducer or demanding his death. But if the themes are unreal the treatment is sober and realistic. 'I do not want anyone to blame me', says our professor, 'for not giving you *loci*. If you want to extend the declamation or to exercise your wits, what you say may perhaps delight the ears, but will be quite irrelevant to the case.'[49] One must stick to the set theme, and not introduce motives that are inconsistent with it.[50] So the outline declamations are strictly to the point, without the forced style, the ingenious and improbable 'colours' and the striking epigrams familiar to us from the elder Seneca.[51]

The analysis is commonly on the traditional lines of *ius* and *aequitas*, the former being often divided into *scriptum* and *sententia*. Careful attention is given to the legal aspect. In one of the declamations a girl who has been raped hangs herself. Her father then produces her twin sister, and makes her exercise the option of the victim of rape and demand the death of the seducer. The trick succeeds, but later the truth comes out and the father is accused of having caused the death of the seducer. 'It is easy and obvious', we read, 'to deal with that side of the old man's case which is concerned with emotional appeal and equity. But unless his defence is founded on law, there is a risk of his being condemned for all his tears. So we must be careful to make the most of the legal case.... We must therefore define what is meant by "cause of death". The whole dispute and the whole point of the case lies in this.'[52]

The characters must be made to behave consistently with the data given by the subject and with the situation in which they find themselves. A father is accused of insanity because he follows his dissolute son weeping through the streets. The father might well be expected to show violent indignation against his son. But we must consider the character we are impersonating. He was not a violent father, for he had not disinherited his son or reviled him; he was not a hard father, for he wept. This character must be preserved.[53] Similarly with the case of the rich man who educated a poor man in oratory at his own expense, and accused him of ingratitude because when acting as the rich man's advocate he failed to secure his acquittal. 'You realise that this young man must show the utmost respect for the rich man. That is the only way of making him appear to have been forced to act as he did if there is any complaint on that score. In all cases based on the law about ingratitude we should be careful to see that the defendant does not show ingratitude in his pleading.'[54]

'One must consider what the theme demands and what suits the characters concerned.' Quintilian's prescription[55] governs the master of the Lesser Declamations. In his hands the *controversia* is a serious exercise, not an occasion for display. He shows us what Quintilian meant when he called declamation the most useful of rhetorical exercises; in spite of the extravagance of the themes it could be made the vehicle of a sober and sensible training.

XII

THE AGE OF THE ANTONINES

Quae nunc sunt aures hominum hoc tempore, quanta in spectandis
orationibus elegantia.

Fronto, *ad M. Caesarem et invicem* 2.2.1

THE AGE of the Antonines was in a sense a golden age for the
art of speech. If little that was said was of any value, seldom
in human history have so many words been uttered in public
and seldom has the spoken word been so highly honoured. It
was the age of the so-called Second Sophistic, of those *virtuosi*
described by Philostratus, who travelled round from city to
city, charming their audiences with their displays and winning
for themselves applause and honour, statues and privileges.

Rhetoricians were honoured in the highest quarters. Hadrian
consorted with them and rewarded them; Antoninus Pius gave
them privileges.[1] Marcus Aurelius was attentive to their words
and their needs; he attended a declamation of Aristeides, and
rewarded Hermogenes and Adrian.[2] He established and endowed the state chair of rhetoric at Athens, and took a personal
interest in appointments.[3] The Emperors' interest was shared
by their subjects; Romans of high position took sides in the
quarrels of rival rhetoricians, and senators left displays of
dancing to hear a star declaimer.[4]

The Second Sophistic was essentially a Greek phenomenon.
The famous performers of the day were Greeks, or, if not Greek,
like Favorinus from Gaul, spoke in Greek. Greek declaimers
were as much at home in Rome as in the eastern parts of the
Empire; they could draw to their audiences even those who did
not understand their language.[5] There was a close connection
between Greek and Roman *literati;* Favorinus and Herodes
Atticus joined in literary discussions with Roman men of learning;[6] Fronto was familiar with Greek and on occasion wrote in

it; Apuleius was eloquent in both languages, and adorned his *Apology* with numerous Greek quotations.[7]

There was of course nothing new about much of this. Educated Romans had always been bilingual and Greek men of learning had always been at home in Rome. Vespasian had founded a chair of Greek rhetoric there along with the Latin chair, and Greek declaimers had performed in the capital before the time of the Antonines.[8] What is new is the weakening of the Roman tradition. It now becomes increasingly hard to recognise a distinctively Roman rhetoric. Apuleius owes little to Rome except his language. An African educated in Athens, he belongs essentially to the cultural tradition of the Greek-speaking world, and his oratory, in so far as it is not purely individual, is that of the Second Sophistic. Fronto, though long resident in Rome, and the tutor of an Emperor, has little of the Roman tradition in him. Quintilian had had his roots in this tradition; to him the political and forensic battles of the Ciceronian age were still living and real. It was not so with Fronto; though he knows and admires the orators of the past, their speeches are for him books rather than events in history. His age has lost touch with the Roman past.

In the field of rhetorical theory the Greeks were now active as ever; Hermogenes, a sophist who lost his powers and took to writing, added new refinements to traditional theory. The only Latin writer of the age who touches on rhetorical theory is Fronto,[9] and his letters provide illuminating evidence of the change that had come over Roman rhetoric. They show epideictic, which had been more or less neglected by earlier theory, and which Cicero's Antonius had dismissed with the words 'Everyone knows what to praise in a man',[10] exalted to a high place of importance.

Roman usage, says Quintilian, gave epideictic a place in the practical affairs of life.[11] Praise and blame were chiefly required in the course of forensic and deliberative speeches, and by Cicero the *genus* was hardly recognised as entitled to independent existence.[12] There was indeed the old established institution of the funeral *laudatio*, but this had its own traditions different from those of the Greek formal panegyric.[13] But under the Empire epideictic oratory begins to creep in. Within the framework of traditional Roman oratory the consular *gratiarum actio* developed into a full-blown eulogy of the Emperor; outside this framework we hear of the praise of Jupiter Capitolinus as a regular feature of the contest in his honour founded by Domitian.[14] Quintilian gives fairly detailed directions for praising gods and men and a brief paragraph on the praise of cities.[15] This is the nearest any Roman writer gets to the elaborate and detailed instructions given by the later Greek writers on epideictic, Menander and pseudo-Dionysius.

Fronto's interest lay less in the topics of eulogy than in the style it required.[16] Its exacting nature, in his view, gave it an especial claim to the attention of the stylist; whereas in other types there was room for all three styles, plain, middle and grand, in epideictic the grand style must be used throughout.[17] Fronto was himself a skilled eulogist; not only was he an admired performer in the senate when the occasion demanded that the Emperor's praises should be sung; he also practised the sophistic art of paradoxical eulogy, and wrote the praises of Negligence, of Smoke and Dust, and the like. This kind of composition was a novelty in Latin,[18] and Fronto, sending to Marcus Aurelius his eulogy of Smoke and Dust, gives his views as to how it should be done. Frequent *sententiae* are required, closely packed together and neatly joined, but there should be no superfluous words. Nothing should be left rough and unconnected; sentences should close with a snap like a brooch. The aim of such speeches is to give pleasure and amusement. But the topic should be treated as if it were grand and important; tales of gods and heroes should be inserted, together with verses, proverbs and ingenious fictions. Finally Fronto claims that it is a sign of a generous disposition to distribute one's praises as widely as possible, in particular to include what has hitherto been neglected as the object of eulogy.[19]

But Fronto has a greater interest for us than as the exponent of the art of eulogy. It fell to his lot as the most eminent orator of his day to tutor the two adopted sons of Antoninus Pius, Marcus Aurelius and Verus. In the correspondence of Fronto and Marcus we can see the tutor at work, and we can see both from the correspondence and from the Emperor's *Meditations* how he lost his pupil's allegiance. Fronto is the last important representative of rhetoric in its age-old fight with philosophy, and it is not difficult to understand how it was that in this case rhetoric was defeated.

Rhetoric was still not without its practical value, for Emperors no less than others needed to be able to express themselves. Indeed they alone perhaps could make full use of the art of speaking. As Fronto writes to his ex-pupil Verus, now a successful military commander, the old ideal of the perfect orator takes shape as the imperial orator. Eloquence to Fronto is the property of *imperium*, command. The word, he writes, 'implies not only power, but also speech, since command is exercised through bidding and forbidding. The commander is false to his name and unjustly so styled, if he does not commend good deeds, blame ill deeds, exhort to goodness and dissuade from evil.'[20] 'Eloquence inspires fear, wins love, encourages effort, puts an end to impudence, commends virtue, confounds vice, persuades, soothes, instructs, consoles.' It is the true sovereign of the human race, and now for the first time is embodied in the sovereign Emperors.[21] Elsewhere, writing in more practical vein to Marcus Aurelius, Fronto points out that the Emperor's duties include giving counsel in the senate, addressing the people, sending out dispatches, and so on. Eloquence is therefore a necessary function of the imperial office.[22]

Rhetoric, the creation of the now far off city-state republics, is thus adapted to the imperial age; Fronto fully recognised the imperial age, and did not delude himself that he was living in the age of Cicero. On the other hand there is nothing practical about his rhetorical teaching. His rhetoric is directed not to persuading but to pleasing; it is the art of elegant self-expression, which has lost touch with the world of politics and power.

So Fronto has much to say about style, and little about the matter of oratory. He found Marcus Aurelius already possessed of nobility of mind and dignity of thought; he therefore exercised him in the beauties of style, and under his guidance the future Emperor collected synonyms and unusual words and paraphrased the older writers, adding refinements, inserting images and figures, producing 'the patina of age'.[23] Old words were indeed Fronto's hobby, almost his passion. He pictures the orator as a commander enrolling an army; not only does he make use of the volunteers, the words, that is, that immediately present themselves; he seeks out the skulkers too, the less obvious words, and presses them into his service.[24] Few of the ancient orators, in Fronto's view, had devoted sufficient pains to seeking out choice words. Cato and Sallust were the chief exceptions; Cicero, for all his beauty and grandeur of style, had very few unexpected words 'such as are not hunted out except with study and care and watchfulness and an extensive familiarity with old poems'.[25]

Fronto made much use of such exercises as the composition of maxims (*gnomae*) and similes (εἰκόνες). In one place he expresses his delight at the brilliance with which Marcus has turned a maxim, and recommends turning the same maxim twice or three times, as well as the copying out of *sententiae* from Sallust.[26] As regards similes, Fronto had been trained in their use by his own rhetoric master and himself attached great importance to them. On one occasion Marcus writes that he has almost completed ten; there is one, however, that is causing him difficulty, and he applies to his master for help.[27] Fronto's method at first was to supply Marcus with the image and leave him to find the application; later he preferred to leave his pupil to discover the image for himself.[28]

Such was the training to which Marcus Aurelius was subjected. Though outwardly he was all that a dutiful and enthusiastic pupil should be, he was not at heart satisfied. Rhetoric's old rival, philosophy, exercised a powerful appeal. With his obstinate conscience he could not reconcile himself to the insincerities of rhetoric.[29] The books of the philosopher Aristo kept him away from his rhetorical tasks and made him disinclined to argue on both sides of a question.[30] He found, too, that whenever he had said anything good he felt pleased with himself, and this to him was a reason for shunning eloquence.[31]

Fronto did his best to secure his pupil's continued allegiance. To the charge that rhetoric encouraged self-conceit he replied that if Marcus's good sayings pleased him too much, he must blame himself rather than eloquence; he should cure himself of self-conceit, not reject the cause of his gratification.[32] He points out, too, that many philosophers had laid down precepts which they did not always live up to in practice; even if Marcus was as wise as Zeno and Cleanthes he would still have to wear the imperial purple, not the philosopher's cloak.[33] Even philosophers, he argues, do not neglect the use of words; Chrysippus does not simply expound, define and explain; he uses the various methods of the orator. Marcus is exhorted to use words worthy of his sentiments; to raise himself and shake himself free of the crabbed style of the dialecticians and to make eloquence the companion of philosophy.[34]

Elsewhere Fronto resorts to the old theme that we found in Quintilian, the easiness of philosophy in comparison with rhetoric. He professes to believe that Marcus has abandoned rhetoric from a dislike of drudgery. In philosophy there is no *exordium* to be carefully elaborated, no *narratio* to be briefly, clearly and skilfully set out, no dividing up of the subject into heads, no arguments to be sought out, no amplification, et cetera.[35] The philosopher's pupil has merely to listen in silence while his master expounds; he has nothing to prepare or write, nothing to recite to his master or say by heart; he need not hunt out words, embellish with synonyms, make translations from the Greek.[36]

Fronto did his best, but it was not good enough. In spite of all the affection and intimacy of their relationship there was a great gulf between master and pupil. In one of his letters Marcus remarked that he was forgetting all that he had learnt. Fronto protests in reply that on the contrary he is speaking better than ever: witness a recent speech which contained, among other virtues, a remarkable example of *paraleipsis*. 'You have shown', the letter ends, 'originality in beginning your speech with this figure; and I am sure you will do many other original and remarkable things in your speeches. So outstanding is your ability.'[37] But Marcus Aurelius had other ambitions than to go down to history as the author of a neat *paraleipsis*. How far Fronto was from understanding him we can see if we turn to the first book of the *Meditations*, where Marcus records what he owes to his various teachers. Looking back on Fronto's teaching he remembers only that he learnt from him 'to observe how vile a thing is the malice and caprice and hypocrisy of absolutism; and generally speaking that those whom we entitle "Patricians" are somehow rather wanting in the natural affections.'[38] From Rusticus, on the other hand, he had learned 'to avoid rhetoric'; and in the closing section of the book he counts it as a blessing owed to the gods that he made no further progress than he did in rhetoric and similar studies.[39]

To conclude this chapter we must turn once more to declamation, for though Fronto shows little interest in this traditional method of rhetorical teaching,[40] there is no doubt that it enjoyed continued popularity in his day and after. This is shown by the declamations of Calpurnius Flaccus, generally supposed to belong to the second century, of which excerpts survive,[41] and by the pseudo-Quintilianic Greater Declamations, a collection which was certainly in existence in the fourth century and may date in part from considerably earlier.[42]

Little need be said about declamation in the later part of the Empire, for there was little development, and the themes and treatment remained much as they were in the Augustan age. When we turn to Calpurnius Flaccus or the Greater Declamations from the elder Seneca we find ourselves in a familiar atmosphere. The same laws and the same situations recur, and though relatively few of the themes are actually identical,[43] there is a strong family likeness between those in the later collections and those of Seneca. Even where a theme appears to be new we cannot assume that it was not current long before. In Calpurnius Flaccus there is a sensational *controversia* about some young men burnt to death in a trap laid by a brothel-keeper; we might well have supposed that this was an invention of later antiquity if it had not been referred to incidentally by Seneca.[44]

There is little realism or contemporary reference in these later declamations. Public affairs are treated on wholly conventional lines. The valiant soldier and the deserter belong to an imaginary world; the tyrant and the pirate are faded stage property. Most of the themes concern private affairs and deal with such occurrences as adultery, incest, rape, remarriage and disinheritance, that had long been the staple of declamation. A number of themes are based on the enmity of rich and poor.[45] A rich man sprinkles the flowers in his garden with poison and so kills the bees of his poor neighbour.[46] This theme, which produces what is perhaps the most attractive of the Greater Declamations is, as far as we know, new. More often the theme of enmity is combined with one of the traditional situations. In one case a rich man adopts the three sons of a poor man. One is caught in adultery and killed; the second is accused of aiming at tyranny; the poor man asks to have the third back.[47]

In another the poor man is put on sale on the ground of being a foreigner, bought by the rich man and made tutor to his son; the son is caught in adultery and killed, and the poor man is sent to be crucified.[48] It is unnecessary to quote at length. We are already familiar with the world of the declamations. We have met the man who raped two virgins, one of whom demanded his hand in marriage, the other his death.[49] We meet him again in Calpurnius Flaccus, but find that the story has developed and a new complication has arisen from the birth of a child to one of the victims and the adoption of the child by the father, now married to the other victim.[50] We may not have met the father who lost his sight from weeping after the death of two of his sons and dreamed that he would recover his sight if the third died too. But we are hardly surprised when his son, hearing of the dream through his mother, kills himself and the father recovers his sight, whereupon he divorces his wife and is accused by her of wrongful divorce.[51] Such complications beset family life as depicted in the rhetorical schools.

There is nothing of interest in the meagre excerpts of Calpurnius Flaccus, but the Greater Declamations, though they make tedious reading on the whole, have at least the interest of being the only complete Roman declamations that have come down to us. They vary in manner. Some are quite sensible and well argued; others are declamatory in the worst sense. On the whole the manner is similar to that of the Augustan declaimers, and by reading them we can obtain some idea of what the declamations from which Seneca quotes were like in completed form. The declamations of Latro and Gallio were probably cleverer and more entertaining than anything in the Greater Declamations; those of the minor Augustan rhetoricians were probably sillier. The outrageous 'colours' preserved by Seneca are little in evidence in pseudo-Quintilian. We have already met the case of the son whose father attempted three times to disinherit him, and who was found mixing a potion which he claimed was poison designed for himself, and we have seen what ingenious 'colours' were used by some of the Augustan declaimers.[52] The declaimer of the Greater Declamations, where the theme recurs, indulges in none of these eccentricities, and confines himself to what may be called the standard 'colour', that used by Latro in the Augustan age, which accepted the son's intention to kill himself and explained it as due to his finding life with his father intolerable.[53]

There is little in the Greater Declamations of the sober legal analysis which, as we saw in the last chapter, belongs to the genuine Quintilianic tradition. Instead we have the forced *sententiae*, the exaggerated descriptions, the highflown emotional outbursts which had become associated with declamation. The tricks are somewhat stale; the tradition, one feels, had lasted too long. Declamation in later antiquity could hardly justify itself as training for the advocate; and as a literary activity in its own right it does not attract. The modern reader of the Greater Declamations is left with the impression of misplaced effort. These declaimers try very hard; but for all their efforts and all their arts, they fail to impress.

RHETORIC IN THE LATER ROMAN EMPIRE

Scis enim bonas artes honore nutriri atque hoc specimen florentis esse reipublicae ut disciplinarum professoribus praemia opulenta pendantur.

Symmachus, *Epistulae* 1.79

A NUMBER of rhetorical writings, mainly belonging to the later Empire, have come down to us, and have been collected under the title *Rhetores Latini Minores*, the lesser Latin rhetoricians.[1] They are justly so called. They are of minor interest, and do not deserve to be read on their own account; but they call for a brief consideration at this point, for at least they provide evidence of the character of rhetorical teaching in the later Roman Empire.

Some of the writers included in the collection confine themselves to figures of speech and of thought. This is the case with Rutilius Lupus, who translated a work of Gorgias, the younger Cicero's tutor at Athens; Aquila Romanus, who probably belongs to the later third century; Julius Rufinianus, who wrote a supplement to Aquila's work; and the anonymous author of the metrical *Carmen de Figuris* (circa A.D. 400). In addition to the works on figures there are complete *artes* by Chirius Fortunatianus, Sulpitius Victor and Julius Victor, all probably belonging to the fourth century, and by Martianus Capella (late fourth or early fifth century);[2] and an incomplete work attributed to St Augustine. There are also commentaries on Cicero's *De Inventione* by Victorinus (fourth century) and Grillius (fifth century); short works containing miscellaneous precepts by Julius Severianus (date uncertain) and Emporius (? fifth to sixth centuries); the rhetorical sections from the encyclopaedists Cassiodorus (sixth century) and Isidore (early seventh century); and finally the rhetorical writings of Bede and Alcuin, which show the classical tradition carried on into the Middle Ages.

The lesser Latin rhetoricians have no literary pretensions.[3] There is no Cicero or Quintilian among them. They write in the bald dogmatic style traditional in the textbook. They proceed by means of technical terms, definitions and examples. They do not discuss or argue; they merely state. One of them, Fortunatianus, uses the method of question and answer, like Cicero in *Partitiones Oratoriae*. This of course precludes any discussion. 'Quid est rhetorica?' is the first question. The answer is *bene dicendi scientia*, and there is the end of it.

Original thought is as lacking as literary charm. Rutilius Lupus, as has already been said, translated Gorgias, Aquila Romanus followed a Greek rhetorician called Alexander Numenius,[4] Capella in his section on figures copies from Aquila, and the author of the *Carmen de Figuris* follows first Rutilius Lupus, whose figures he arranges in alphabetical order, then Alexander Numenius. Sulpitius Victor follows in the main a Greek called Zeno, though he allows himself to omit, alter and add from other authorities;[5] Julius Victor's sources are given in the heading to his work,[6] and we can observe in numerous places his dependence on one of them, Quintilian.

But though they show little or no originality, they are not all of one pattern. There was no standard doctrine. This was so even in the matter of the arrangement of material. The traditional framework was that provided by the functions of the orator, *inventio, dispositio, elocutio, memoria* and *pronuntiatio;* there were also other divisions—the parts of a speech (proem, *narratio*, etc.) and the three kinds of oratory (forensic, deliberative and epideictic)—which had to be fitted in somehow, not to mention much highly detailed theoretical matter concerning the *status*, topics of argument, etc, which had been developed more or less independently of the traditional schemes. The later *artes* show that there was no recognised method of combining this matter into a single scheme. While Fortunatianus, Julius Victor and Capella use as their framework the five functions of the orator, and include the *status* doctrine under *inventio*, Sulpitius departs from the traditional division, postulating three functions—*intellectio, inventio* and *dispositio*, the last including *elocutio* and *pronuntiatio*[7]—and treats the doctrine of *status* at the end. This section, which occupies about two-thirds of the whole, was evidently what interested his authority, Zeno. The parts of the speech are handled by Fortunatianus and Julius Victor under *inventio*, after the *status* doctrine; in Capella they come right at the end, and in Sulpitius they are inserted after the functions of the orator and before the *status*. The three *genera causarum* have almost completely dropped out; they do not appear in Fortunatianus, Julius or Sulpitius, and have only an unimportant place in Capella's scheme. Capella is much fuller than the others on *elocutio;* Julius is peculiar in adding at the end of his work sections on practice (*exercitatio*), conversation (*sermocinatio*) and letter writing (*epistolae*).

In details, too, there is considerable variation. The *artes* seldom agree with one another completely and seldom disagree completely.[8] The general outlines of rhetoric were fixed, but there were many minor variations of doctrine. Any rhetorician who wished to make a name for himself would make some innovation in terminology or classification, or at least some new selection from existing doctrine. Quintilian noted the 'endless disagreements of the authorities, as each writer altered even what was correct in the hope of showing originality';[9] and the same spirit continued after Quintilian.

It was the Greeks as always who were foremost in theorising, and Greek influence remained strong. Cicero and Quintilian were not the only or the undisputed authorities. Hermagorean doctrine came down to the lesser rhetoricians independently of earlier Roman rhetoric; there was added the influence of Hermogenes, the ablest Greek rhetorician of the imperial period. Other minor Greek masters, known and unknown, contributed something. The result is a rhetoric more Greek in character than that of Cicero or Quintilian.

The practical side is very much in the background. Rhetoric is now only to a small extent a training for the courts. Only one of the lesser rhetoricians, Julius Severianus, has a practical aim in view, and even ventures to suggest that too much learning is harmful to the speaker.[10] The rest are purely men of the schools,[11] whose chief interest is in theoretical analysis, and who, so far as they have practice in mind, are thinking as much of the declamation hall as the forum.[12] There is in these later rhetoricians nothing of the commonsense attitude of earlier Roman writers on rhetoric who left out what seemed useless or over-subtle. They include portions of Greek theory which were ignored even by Cicero in *De Inventione* and by Quintilian. For example Fortunatianus has a detailed consideration of ἀσύστατα (sc. ζητήματα), cases which for one reason or another did not fit the definition of a *controversia*. This was part of Hermagoras's doctrine which Cicero and Quintilian had left alone. But interested though they are in theoretical analysis these lesser rhetoricians have not the thoroughness and acuteness of the better Greek masters. Fortunatianus, the most elaborate of them, does not arouse even that reluctant admiration which one gives to the subtleties of Hermagoras and Hermogenes.

The existence of these treatises is sufficient to show the continued life of the Roman rhetorical schools, but even apart from them there is plenty of evidence to show that rhetoric flourished in the later Empire. The rhetorician had charge of higher education, and in this capacity he had an honoured place in the social system. The Flavian and Antonine policy of exempting teachers from burdensome obligations was continued and extended.[13] Schools and teachers enjoyed official encouragement. In 297 Constantius Chlorus sent the rhetorician Eumenius to Autun to restore the schools there. The letter of appointment is quoted in the speech delivered by Eumenius on the occasion.[14] The Gauls of Autun, says Constantius, 'deserve that we should take thought for the education of their children's talents, and what gift is more fitting to be bestowed than that which fortune can neither give nor take away?'[15] Eumenius is therefore exhorted to undertake the restarting of the school of rhetoric, with a fixed salary to be provided out of public funds. With Julian official encouragement developed into official control, when Christians were forbidden to teach in the schools of grammar and rhetoric.[16] A later Emperor, Gratian, in 376 found it necessary to remind local authorities of their educational duties, and to require the larger towns to appoint the best grammarians and rhetoricians to teach their young.[17] The old Roman prejudice against state control of education[18] had completely disappeared. The Hellenistic faith in παιδεία had become accepted doctrine. It was the belief not only of men of letters but also of legislators that literary culture was the greatest of virtues.[19] And this literary culture was embodied in an educational system of which rhetoric was the crown.

The rhetorician owed his position in society not only to a disinterested admiration for his accomplishments, but also to the fact that it was he who trained men for the imperial service.[20] The rhetorical school led, as in the past, to the bar, and the bar to posts in the administration. An anonymous fourth-century rhetorician refers to members of his school who have gone out to the forum, to positions at court and to the administration of provinces.[21] Ausonius says that his master Minervius gave a thousand young men to the forum and twice as many to the senate.[22] The poet Prudentius is an example of one who, after a training in rhetoric and a period of practice as an advocate, held important administrative positions. Moreover it often happened that the professional rhetorician himself rose to high office. Ausonius became consul and governor of Gaul; two contemporaries of his, Nepotianus and Exuperius, held provincial governorships,[23] and St Augustine while teaching at Milan had ambitions of attaining a similar honour.[24] Finally, at the end of the fourth century, the rhetorician Eugenius became Emperor.

The rhetorician was not only trainer of administrators and sometimes himself an administrator; he was also imperial propagandist.[25] It was expected of him that he should sing the praises of the Emperor on suitable occasions. Augustine while at Milan wrote such a panegyric, full, he tells us, of untruths.[26] Minervius, according to Ausonius, was a practised panegyrist.[27] There survive in the collection of *Panegyrici Latini* a number of speeches which show us the rhetoricians of the fourth century displaying all their arts for the glory of their imperial master. In fulsome flowery periods they say what was expected of them, prove their loyalty and show that, if rhetoric no longer wielded power itself, it could at least grace and dignify power with fair words.[28]

Most of the panegyrists, like other eloquent men of the imperial period, were Gauls. For Roman rhetoric had long since ceased to be confined to Rome. The provinces had their own schools and their products outshone those of the capital in eloquence. Where Roman arms penetrated, the language and culture of Rome followed, and rhetoric was an essential part of that culture.

> Nunc totus Graias nostrasque habet orbis Athenas.
> Gallia causidicos docuit facunda Britannos,
> de conducendo loquitur iam rhetore Thule.[29]

The process had begun early. It was partly deliberate policy, partly a spontaneous development. In the first century B.C. Sertorius in Spain had had the sons of local chieftains educated in Greek and Roman culture.[30] At a later date Agricola encouraged the Britons to learn Latin.[31] This was part of the policy of Romanisation. But apart from official policy the prestige of Roman culture and its usefulness in opening the way to a career naturally caused the provincials to adopt the Latin language and the Latin rhetorical education. They adopted it wholeheartedly. Soon they were declaiming as fluently as any Italian, taking a lively interest in the oratorical celebrities of the day and in the latest *sententiae* from the Roman schools.[32] And it was not long before they ceased to be learners and became masters.[33] Spaniards were teaching in Rome as early as the time of Augustus, and there are few of the famous rhetoricians of the Empire who did not have a provincial origin.

Though there is no reason to doubt the truth of Juvenal's line about Gaul teaching rhetoric to Britain, our island was never particularly famous for eloquence. There is only one recorded case, and that a doubtful one, of a British rhetorician.[34] It was, as we should expect, in the more thoroughly Romanised provinces that rhetoric flourished most. The fame of Spain in the rhetorical field belongs mainly to the Augustan age and the early Empire. Marullus, the teacher of the elder Seneca, was a Spaniard; so were Porcius Latro and, probably, Junius Gallio, who figure so prominently in Seneca's pages, as well as lesser men such as Statorius Victor and Clodius Turrinus.[35] Not all the Spaniards of this period learnt their rhetoric in Spain. The elder Seneca completed his education in Rome, and the other famous members of his family, the younger Seneca and Lucan, came to the capital at an early age. Quintilian too was almost certainly a product of the Roman rather than the Spanish schools, though his contemporary Martial received the whole of his education, including the study of rhetoric,[36] in Spain. There were certainly Spanish schools of rhetoric in the first century; and there is evidence for the existence of such schools in later times. In the fourth century one of Ausonius's Bordeaux professors went to teach at Lerida, and a panegyrist of the same period can mention eloquent orators as among the products of Spain.[37]

Africa was called by Juvenal the nurse of pleaders.[38] One of these pleaders, Septimius Severus, from Leptis, is celebrated in a poem by Statius, and before his day another native of Leptis, Cornutus, had made a name as a writer on rhetoric as well as philosophy.[39] Africa produced in the person of Fronto the leading orator of his day and the tutor of a future Emperor; at a later date the African Caelianus taught rhetoric to the Emperor Diadumenianus.[40] African writers on rhetoric include Victorinus and Martianus Capella, both mentioned earlier in this chapter. The great African fathers Cyprian, Arnobius, Lactantius and Augustine all taught rhetoric. Apart from these names there are a number of inscriptions commemorating advocates and men of eloquence which attest the existence of flourishing native schools of rhetoric.[41] The most famous rhetorical school was that of Carthage. Apuleius, who began his education there, proclaimed it as *provinciae nostrae magistra venerabilis*.[42] Here Augustine came at the age of sixteen, after beginning his rhetorical studies at Madaura, and remained to teach, until the rowdiness of the students prompted him to move to Italy.[43]

The fame of Africa as a home of eloquence was equalled by that of Gaul, *Gallia facunda*, as Juvenal calls it.[44] Suetonius describes how at an early date teachers of 'grammar' set up in Cisalpine Gaul;[45] it may be assumed that they soon penetrated beyond the Alps and that they were followed by teachers of rhetoric. Soon Gauls were playing their part in rhetorical teaching. We know the names of a number of rhetoricians of the first century A.D. who either taught in Gaul or came from there to Rome. There was Claudius Quirinalis from Arles, Julius Gabinianus, whom the *scholastici* of the day rated above Cicero, Julius Florus, Statius Ursulus from Toulouse and the great Domitius Afer, from whom Quintilian learned.[46] Further evidence of the rhetorical interests of Gaul is provided by Caligula's games at Lyons, where there were contests of Greek and Latin

eloquence, with novel rewards and punishments.[47] Finally we
have Tacitus's picture of Aper in the *Dialogue*; of Gallic origin,
he is a typical provincial on the make, pushing, self-confident,
with little respect for tradition.

The oldest centre of culture in Gaul was Marseilles, a Greek
foundation, which retained its Greek character, and to which
some Roman parents sent their children in preference to Athens.[48]
Autun was a seat of education as early as the first century
A.D.; the reopening of the schools there at the end of the third
century is the theme of the speech by Eumenius already referred
to.[49] Other known centres of rhetorical teaching are Bordeaux,
Toulouse, Narbonne, Lyons, Besançon, Trèves, Poitiers, Angoulême and Saintes.[50]

Of these centres it is Bordeaux that is best known to us,
thanks to Ausonius who taught and studied there and celebrated its professors in a series of poems not without interest
and charm as an expression of the *pietas* of the scholastic world
of fourth-century Gaul. Of the rhetoricians he celebrated some
lived and worked at Bordeaux; others transferred their talents
elsewhere. Arborius and Sedatus held chairs at Toulouse;
Minervius taught at Constantinople and Rome before returning
to his home town.[51] Dynamius had to leave Bordeaux owing to a
scandal; he went to Spain, where he married a rich wife,
changed his name and set up as a rhetorician.[52]

Of some of the rhetoricians it is recorded that they practised
in the courts.[53] Some sought a career in public life. Nepotianus
and Exuperius, as has already been mentioned, held provincial
governorships. Delphidius experienced the dangers rather than
the rewards of a public career; he narrowly escaped disaster and
thereafter resigned himself to teaching.[54] Others like Alethius were
content with the tranquil life of the teacher and man of letters.

Some of the rhetoricians practised poetry and other forms of
literature as well as oratory.[55] They were, we may suppose,
possessed of the elegant culture and fluent versatility which
we see displayed in Ausonius himself. Their oratory was also
no doubt fluent and elegant. Minervius is credited with a
rushing flood of eloquence, rolling down not mud but gold;
Exuperius on the other hand had only a superficial charm; his
words sounded well enough, but if you analysed them you found
there was no solid matter in them.[56]

Ausonius's poems on the professors leave us with the impression of a pleasant academic society, friendly and sociable, devoted to the traditions of Greco-Roman culture and to the arts of self-expression. Theirs is an elegant and harmless, if somewhat lifeless culture, nourished on the mutual admiration of their professional circle and the recognition which society in general accorded to their accomplishments. A generation or so after the death of Ausonius, in the early fifth century, the foundations of this culture were shaken by the barbarian invasions of Gaul. The society which supported the rhetorician was shattered, and the rhetorical culture gradually declined until it all but disappeared in the sixth century.[57]

RHETORIC AND CHRISTIANITY

Daemonum cibus est carmina poetarum, saecularis sapientia, rhetoricorum pompa verborum.

St Jerome, *Epistulae* 21.13

IN A famous passage in one of his letters St Jerome tells how when he was on his way to Jerusalem to adopt the life of an ascetic he found it impossible to do without his library. Fasting and penance alternated with the reading of Cicero and Plautus, and when he took up the prophets he was disgusted by their style. Then he fell ill, and in a feverish dream seemed to be brought before the seat of judgment. Asked to give an account of himself he replied: 'I am a Christian.' 'You lie', answered the judge. 'You are a Ciceronian, not a Christian. For where your heart is, there shall your treasure be.' 'I was silent at once', Jerome goes on, 'and amid my stripes (for he had ordered me to be beaten) I was even more tortured by the burning of my conscience. . . . Finally those present threw themselves at the feet of the judge and besought him to make allowances for youth and to allow time for penitence to the sinner, punishing me thereafter if I should ever read the books of the Gentiles again. And I who at this moment of crisis would have promised even more, began to swear an oath: "Lord, if ever I possess or read secular books, I shall have denied thee." '[1]

St Jerome's dream gives a vivid picture of the conflict between the new religion and the old learning. Christianity demanded a whole-hearted allegiance which left no room for Cicero and the poets. The old literary and rhetorical education by which many generations had been brought up on the study of the classical authors and the practice of fine writing and effective speaking, was subjected to a new and powerful threat.

In a sense, perhaps, the conflict was not a new thing, but only

a revival in a new form of an old conflict. Plato had expelled
the poets from his ideal state. Marcus Aurelius had turned away
from rhetoric to philosophy. Many of the criticisms which the
Christians directed against pagan culture had been made
before by the philosophers. None the less Christianity presented
a challenge to traditional culture that was both stronger than,
and different in character from, that offered by philosophy.
For the philosophers belonged to the Greco-Roman world,
whereas Christianity came in a sense from outside. The
Christians brought with them not only certain religious and
ethical ideals by comparison only weakly represented in the
Greco-Roman tradition; they also brought with them their
sacred books. The Christian priest was not, like the priest of
the mystery religions, a mere performer of a ritual; he was
teacher and preacher. Thus he had to be an educated man, but
an educated man in a new sense, learned not in the poets and
prose writers of Greece and Rome, but in the Scriptures.
Christianity was not only a religion competing with a culture;
it was itself a new culture.

The existence of the Bible and its supreme importance for
Christians sharpened the conflict with pagan culture. The
Englishman brought up on the Authorised Version is accustomed to regard the Bible as a literary masterpiece; the Roman
brought up on Cicero thought far otherwise. The earliest Latin
translations of the Bible were unpretentious unskilful versions,
which in their anxious desire to represent the original literally
often departed from correct Latin usage.[2] They were an
inevitable stumbling-block to the educated man. Augustine in
his early days found them unworthy to be compared with
Cicero;[3] Jerome, as we have seen, was disgusted by the style
of the Old Testament prophets. The main cause, according to
Lactantius, of the failure of the Scriptures to convince the
educated was that the prophets wrote in ordinary simple
language and were therefore despised by those 'who will not
listen to or read anything which is not polished and eloquent,
and will allow nothing to enter their hearts which does not
charm the ears with its pleasing sound'.[4]

Yet though rhetoric and Christianity might thus come into
conflict, there was a sense in which Christianity can be called
a rhetorical religion. The massive works of the Latin Fathers

show us that a Christian leader in the early centuries was a writer and speaker, teacher, controversialist, letter writer, preacher, one who used to the full the written and spoken word. The Fathers did all this as a matter of course; they had been brought up in the pagan schools, had in many cases taught rhetoric. They had learnt the art of persuasion and self-expression, and this art they used to the full in the service of their religion.[5]

This is not the place for a full study of the relations between Christianity and classical culture. Rhetoric was only a part of that culture, and not the part which was most open to attack.[6] It will suffice here to confine ourselves to the greatest of the Latin Christian writers, St Augustine, and to outline his attitude to the rhetoric to which he had been brought up, and which he taught with distinction until the time of his conversion.[7]

As Augustine looks back on his education, whose sole aim was to make him a good speaker, he is struck by its futility and neglect of essentials. His models were men who were confounded when they uttered a solecism; they would pride themselves on the beauties of their style even if the subject were their own vices. They observed with care the laws of letters and syllables handed down to them from previous speakers, while neglecting the laws of eternal salvation.[8] Not only were these studies vain; they were also dishonest. Not so by the ordinary standards of the day. 'In all innocence I taught my pupils crafty tricks, not to enable them to secure the death of an innocent man, but on occasion to acquit a guilty one.'[9] This was the traditional morality of rhetoric. It was not good enough for a Christian. To Augustine the whole rhetorical system was bound up with dishonesty. The greater the deceit the more the praise.[10] Rhetoric was 'mendacious folly', oratory 'wordy and polished falsehood'.[11]

Moreover the rhetorical education was aimed solely at worldly success. The object of his parents, says Augustine, was that he should be successful in this world and excel in the art of speech which ministers to human honour and false riches.[12] He himself for long accepted these values, and while at Milan was still greedy for success and gain.[13] But as a Christian he rejected worldly success. 'Why did you go to school?' he asks in one of his later works, and he answers: 'To gain money or to attain to honour and to the heights of esteem. But what you learned with such pains and punishments is a mortal thing, as are you yourself and as is the aim of your learning.'[14] And rhetoric, as well as being directed towards a vain end, encouraged an attitude far removed from Christian humility. 'I studied the authorities on rhetoric', writes Augustine, '. . . . and desired to excel therein, an aim leading to damnation and puffed up with the joys of human vanity.'[15] Writing of the period shortly after his conversion, when he retired to Cassiciacum, he refers to his writings of that period as 'still breathing the pride of the schools'.[16]

So much for Augustine's criticisms of rhetoric. But he was not content with mere criticism. He was aware that rhetoric had its uses, and in his later life, when he was now fully committed to the Christian life and doctrine, he set himself to produce a new theory of rhetoric adapted to the needs of the Christian teacher.[17] The *De Doctrina Christiana* is a treatise on the uses of the Scriptures; the subject is divided into two parts, firstly how to understand them and secondly how to communicate to others the fruits of one's understanding. The second part, which is treated in the fourth book, may be described as a Christian *Ars Rhetorica*, or better, a Christian *De Oratore*, for the work has more in common with Cicero than with the scholastic tradition.[18]

The tone is serene and uncontroversial. There is no hostility to rhetoric, which is recognised to be not without its uses. 'It is true that the art of rhetoric is used for the purpose of commending both truth and falsehood, yet who would venture to say that truth should remain defenceless in the hands of its champions . . .? The faculty of eloquence is something neutral, which has great persuasive effect whether for good or for evil; why then should not the good acquire it for use in the championship of truth, if the bad use it to win their perverse and vain causes in the interests of wickedness and error?'[19] Or, as he says elsewhere, 'The rules of rhetoric are none the less true, although they can be used in the interests of falsehood; but because they can also be used in the interests of truth, rhetorical skill is not in itself to be blamed, but rather the perversity of those who misuse it.'[20]

Augustine disclaims any intention of writing an art of rhetoric as it was taught in the schools; that can be learned elsewhere, by those that have the time.[21] It is unnecessary for those who have not learned the rules when young to spend time over them. Natural genius combined with reading, listening and practice will more easily produce eloquence than an attention to rules. Good speakers who know the rules seldom make use of them when speaking; their speeches may be in accordance with rhetorical doctrine, but this can be the case even when they have not learned the doctrine. Rules do not make eloquence; they derive from eloquence.[22]

This last remark can be paralleled from Cicero's *De Oratore*.[23] From Cicero, too, Augustine derives his doctrine of the three aims of the orator, to instruct, to please and to win over.[24] For him, however, the first is the most important, and he finds it necessary to give a warning against paying too much attention to giving pleasure. 'A serious-minded audience will not find pleasure in that sweetness which, while it does not speak of wicked things, adorns slight and trivial goods with a frothy parade of words.'[25] The ornamental eloquence of the Second Sophistic was not unknown even in the Fathers of the Church, and Augustine quotes a passage from Cyprian which he condemns, not without reason, for its excessive profusion.[26]

Augustine also follows Cicero in connecting the three purposes of the orator with the three styles, the plain, the middle or mixed and the grand.[27] It is true that the ecclesiastical orator always deals with great themes, but they need not always be handled in the grand style. When he instructs, his style is plain; when he uses praise or blame it is mixed; when he wishes to rouse to action, then he will bring the grand style into play.[28] On the other hand it is a mistake to connect the three aims of the orator too closely with the three styles; he should as far as possible fulfil all three aims even when using only one of the three styles. When we speak plainly we wish to be heard willingly and to ensure obedience, and simple explanation and argument, especially when it has a natural unsought charm, often arouses such applause that it hardly seems to be the plain style. So with the other two styles. Pleasure may be the chief aim of the mixed style, but the speaker wishes to be understood and obeyed also; and in the grand style persuasion cannot be achieved unless the speaker is understood and heard with pleasure.[29] Finally Augustine emphasises that the speaker's life is more influential than his words, however eloquent they may be. This is the old doctrine of ethos, which naturally and rightly assumes a new importance when the orator is transformed to a religious and moral teacher.[30]

So far Augustine follows Ciceronian doctrine. But the differences from Cicero are as remarkable as the resemblances. Augustine has freed himself more completely than Cicero ever did from the school tradition, and more than Cicero he emphasises the supreme importance of clarity and truth.[31] Moreover Augustine's orator is a very different person from Cicero's; he is not the orator of the forum and the senate house, but the interpreter of the Scriptures and the defender of the faith.[32] He is thus a sort of combination of the *grammaticus*, the philosopher and the orator of the pagan world. He studies his texts like the *grammaticus*, he teaches his doctrine like the philosopher and he persuades his hearers like the orator. His texts are of course the Scriptures, and this brings Augustine up against the question whether eloquence is to be found in the sacred writings. His answer is interesting. We have seen how many saw in them nothing but uncouthness. Augustine finds in the sacred authors an eloquence of their own, one which does not avoid the methods of rhetoric, but does not consciously make use of them. The words are not a detachable ornament, but arise spontaneously from the matter.[33] None the less he cannot forbear to point out that even judged by the traditional standards of pagan literature, there is eloquence in the Christian authors.[34] He quotes from St Paul's Epistle to the Romans an example of a climax (in the rhetorical sense of the word) and of κῶλα and κόμματα followed by a period,[35] and a longer passage from the first Epistle to the Corinthians, the structure of which he carefully analyses.[36] Even the prophets, whose style Jerome had found so distressing, provide him with an example of eloquence in a passage of Amos, of which he triumphantly asks: 'Would those who priding themselves on their learning and eloquence despise our prophets as unlearned and ignorant of style, have desired to express themselves otherwise if they had had to say something of this sort?'[37] Thus the Scriptures were vindicated. Only in one respect is Augustine a trifle apologetic; he has to admit that they are lacking in rhythmical *clausulae*.[38]

In pointing to the formal beauties of scriptural passages

Augustine seems to be accepting the standards of pagan culture, and bringing the biblical writings as it were into the canon of stylistic models accepted by the secular tradition. But this was not his purpose. It is clear that for him the Scriptures are to take the place of the pagan writers. The cultural background of the Christian teacher is to be completely different from that of the pagan. The Scriptures and the Christian Fathers provide the models to be studied and imitated,[39] and if any non-Christian writers are to be studied, it is only to assist in understanding the Scriptures. Pagan learning is of use, so far as it is not connected with falsehood and superstition,[40] but its usefulness is very limited. It is small compared with the learning of the Scriptures. 'Whatever a man has learned outside is, if it is harmful, condemned in the Scriptures; if it is useful, it is found in them.'[41]

Augustine might draw up a programme of Christian studies, but he did not establish a Christian educational system. The pagan schools of literature and rhetoric continued to function until the disruption of ancient society by the barbarians. Christians sent their sons to them, because there were no other schools;[42] they even taught in them themselves, as is shown by the fact that Julian tried to exclude them from the teaching profession. Nor, it seems, did they attempt to reform the schools from within; Julian's objection to them was the negative one that they did not believe what they taught and that they did not honour the gods honoured by the authors they expounded.[43] Christian teachers went on with the old curriculum, and they do not seem to have attempted to modify it at all in the interests of their religion.[44] A Christian rhetorician in his capacity of rhetorician would differ little if at all from a pagan one. Victorinus did not consider it necessary to resign from his chair of rhetoric at Rome on his conversion, and he presumably went on giving the same lectures after as before his change of religion.

Thus rhetoric remained part of the cultural background of the educated Christian, and not only of nominal Christians like Ausonius, but even of those who adopted the new faith without reserve. A letter to Augustine of the year 412 gives us a picture of a group of educated Christians engaged in intellectual discussion. We find them beginning with questions of rhetorical theory and technique on traditional lines. They pass on to poetry and philosophy, and were it not that they end up with theology, they might well be a group of pagan men of learning.[45] The old tradition was too strong for any radical change to take place in society as a whole.

We have to pass on to the very end of ancient civilisation before we find any attempt made to found a Christian system of education. In the sixth century Cassiodorus observed that whereas the study of secular writers flourished—for the public schools of literature and rhetoric still survived under Theodoric[46]—there was no public teaching of the Scriptures, and proposed the setting up of Christian schools, 'from which the soul could attain to everlasting salvation and the tongue of the faithful be adorned with a chaste eloquence'.[47] The disturbances of the times prevented the fulfilment of this design. Later, however, when he retired to the monastery of Vivarium Cassiodorus compiled, to guide his monks in their studies, an encyclopaedia of sacred and secular learning, the *Institutiones Divinarum et Saecularium Litterarum*. Among the secular arts which he summarises is rhetoric; even in the monastic life, which might seem the very antithesis of the rhetorical ideal, something of the old secular tradition was allowed to survive. Cassiodorus even discovers that certain aspects of the art of rhetoric—memory, delivery and voice production—have their uses for the monk.[48] But apart from this, he regards rhetoric, like the other arts, as strictly subordinate to sacred studies and justified only by its usefulness in explaining the Scriptures.[49] In this way the art of rhetoric, shrunk to a meagre summary and reduced to one of a number of arts ancillary to the study of the Scriptures, found a place in monastic studies.

Cassiodorus through his *Institutiones* has an important place in history as one of the channels through which classical learning was passed on to the Middle Ages. In another way, too, he marks the transition to the new society. In his earlier life he was quaestor to Theodoric, and under an Ostrogothic king a quaestor's duty was to draft official documents. Cassiodorus in this capacity sees himself as the embodiment of the Ciceronian ideal orator.[50] Rhetoric had become what it was to be to a large extent in the Middle Ages, the art of writing letters. The orator has developed into the civil servant.

While Cassiodorus looks forward to the future, an older contemporary of his, Ennodius, looks back to the past, and it is with him as the last representative of the secular tradition that we may suitably end this survey. Born in Gaul, he studied in Italy, and was bishop of Pavia from 511 to his death in 521. His clerical calling did not prevent him from pursuing pagan letters and pagan rhetoric,[51] and we find among his works declamations in the old school tradition. There are *Dictiones Ethicae*, imaginary speeches of mythological characters,[52] and *controversiae*, in which the familiar figures of declamation, the stepmother, the tyrant and the disinherited son, make their last appearance. One of the declamations[53] is on a theme also found in the Greater Declamations, and Ennodius, with apologies for his presumption, takes the opposite side to that taken in the Quintilianic declamation. Thus the old tradition of declamation survived almost without change from Augustus to the Ostrogothic kingdom.[54]

Ennodius's works also include a curious letter of instruction to two young friends, in which Modesty, Chastity and Faith are somewhat incongruously combined with Grammar and Rhetoric, and each in turn is made to speak to the young men.[55] Rhetoric advances all her old high-flown claims, first in prose, then in some lines of verse of which the following is a translation.

> He whom I take in charge unscathed remains,
> It is my art that blots out all life's stains.
> The man of spotless fame I can compel
> All to acknowledge sprung from darkest hell.
> My lips can ruin and my lips can save;
> My words draw judgment captive and a slave.
> Jewels, fine wool, pride of Tarentum's town,
> And power, are brought to nothing by my frown.
> Dominion o'er the world my precepts bring;
> My art fears nothing; with its aid I'm king.

The words sound like an echo from the distant past. They recall the age of the sophists, with its proud proclamation of the power of words. But power had long ago passed from the orator to the man of arms. Rhetoric as statesmanship was dead; rhetoric as persuasion was dead too, for a rhetorician like Ennodius had nothing worth saying to say, nothing of which to persuade his hearers. There remained only rhetoric as the art of words, a laboured and feeble art by now, but faintly preserving, in an age that cared little for such things, something of the old Greek love of beauty.

XV

CONCLUSION

Sequitur quaestio an utilis rhetorice.
Quintilian, *Institutio Oratoria* 2.16.1

'RHETORIC', SAID Renan, 'is, with poetic, the only mistake
the Greeks made.'[1] If this is so, it was a costly mistake for their
pupils, the Romans. For of all the arts and sciences invented by
the Greeks rhetoric was the one which the Romans adopted
most whole-heartedly. It formed the basis of their education,
it absorbed the interests of some of their best men and it deeply
influenced their literature. Was it all a mistake?

Let us first consider the most obvious function of rhetoric,
to teach men how to speak well. If Roman rhetoric succeeded
at all in doing this, it was to some extent justified. And undoubtedly it did succeed. The intensive training in speaking
which the Roman received made him a ready speaker, a good
debater, quick to see the pros and cons in any situation, able to
put his material in order, to hold it in his mind and produce it
as required. The advocate in the forum, the politician in the
senate or outside it, the commander among his troops, the
man of letters in conversation, could say what he wanted to say
easily and effectively.

The influence of rhetoric was of course felt outside speaking
in most branches of writing, and its influence was in many respects good. It developed the capacities of the Latin language
as an effective instrument, disciplined its rough vigour, modified its stiffness, taught it new rhythms and turns of expression. It encouraged a care for form and artistry, and discour-
aged waywardness and eccentricity and incoherence. It imposed
a standard of literary Latin which enabled educated men of
different ages and races to understand one another.

On the other hand one may well ask whether equally good
results could not have been achieved with less expenditure of

effort. One must study, says Quintilian, at all times and in all places.[2] Was such an exacting training really necessary? In fact there is evidence that, at any rate under the Empire, the rhetorical education did not always result in that facility of speech at which it was aimed. Some pupils of the Roman schools seem to have been rather reduced to silence by the training they received, and Quintilian ruefully contrasts the ease with which the uneducated spoke with the anxious self-criticism which afflicted some of those who had been elaborately trained in the art of speech.[3]

Moreover, an excessive concentration on the art of writing has other dangers. There was a tendency to avoid the direct and straightforward and to resort to the involved and far-fetched and unnatural.[4] Even in Augustan times, or perhaps earlier, there was a teacher who, when his pupils' compositions were too clear, used to say Σκότισον, Darken it.[5] In Quintilian's day there were many who were convinced that one could not write elegantly unless what one wrote required interpretation.[6] Some of the least attractive writing in Latin is that of professed teachers of style, the rhetoricians whose work is preserved by the elder Seneca. Even Cicero perhaps is not at his best when the rhetorical note sounds loudest; there are passages in his speeches which remind one of the Emperor Augustus's characterisation of the Asiatic style, 'a flow of words without meaning'.[7] The cultivation of the art of words for its own sake was apt to lead to neglect of words as a means of conveying meaning.

Among the bad influences must be reckoned the cult of *ornatus*. No doubt it was easier to teach this than the other virtues of style. The figures of speech and of thought which were considered to contribute so powerfully to *ornatus* had been conveniently classified; whereas nothing of the sort had been done for clarity and appropriateness. Thus overmuch attention was paid to writing in a distinguished and elevated manner, and it was generally believed that distinction and elevation could be produced by the mechanical use of certain tricks of style. Rhetoric tended to teach the Roman to write finely before he could write simply and clearly. The easy natural manner which the men of the Ciceronian age had at their command in addition to the grand style was lost as time went on, and in the final decay of Roman culture we find Sidonius so anxious to write elegantly that he can hardly write intelligibly.

Declamation, as we have seen, encouraged many faults. The taste for epigram, though it produced much poor stuff, was not perhaps the most serious of these. Lucan and the younger Seneca, the two writers other than professional rhetoricians most influenced by the fashion, were in their way powerful writers, who added something to Latin literature. More serious perhaps was the enfeeblement of the Latin language which the schools of declamation encouraged. In the interests of refinement any words which might possibly be objected to were disallowed, and thus, according to Quintilian, a large proportion of the vocabulary of Latin was excluded.[8]

It was not only in the matter of style that the influence of rhetoric was felt. It taught *inventio* as well as *elocutio*, and thus influenced habits of thought as well as of expression. From an early age the Roman was taught to find the materials for his compositions and practice speeches according to certain rules. He was taught the topics to be drawn on and the arguments to be used. He was not taught to think for himself; all his material was drawn from outside himself, from the theme with which he was presented and from the traditional topics of the schools. Rhetoric would thus inevitably encourage a certain conventionality of thought.

Moreover, though the topics were ultimately based on experience, generations of teachers had reduced them to a system, so that observation and personal experience played little or no part in rhetorical *inventio*. Rhetoric provided a ready-made set of arguments and modes of treatment, and the danger was that those who were brought up on it might go through life without enlarging and deepening the inherited common stock from their own experience and observation. Rhetoric thus tended to destroy curiosity. If the old Greek spirit of enquiry is so weak in later antiquity, it is partly the effect of the all-pervading influence of rhetoric.

Nor did rhetoric encourage a love of truth. It is no doubt wrong to suppose that rhetoric inevitably involves insincerity; it is only an instrument, which can be used by the sincere and the insincere, in the service of truth and of falsehood. None the less the practice of speaking on either side of a case and of saying what the occasion demanded, if it was not modified by other influences, could hardly fail to blur the distinction between true and false. To give a small example, Quintilian records two images that were particularly popular with the *scholastici* of his youth: 'Even the sources of mighty rivers are navigable.', and 'The generous tree bears fruit when it is still a sapling.'[9] This may seem trivial, but it is symptomatic of the reckless disregard for facts that rhetoric encouraged. Augustine described his panegyric of the Emperor as full of falsehoods. Probably it was no more false than others of its kind. But how many panegyrists were really conscious of their falsehood? For the complete rhetorician truth is irrelevant. It is enough for him if he makes his case effectively or treats his theme with elegance and eloquence.

It might be maintained, however, that the rhetorical education should be judged mainly as a practical training for public life. Its uses under the Republic, when speaking was such an important accomplishment for the politician, are more obvious than its uses under the Empire. Yet even in the later Empire the rhetorician prided himself on educating men for the public service, and the fact that the system was accepted without question for so long suggests that it served its purpose well enough. The administrator does not require to be a philosopher or a scientist or a creative artist. He needs to be able to see the relevant factors in a situation or a problem and to express himself clearly and accurately, and a rhetorical education, if well conducted, is perhaps as good a training as any for such a career. One may well suppose that the habits of accurate thought and expression which would be learnt in Quintilian's school would stand a man in good stead in a public career. But whether other schools provided so good a training is open to question. The flowery language, the false sentiment and the studied ambiguities of declamation as it was so often practised seem to be a poor preparation for the official dispatch. We learn from Quintilian that the young man who had practised giving advice in the *suasoriae* had a good deal to unlearn before he could give real advice in the senate or elsewhere.[10] Yet the Empire continued to be administered, and those who administered it were products of the rhetorical schools. Perhaps their education mattered little in comparison with what they imbibed from tradition. The Romans had administrative capacity in their bones, and it could survive even the follies of the lesser rhetoricians.

To some extent, perhaps, criticism of ancient rhetoric on intellectual or practical grounds is beside the mark, for there is an element in it which is impervious to such criticisms, an element of pure art. When one reads of the triumphant progress from city to city of some famous sophist, the applause he arouses and the rewards he receives, one is reminded of a popular operatic singer of today.[11] The singer's audience do not judge him by the quality of his libretto; it is the music and the voice which charm. So with the ancient sophist, the speaker for display. The meaning was unimportant; it was the sound of the words and the delivery that produced the effect. The speech was a work of art in itself; that was enough. Whether the words made sense or nonsense, were true or false, was indifferent. Such was the oratory of the Greek Second Sophistic and of Apuleius's *Florida*. The element of pure art entered even into speeches like those of Cicero, where the meaning was by no means unimportant. It entered, too, into school declamation. And if one considers such declamation as playing a part not unlike that of the school play or the singing class today, one can better understand its popularity. The aesthetic side of human nature, having no other outlet, was satisfied through the medium of speech. So much we may allow. We may admit the enjoyment of the beauty of words and the pride in their artistic use to be in some degree legitimate and understandable. But the primary purpose of speech and writing is to express thought and feeling, and in so far as this was forgotten the culture of the ancient world lost its vitality. It is easy to understand how in the fourth century men like Augustine reacted against a culture which overvalued the aesthetic side of self-expression.

There is yet another aspect of rhetorical education that remains to be considered. The pupil in the schools, in addition to showing off on the platform, had to put in a good deal of hard work on rhetorical theory. Besides the excitements of declamation there was the hard narrow discipline of formal rhetoric; there were the endless divisions and subdivisions to be learned and the obscurities of the *status* doctrine to be mastered. This certainly provided a mental exercise, and in so far as it was taught thoroughly and followed intelligently it must have been of value educationally. And yet, would not all the mental energy that went into rhetorical theory have been better employed on something else? If the verdict of posterity is to be trusted, rhetoric was one of the least valuable intellectual creations of the ancients. The Greek achievements in other arts and sciences are recognised as the foundation of modern developments, whereas rhetoric has led to nothing and is now more or less forgotten. What was valuable in the system was small in comparison to what was of no real importance. It is safe to say that the world would have been none the worse without the *status* doctrine. Much of ancient rhetoric seems to be little more than what Quintilian calls a ματαιοτεχνία, 'an unprofitable imitation of a science, which is neither good nor bad, but merely involves a useless expenditure of labour'.[12]

Even if rhetoric was of more value than these criticisms would suggest, it can hardly be denied that it was given an excessively large place in the system of Roman education. The medieval system was better balanced. In this one began by learning the three subjects of the *trivium*, grammar, logic, and rhetoric, and then went on to the *quadrivium*, arithmetic, music, geometry and astronomy. One thus first equipped oneself with the instruments of thought and expression and then went on to the various branches of science as they were then understood. The division of the two branches of study recalls Aristotle's distinction of dialectic and rhetoric from the ἐπιστῆμαι, the sciences with their own specific subject matter. Indeed the medieval system, based as it was on the liberal arts handed down by the encyclopaedists of later antiquity, was a return to a Greek ideal of general education which had never been adequately represented in the Roman system. The Roman education was founded on two only of the liberal arts, grammar and rhetoric.

So much may be said in criticism of the rhetorical education of the Romans. But it should always be remembered that there was more in Roman culture than was embodied in the educational system. There was philosophy, independent of rhetoric and at times in opposition to it; there were also the various branches of literature other than oratory, which the rhetoricians might analyse according to their rules and subordinate to their purposes, and which might themselves adopt much of the rhetorical manner, but which were never wholly absorbed by rhetoric. The vitality of Roman culture, it may be suggested, depended on the survival of independent influences to counteract the dominance of rhetoric in the school system. If we regard the last century before Christ as the golden age of Latin literature, it is surely in part due to the fact that rhetoric was then kept in its place and that other studies flourished by its side. Cicero studied in the Academy as well as under the rhetoricians; Lucretius was an adherent of a school which regarded rhetoric with hostility. Virgil had experience of the same school; he passed from his rhetoric master to the Epicurean Siro, and who can doubt that he profited by the variety in his education? Horace, if we can judge from his own account, missed the rhetoric school and passed straight from studying literature at Rome to studying philosophy at Athens. It is doubtful whether for all the learning and love of literature which flourished among the educated in the imperial period the general level of culture was ever so high as in the first century before Christ. Pliny's range of interests is narrower than Cicero's, and Fronto's is narrower than Pliny's. The decline reflects the growing influence of rhetoric and the weakening of other elements in Roman culture.

The answer to the question with which this chapter began would then appear to be something like this: Rhetoric is well enough, if kept within limits. But it should not be allowed to dominate the educational system and absorb the interests of the educated man so far that other more valuable studies languish. In short, as the Emperor Julian put it: 'Do not despise the art of words; do not neglect rhetoric, do not give up your familiarity with the poets. But devote more attention to the sciences.'[13]

NOTES

Greek authors and works are abbreviated as in H. G. Liddell, R. Scott, H. Stuart Jones and R. McKenzie (eds), *A Greek-English Lexicon*[9] (Oxford, 1968); Latin authors and works as in P. G. W. Glare (ed.), *Oxford Latin Dictionary* (Oxford, 1982); and periodicals (with some minor exceptions) as in Marouzeau's *L'Année philologique*. Full details of books referred to in abbreviated form may be found in the bibliography.

CHAPTER I

[1] Arist. ap. Cic. *Brut.* 46. Another tradition made Empedocles the founder of rhetoric. But Quintilian, who records it, is very vague on Empedocles' alleged contribution (*movisse aliqua circa rhetoricen Empedocles dicitur*), and he goes on: *artium autem scriptores antiquissimi Corax et Tisias* (*Inst.* 3.1.8). Cf. S.E. *adv. Dogm.* 1.6; D.L. 8.57.

[2] Cic. *Brut.* 46. This is to be preferred to the tradition that it arose from political oratory. See D. A. G. Hinks, *CQ* 34 (1940), 61–9. S. Wilcox (*HSCP* 53 (1942), 121–55) argues against the view that the early rhetoricians concentrated on judicial oratory. G. A. Kennedy (*AJP* 80 (1959), 177) considers that Corax was probably concerned with deliberative oratory, while Tisias' theory was mainly intended to help those who spoke in court.

[3] Plat. *Phdr.* 273 a–c; Arist. *Rh.* 2.24.11.

[4] Plat. *Phdr.* 266 e–267 d.

[5] Euenus of Paros (Plat. *Phdr.* 267 a).

[6] Plat. *Prt.* 318 e–319 a; Arist. *Rh.* 2.24.11; Cic. *Brut.* 46; D.L. 9.53.

[7] Plat. *Phdr.* 267 a.

[8] *ibid.* Attributed to Tisias and Gorgias, but one would suspect the latter to have been responsible.

[9] Plat. *Grg.* 459 b–c, 463 a.

[10] Kroll, *Rhetorik*, § 12. Quintilian refers to those who are content to read a few passages from the *Gorgias* put together by clumsy excerptors, and do not trouble to read the whole work or other works of Plato (*Inst.* 2.15.24).

[11] Plat. *Phdr.* 259 e, 271 d.

[12] Arist. *Rh.* 1.1.1, 1.2.1, 1.4.5–6.

[13] Arist. *Rh.* 1.1.12–13.

[14] Cic. *de Orat.* 3.141; *Tusc.* 1.7; Quint. *Inst.* 3.1.14; Gel. 20.5.2. He was considered to be the founder of a method of teaching by which the pupils were made to handle theses, or general questions, and argue them on both sides: see Cic. *de Orat.* 3.80; *Orat.* 46; *Fin.* 5.10; D.L. 5.3.

[15] Arist. *Rh.* 1.1.14; cf. 1.2.1.

[16] Arist. *Rh.* 2.22ff.

[17] Arist. *Rh.* 2.1–11. This is the main sense in which Aristotle uses the term *ethos*. Other aspects of *ethos* handled by him are the adapting of the speech to the differing ages, classes etc. of the audience (2.12ff.) and the representation of character through appropriate speech (3.7.6–7). For the various senses the term *ethos* came to bear in later theory see Quint. *Inst.* 6.2.8ff.

[18] Arist. *Rh.* 1.2.7.

[19] See F. Solmsen, *AJP* 62 (1941), 35–50, 169–90.

[20] We hear of treatises on *enthymemata, atechnoi pisteis, gnomai* and *paradeigmata*, all Aristotelian themes (D.L. 5.42–50).

[21] See J. Stroux, *De Theophrasti virtutibus dicendi* (Leipzig, 1912).

[22] D.H. *Dem.* 3 'a mixture formed by combining the other two'.

[23] G. L. Hendrickson, *AJP* 25 (1904), 125–46; but see Kroll, *Rhetorik,/§* 17. See also G. A. Kennedy, *HSCP* 62 (1957), 93–104.

[24] Cic. *Brut.* 37–8; Quint. *Inst.* 10.1.80.

[25] Quint. *Inst.* 2.4.41–2.

[26] Our knowledge of the *progymnasmata* comes from the writers of the empire, but the system no doubt took shape earlier, perhaps in the second century B.C. See K. Barwick, *Hermes* 63 (1928), 283.

[27] Tac. *Dial.* 19.3. On Hermagoras see D. Matthes, *Lustrum* 3 (1958), 158ff.

[28] Cic. *Fin.* 4.7.

[29] Cic. *Brut.* 309; Quint. *Inst.* 12.2.25; D.L. 7.59. But see Cic. *de Orat.* 3.66.

[30] S.E. *adv. Rhet.* 20–42.

[31] Cic. *de Orat.* 1.45ff. Rather surprisingly the Peripatetic Diodorus joined in the game (*ibid.*). His master Critolaus had been hostile to rhetoric (S.E. *adv. Rhet.* 12).

[32] D.L. 4.28.

[33] D.L. 4.62.

[34] Cic. *Tusc.* 2.9.

[35] Cic. *Inv.* 1.8.

[36] Cic. *de Orat.* 1.86, 2.78, 3.110.

[37] Cic. *Inv.* 1.8. It seems likely that the immediate source for Cicero's criticism of Hermagoras was rhetorical rather than philosophical.

[38] Plut. *Pomp.* 42.5.

[39] Cic. *de Orat.* 3.110. Barwick (*Das rednerische Bildungsideal Ciceros*, 39) maintains, not in my opinion convincingly, that Philo's teaching did not involve declamatory exercises. He considers it unlikely that Philo was the first Academic philosopher to teach rhetoric.

CHAPTER II

[1] Suet. *Rhet.* 1; cf. *Gram.* 1. The earliest reference in Latin literature to rhetoric is in Ennius (*Var.* 28 Vahlen).

[2] Cic. *de Orat.* 1.14.

[3] Suet. *Rhet.* 1. In the fragments of Philodemus we find Rome coupled

with Sparta as a country which had expelled the rhetorician and managed its affairs without him: Phil. *Rhet.* 1.14 Sudhaus (fr. 5); cf. 2.65 Sudhaus (fr. 2).

⁴ See F. Leo, *Geschichte der römischen Literatur* 1 (Berlin, 1913), 279.

⁵ Quint. *Inst.* 3.1.19.

⁶ Plut. *Aem.* 6.5; Cic. *Brut.* 100, 104, 125; Plut. *TG* 8.4.

⁷ There is evidence in the fragments of Lucilius of an interest in rhetorical matters: see lines 26, 181, 383, 385, 603, 1133 (Marx), with F. Marx's notes (edition, Leipzig, 1904–5). See also Cic. *de Orat.* 1.72.

⁸ F. Marx regarded Coelius Antipater, the historian who flourished in the latter part of the second century, as a rhetorician, and surmised that much of the doctrine of *ad Herennium* and Cicero's rhetorical works goes back to him (*Incerti auctoris De ratione dicendi ad C. Herennium Libri IV* (Leipzig, 1894), 136–8; cf. M. Schanz and C. Hosius, *Geschichte der römischen Literatur bis zum Gesetzgebungswerk des Kaisers Justinian* 1⁴ (Munich, 1927), 200). But it is by no means certain that he taught rhetoric: Cicero's words in *Brut.* 102 would naturally mean that he taught law, not rhetoric.

⁹ Suet. *Rhet.* 1.

¹⁰ Cic. ap. Suet. *Rhet.* 2. Aurelius Opilius, who accompanied Rutilius Rufus into exile in 92, taught rhetoric before that date (Suet. *Gram.* 6). Whether he should be classed with the Latin rhetoricians we do not know.

¹¹ Suet. *Rhet.* 2.

¹² Cicero in *de Oratore* makes Crassus wholly responsible. That *de Oratore* was largely directed against Plotius and the Latin rhetoricians was a view once held by some (e.g. Norden, *Kunstprosa*, 1.222–4). It is discussed and rightly rejected by L. Laurand, *De M. Tulli Ciceronis studiis rhetoricis* (Paris, 1907), 7ff.

¹³ Cic. *de Orat.* 3.93–5.

¹⁴ Cic. *Arch.* 20; Sal. *Jug.* 63.3, 85.32; Plut. *Mar.* 2.2.

¹⁵ Marx, *op. cit.* (n. 8), 147–50; Schanz-Hosius, *op. cit.* (n. 8), 209; Gwynn, *Roman Education*, 62–9.

¹⁶ For censorial interest in the upbringing of the young see D.H. *Ant. Rom.* 20.13 (20.3).

¹⁷ Marx believed that *ad Herennium* was written *ab adulescentulo immaturo et satis indocto* (*op. cit.* (n. 8), 82).

¹⁸ In the introductory passage to Book 4 (4.10) the author of *ad Herennium* remarks on the unfamiliarity of the Latin technical terms which he is using, but elsewhere one does not get the impression that he is creating his own terminology.

¹⁹ Quint. *Inst.* 3.1.19.

²⁰ Cic. *Brut.* 163; Quint. *Inst.* 3.1.19; cf. Cic. *de Orat.* 1.94.

²¹ Cic. *de Orat.* 1.208.

²² Quint. *Inst.* 3.6.45.

²³ Two orators of the first century B.C., C. Sicinius and T. Accius Pisaurensis, are mentioned by Cicero as having been trained according to the method of Hermagoras (*Brut.* 263, 271).

²⁴ Marx, *op. cit.* (n. 8), 155. W. Warde Fowler (*Roman Essays and Interpretations* (Oxford, 1920), 98) argues that the *terminus post quem* can be

brought down to 84 B.C.; cf. H. Caplan's Loeb edition of *ad Herennium* (1954), p. xxvi. A. E. Douglas (*CQ* n.s. 10 (1960), 65–78) argues that the date of publication could be considerably later than 82 B.C.

[25] Cic. *de Orat.* 1.5.

[26] See Schanz-Hosius, *op. cit.* (n. 8), 588 for a summary of various theories. See also Caplan's edition (n. 24), pp. xxvi–xxviii. D. Matthes (*Lustrum* 3 (1958), 58–214) has argued that the two works derive from two Latin teachers both of whom used, in the main, a Latin version of a Greek treatise.

[27] See the arguments in Marx, *op. cit.* (n. 8), 69–73. These have not however finally disposed of Cornificius as author.

[28] *Rhet. Her.* 1.1.

[29] *Rhet. Her.* 1.18. On the other hand he was old enough to be occupied with family affairs (1.1).

[30] Plut. *Mar.* 5.4.

[31] Marx, *op. cit.* (n. 8), 150–3.

[32] e.g. *Rhet. Her.* 4.31, 4.68. The evidence for popular sympathies is not strong. See Caplan's edition (n. 24), pp. xxiii–xxiv.

[33] *Rhet. Her.* 1.1.

[34] Suet. *Gram.* 4; *Rhet.* 1.

[35] Antonius Gnipho in the time of Cicero used to lecture daily on rhetorical theory (Suet. *Gram.* 7). Quintilian implies that *de Inventione* was based on lecture notes (*Inst.* 3.6.59); but Cicero also used written authorities (*Inv.* 2.4). Cf. Cic. *Fam.* 16.21.8 for lecture notes.

[36] Cic. *Part.* 2.

[37] Suet. *Rhet.* 1.

[38] Diomedes 1.310 Keil; cf. Quint. *Inst.* 1.9.5, with F. H. Colson's note (edition, Cambridge, 1924).

[39] Suet. *Rhet.* 1.

[40] *Rhet. Her.* 4.54ff. Some of the themes of this exercise can be traced in Cicero's speeches (*Sest.* 47–8; *Phil.* 10.20, 14.31).

[41] *Rhet. Her.* 4.56–7. A very similar scheme was recommended by the later Greek rhetoricians for the development of the *chria* (Aphthonius *Prog.* 3 (23 Spengel); [Hermogenes] *Prog.* 3.21 (6 Spengel)).

[42] Quint. *Inst.* 2.1.1ff.

[43] Quint. *Inst.* 2.1.9; cf. 2.4.41.

[44] See M. L. Clarke, *CQ* n.s. 1 (1951), 159–66.

[45] Cic. *de Orat.* 1.149, 1.244.

[46] Cic. *de Orat.* 2.100.

[47] See Marx, *op. cit.* (n. 8), 102–11 for those in *ad Herennium*.

[48] Cic. *Inv.* 2.72–8.

[49] Cic. *Inv.* 2.78–86; cf. Quint. *Inst.* 3.6.76.

[50] Cic. *Inv.* 2.87–91.

[51] Cic. *Inv.* 2.95–102.

[52] In *Rhet. Her.* 1.25, where the case also occurs, the commander's name is given. The incident took place in 107 B.C.

[53] Cic. *Inv.* 2.118 *nihil enim prohibet fictam* (sc. *legem*) *exempli loco ponere quo facilius res intelligatur.*

[54] Cic. *Inv.* 2.153–4. There is a simpler variant in *Rhet. Her.* 1.19.

[55] Cf. Cic. *de Orat.* 2.99.

[56] *Rhet. Her.* 3.2; Cic. *Inv.* 1.11, 1.17, 1.71.

[57] *Rhet. Her.* 3.2.

[58] Juv. 7.160ff.

[59] Cic. *Brut.* 127, 164.

[60] Cic. *de Orat.* 1.154.

[61] Cic. *de Orat.* 3.74.

[62] Tac. *Dial.* 34.1–2.

[63] Cic. *Amic.* 1; *Cael.* 9.

[64] Cic. *Brut.* 320.

[65] Cic. *Tusc.* 1.7.

[66] Suet. *Rhet.* 1.

[67] Cic. *Brut.* 310; Cic. ap. Quint. *Inst.* 6.3.73; Sen. *Con.* 1 pr. 11; Suet. *Rhet.* 1.

[68] Suet. *Rhet.* 1; cf. Cic. *Phil.* 2.42 for Antonius.

[69] Cic. *Brut.* 305ff.

[70] Cic. *Brut.* 310. Cicero's son at Athens declaimed in both Greek and Latin (Cic. *Fam.* 16.21.5).

CHAPTER III

[1] Cic. *Part.* 139.

[2] Kroll, *Rhetorik*, § 24.

[3] *Rhet. Her.* 1.2; Cic. *Inv.* 1.7; Quint. *Inst.* 3.4.1ff. The division goes back to Aristotle (*Rh.* 1.3.1–3), though he probably did not invent it himself (see D. A. G. Hinks, *CQ* 30 (1936), 172). Cicero in *Part.* 10 follows Aristotle in relating the three types to three different kinds of audience. Cf. Mart. Cap. 8 (456 Halm).

[4] Quintilian (*Inst.* 3.3.11–15) discusses the question whether they are *partes rhetorices* or *opera oratoris*. Cic. *Part.* 3 treats them as different aspects of the *vis oratoris*.

[5] *Rhet. Her.* 1.3; Cic. *Inv.* 1.9.

[6] Cic. *de Orat.* 1.145; Quint. *Inst.* 3.3.4.

[7] *Rhet. Her.* 1.4; Cic. *Inv.* 1.19; cf. *de Orat.* 1.143.

[8] Cic. *de Orat.* 2.79. Cicero himself gives four in *Part.* 4 and 27, *Orat.* 122 and *Top.* 97.

[9] Quint. *Inst.* 3.9.1–3.

[10] *Rhet. Her.* 1.5. Cicero adds another, *admirabile* (*Inv.* 1.20). Quintilian omits *turpe*, includes *admirabile* and adds *obscurum* (*Inst.* 4.1.40).

[11] *Rhet. Her.* 1.6; Cic. *Inv.* 1.20; Quint. *Inst.* 4.1.42ff.

[12] *Rhet. Her.* 1.6–8; Cic. *Inv.* 1.22–3; *Part.* 28–30; Quint. *Inst.* 4.1.5ff.

[13] *Rhet. Her.* 1.8; Cic. *Inv.* 1.22.

[14] *Rhet. Her.* 1.9ff.; Cic. *Inv.* 1.23ff.; Quint. *Inst.* 4.1.48.

[15] *Rhet. Her.* 1.12ff.; Cic. *Inv.* 1.27; *Part.* 31–2; Quint. *Inst.* 4.2.

[16] Those concerned with things were divided into (i) *fabula*, (ii) *historia*, (iii) *argumentum* (*Rhet. Her.* 1.12; Cic. *Inv.* 1.27).

¹⁷ *Rhet. Her.* 1.14.

¹⁸ Cf. Cicero's *narratio* in *pro Milone*, where we are in the fortunate position of being able to check it by Asconius' account.

¹⁹ *Rhet. Her.* 1.16.

²⁰ Cic. *Inv.* 1.30.

²¹ *Rhet. Her.* 1.17; Cic. *Inv.* 1.31–3.

²² *De Inventione* introduces it before the *partes orationis* (1.10).

²³ *Stasis* in Greek. The Latin term *status* became the accepted one in preference to *constitutio* which is used in *ad Herennium*.

²⁴ Quint. *Inst.* 3.6.5. Cf. Cic. *Inv.* 1.10 *prima conflictio causarum ex depulsione intentionis profecta. Rhet. Her.* 1.18 defines *prima deprecatio defensoris cum accusatoris insimulatione coniuncta.*

²⁵ *Rhet. Her.* 1.18.

²⁶ Quint. *Inst.* 3.6.

²⁷ Cicero, who in *Inv.* had followed the fourfold classification (1.10), followed the threefold in his later works: *de Orat.* 2.104, 113, 132; *Part.* 33, 101ff.; *Orat.* 45; *Top.* 92. See L. Laurand, *De M. Tulli Ciceronis studiis rhetoricis* (Paris, 1907), 94ff.

²⁸*Rhet. Her.* 1.26; Cic. *Inv.* 1.18–19. *Inv.* uses *firmamentum* in a different sense.

²⁹ Quint. *Inst.* 3.11.21–2.

³⁰ *Rhet. Her.* 2.3–26; Cic. *Inv.* 2.14–115; *Part.* 34–43.

³¹ *Rhet. Her.* 2.3ff.

³² In *Rhet. Her.* (2.9) *communes loci* are those *qui alia in causa ab reo alia ab accusatore tractantur.* In *Inv.* (2.48) they are *argumenta quae transferri in multas causas possunt.*

³³ Cic. *Inv.* 2.48.

³⁴ *Rhet. Her.* 2.12.

³⁵ *Rhet. Her.* 1.19–23.

³⁶ Cic. *Inv.* 2.116–54.

³⁷ Cic. *Inv.* 1.16. It was pointed out that Roman practice meant that such cases did not normally come into court (*Rhet. Her.* 1.22; *Inv.* 2.57).

³⁸ Cic. *Inv.* 1.10; cf. *Part.* 41. At *de Orat.* 2.110 Cicero includes disputes arising from the interpretation of documents *in eo genere in quo quale sit quid ambigitur*, and classes all such disputes under ambiguity.

³⁹ *Rhet. Her.* 2.14. The arguments on this theme in *Inv.* are more subtle and interesting, but too long for quotation: see Cic. *Inv.* 2.138–41.

⁴⁰ *Rhet. Her.* 1.24. In *Inv.* the third *constitutio* is *generalis*, divided into *iuridicialis* and *negotialis*. The subdivisions of the former follow those in *Rhet. Her.* except that *comparatio* is differently defined (Cic. *Inv.* 1.14–15).

⁴¹ *Rhet. Her.* 2.19 *natura, lege, consuetudine, iudicato, aequo et bono, pacto.*

⁴² *Rhet. Her.* 1.24, 2.23; Cic. *Inv.* 1.15, 2.94.

⁴³ *Rhet. Her.* 2.24; Cic. *Inv.* 2.99.

⁴⁴ *Rhet. Her.* 1.24, 2.26; Cic. *Inv.* 2.105.

⁴⁵ *Rhet. Her.* 1.25, 2.22. In *Inv.* (2.71) it is called *relatio criminis.*

⁴⁶ *Rhet. Her.* 1.25, 2.26.

⁴⁷ *Rhet. Her.* 1.25, 2.21; Cic. *Inv.* 1.15, 2.72–8. In *Inv.*, *comparatio* is the defence of a deed not itself to be approved on the ground that it is the means

to a desirable end.

[48] *Rhet. Her.* 2.27ff.

[49] *Rhet. Her.* 2.28. Cic. *Inv.* (1.57–9, 67–9) gives different types of quinquepartite argument.

[50] Cic. *Inv.* 1.34ff.

[51] Cic. *Inv.* 1.39.

[52] *Rhet. Her.* 2.31–45; cf. Cic. *Inv.* 1.78–96; *Part.* 44. Quint. *Inst.* 5.13 is more practical.

[53] *Rhet. Her.* 2.47–50; Cic. *Inv.* 1.98–109; *Part.* 52; Quint. *Inst.* 6.1.

[54] According to Quintilian, most Athenians and almost all philosophers who had written on oratory held that the peroration should be confined to recapitulation (*Inst.* 6.1.7). There is no trace of this view in the Roman republican writings.

[55] See Quint. *Inst.* 8.4.

[56] Attributed in *Inv.* 1.109 to the rhetorician Apollonius.

[57] *Rhet. Her.* 3.1–9; cf. Cic. *Inv.* 2.155–76; *de Orat.* 2.333–40; *Part.* 83–97; Quint. *Inst.* 3.7.

[58] *Rhet. Her.* 3.2. The philosophic origin of the second classification is clearer in *Inv.* (2.157) than in *Rhet. Her.*

[59] According to Cic. *Inv.* 2.156 it is *honestas* as well as *utilitas*. *Part.* 83 and *Top.* 91 agree with *Rhet. Her.* Cic. *de Orat.* 2.334 and Quint. *Inst.* 3.8.1 hold that the aim is primarily connected with what is honourable.

[60] *Dolus.* In the actual speech this should be called *consilium* (*Rhet. Her.* 3.8).

[61] *Rhet. Her.* 3.3.

[62] See W. Kroll, *Philologus* 90 (1938), 206.

[63] Cic. *Part.* 90 distinguishes between two different kinds of audience, the uneducated which prefers utility to honour and the educated which puts honour above everything. One's speech should be adapted to one's audience, and before the uneducated one may even praise pleasure.

[64] *Rhet. Her.* 3.6.

[65] *Rhet. Her.* 3.8–9. Aristotle (*Rh.* 1.6.1) had held that the aim was *to sympheron* (the advantageous); for him *to sympheron* was *agathon* (a good).

[66] *Rhet. Her.* 3.10–15; Cic. *Inv.* 2.177–8; *Part.* 70–82; *de Orat.* 2.340–9; Quint. *Inst.* 3.7.1–28.

[67] *Rhet. Her.* 3.15; cf. Cic. *de Orat.* 2.341.

[68] Cic. *de Orat.* 2.47, 341.

[69] *Rhet. Her.* 3.16–18; Cic. *Part.* 9–15; *de Orat.* 2.307–15; Quint. *Inst.* 7.

[70] *Rhet. Her.* 3.16. Cicero (*de Orat.* 2.307) divides into the order which the nature of the pleading produces, i.e. the textbook order of the *partes orationis*, and that produced by the orator's judgment, the latter being confined to the arrangement of arguments.

[71] *Rhet. Her.* 3.18; Cic. *de Orat.* 2.314; Quint. *Inst.* 7.1.2–31, esp. 2–3, 11.

[72] Quint. *Inst.* 7. The book however includes much that one would not expect to find under this head.

[73] See p. 6.

[74] *Rhet. Her.* 4.11.

[75] See p. 82. Quintilian (*Inst.* 12.10.58) follows Cicero. It is to be noted

that he deals with this theme apart from his main consideration of *elocutio*.

[76] Cic. *de Orat.* 3.37 *ut Latine, ut plane, ut ornate, ut ad id quodcunque agetur apte congruenterque dicamus*; cf. Quint. *Inst.* 8.1.1.

[77] *Rhet. Her.* 4.17. Cic. *Part.* 18 adds *breve* (of Stoic origin; see p. 8) and *suave*.

[78] Quint. *Inst.* 9.1.1–25.

[79] See D'Alton, *Roman Literary Theory*, 106–9.

[80] Cicero distinguishes (1) *ornatus verborum*, (a) *simplicium*, (b) *collocatorum*; and (2) *ornatus rerum* (*Orat.* 80). His favourite word for figures is *lumina*. *Figura* is common in Quintilian. The term *trope* was not yet naturalised in Latin in the republican period. Cicero refers to it as a Greek term in *Brut.* 69. See H. Bornecque, *RPh* (sér. 3) 8 (1934), 143.

[81] His illustrations are not derived from existing works of literature, but are invented, at least allegedly (see F. Marx, *Incerti auctoris De ratione dicendi ad C. Herennium Libri IV* (Leipzig, 1894), 114), by himself. See *Rhet. Her.* 4.1–10.

[82] There is a convenient list in A. S. Wilkins' edition of Cicero, *de Oratore* (Oxford, 1882–92), 1.62–4.

[83] *Rhet. Her.* 4.19.

[84] *Rhet. Her.* 4.38. Cf. Cic. *de Orat.* 3.206 and, for both *anaphora* and *anadiplosis*, *Orat.* 135; *Part.* 21, 54, 72; Quint. *Inst.* 9.3.28–30.

[85] *Rhet. Her.* 4.53.

[86] *Rhet. Her.* 4.39.

[87] *Rhet. Her.* 4.51.

[88] *Rhet. Her.* 4.68.

[89] *Rhet. Her.* 4.66; Cic. *Orat.* 85.

[90] Cic. *de Orat.* 3.205 *vel gravissimum lumen augendi*; cf. *Orat.* 138; Quint. *Inst.* 9.2.29.

[91] *Rhet. Her.* 4.59–62; Cic. *de Orat.* 3.205; *Orat.* 138.

[92] *Rhet. Her.* 4.61; Quint. *Inst.* 8.3.72ff.

[93] *Rhet. Her.* 4.62.

[94] Cic. *de Orat.* 3.205; cf. *Orat.* 138.

[95] *Rhet. Her.* 4.22; cf. Cic. *Orat.* 135.

[96] *Rhet. Her.* 4.28; cf. Cic. *de Orat.* 3.206; *Orat.* 38, 84, 135, 220.

[97] *Rhet. Her.* 4.29ff.

[98] *Rhet. Her.* 4.32; cf. Demetr. *Eloc.* 27.

[99] *Rhet. Her.* 4.25.

[100] See *Rhet. Her.* 3.28ff.; Cic. *de Orat.* 2.350–60; *Part.* 26; Quint. *Inst.* 11.2.

[101] *Rhet. Her.* 3.19ff.; Cic. *de Orat.* 1.18, 3.213; *Orat.* 56; Quint. *Inst.* 11.3.2ff.

[102] *Rhet. Her.* 3.19.

[103] Quint. *Inst.* 11.3.

[104] *Rhet. Her.* 3.20ff.

[105] *Rhet. Her.* 3.23–4.

[106] *Rhet. Her.* 3.26–7.

[107] Cf. Cic. *de Orat.* 1.230, 2.47, 2.220; *Brut.* 141, 158.

[108] Cf. Cicero's description of Calidius' delivery: *non frons percussa, non femur* (ap. *Brut.* 278).

CHAPTER IV

1 As was observed in antiquity. See Quint. *Inst.* 2.17.6.

2 Cic. *Brut.* 61–2. Though Appius' speech was extant Cicero infers its author's eloquence not from the speech itself, but from the effect it had on the senate (*Brut.* 55). At *Sen.* 16 he quotes from Ennius' poetical version in preference to the original.

3 Cic. *Brut.* 52–60.

4 F. Leo, *Geschichte der römischen Literatur* 1 (Berlin, 1913), 30–31.

5 Leo, *op. cit.* (n. 4), 31. There are various references to the *patronus* in Plautus: *Men.* 581; *Poen.* 1244; *Rud.* 705; *Vid.* 60, 62.

6 D.H. *Ant. Rom.* 5.17.

7 Quint. *Inst.* 8.6.75.

8 See J. B. Hofmann, *Lateinische Umgangssprache*² (Heidelberg, 1936), 1.

9 Hofmann, *op. cit.* (n. 8), 58ff.

10 Cic. *Brut.* 65; cf. 69. Cicero was somewhat deflected from the course of impartial criticism by his desire to score a point against the Atticists. He discovers a resemblance between Cato and Lysias, and asks why the imitators of the latter do not extend their admiration to the former (*Brut.* 67).

11 For the former view see Norden, *Kunstprosa*, 1.165ff.; A. Cima, *L'eloquenza latina prima di Cicerone* (Rome, 1903), 93; for the latter Leo, *op. cit.* (n. 4), 286.

12 ap. Gel. 6.3.12–13, 15, 27, 34.

13 Gel. 6.3.52.

14 See, e.g., fr. 167 Malcovati.

15 ap. Gel. 10.3.17, fr. 66 Malcovati.

16 Cic. *Brut.* 69.

17 e.g. frr. 22, 243 Malcovati.

18 See *Rhet. Her.* 4.18.

19 Cato frr. 23, 52, 61, 162 Malcovati; cf. Plaut. *Pseud.* 385; *Trin.* 1096. See Hofmann, *op. cit.* (n. 8), 93–4. Norden (*Kunstprosa*, 1.167) is surely wrong in finding a Greek origin for Cato's use of synonyms.

20 Cic. *Tusc.* 1.5. He is *studiosus* as opposed to *doctus*. In *de Oratore* (3.135) he is said to have lacked *haec politissima doctrina transmarina atque adventicia.* Plutarch (*Cat. Ma.* 2.4) refers to traces of Greek influence in his speeches and other writings. The tradition was, of course, that he learned Greek in old age.

21 Cic. *Brut.* 68; cf. *Orat.* 152; Gel. 6.3.53.

22 Cic. *Brut.* 83. But at *de Orat.* 3.28 *gravitas* is ascribed to Scipio, *lenitas* to Laelius. To Quintilian both are equally *horridus*: *Inst.* 12.10.10.

23 Cic. *Brut.* 96 *hoc in oratore Latino primum mihi videtur et levitas apparuisse illa Graecorum et verborum comprehensio et iam artifex, ut ita dicam, stilus.*

24 Lucil. 84ff.

25 Cic. *Brut.* 82.

26 Cic. *Brut.* 92. At *Tusc.* 1.5 Cicero describes Galba as *doctus*. But the thoughtful discussion in the *Brutus* is to be preferred to the hasty sentence of the *Tusculans*.

27 Cic. *Brut.* 82, 93.

[28] Cic. *Brut.* 89–90; V. Max. 8.1.2; Quint. *Inst.* 2.15.8. Appian (*Hisp.* 60) says Galba used bribery.

[29] Cic. *Har.* 41; *de Orat.* 1.38; *Brut.* 103. In early life Cicero was more favourably disposed to the politics of the Gracchi. In *Inv.* (1.5) they are bracketed with Cato, Laelius and Africanus as men in whom was *summa virtus et summa virtute amplificata auctoritas et quae et his rebus ornamento et reipublicae praesidio esset eloquentia.*

[30] Plut. *TG* 2.2.

[31] Plut. *TG* 9.4; *TG* 15.

[32] ap. Gel. 10.3.3, fr. 45 Malcovati.

[33] Cic. *de Orat.* 3.214, fr. 58 Malcovati; cf. Quint. *Inst.* 11.3.115.

[34] *Rhet. Her.* 4.33–4. The example from Gracchus belongs to the second type mentioned by *ad Herennium,* and is closely parallel to his imaginary example, *nam quid me facere convenit* etc. For the figure see Volkmann, *Rhetorik,* 493; M. Bonnet, *REA* 8 (1906), 40–6.

[35] Gel. 11.13.1–5, fr. 30 Malcovati.

[36] Cic. *Orat.* 233.

[37] Cic. *Brut.* 106.

[38] *ibid.*

[39] Cic. *de Orat.* 1.40; *Brut.* 105.

[40] Cic. *de Orat.* 2.106.

[41] Cic. *de Orat.* 2.165, 169.

[42] Cic. *Brut.* 122, 124.

[43] Cic. *Brut.* 110, 111, 116.

[44] Cic. *Brut.* 114.

[45] Cic. *de Orat.* 1.228.

[46] Cic. *de Orat.* 1.227–30; *Brut.* 115. One of his advocates was Q. Mucius Scaevola, also a Stoic, whose sober legal arguments proved ineffective against Crassus' mockery in the *causa Curiana.* See p. 47.

[47] Cic. *de Orat.* 1.230. Other Stoic orators were Q. Aelius Tubero, whose mode of speaking, according to Cicero, matched the harshness and uncouthness of his way of life (*Brut.* 117; *Off.* 3.63), Mummius (*Brut.* 94; cf. *Rep.* 5.11) and Fannius (*Brut.* 101).

[48] Cic. *Brut.* 138.

[49] Fimbria: Cic. *Brut.* 129; Scaevola: *de Orat.* 1.180; *Brut.* 145; Catulus: *de Orat.* 2.28; *Brut.* 132–4, 259; Philippus: *de Orat.* 2.316; *Brut.* 173.

[50] Cic. *Arch.* 6; *de Orat.* 1.45, 1.155, 2.1–4, 3.75; *Brut.* 145.

[51] Cic. *de Orat.* 2.1–4.

[52] Cic. *de Orat.* 1.82, 172, 248.

[53] Cic. *de Orat.* 2.3.

[54] Cic. *de Orat.* 2.8; *Brut.* 163; *Orat.* 132; *Clu.* 140.

[55] Crassus' first speech was apparently an attack on the political career of the turncoat Carbo (Cic. *de Orat.* 2.170).

[56] See Cic. *de Orat.* 2.200–1.

[57] Cic. *de Orat.* 2.108–9.

[58] Cic. *de Orat.* 2.201.

[59] Cic. *Brut.* 139; *de Orat.* 2.203.

[60] Cic. *Brut.* 145.

[61] Cic. *Brut.* 143.

[62] Cic. *de Orat.* 2.199.

[63] Cic. *de Orat.* 2.220, 228; *Brut.* 158. Examples are quoted in *de Orat.* 2.222ff., 240, 242, 267, 269.

[64] Cic. *de Orat.* 1.243.

[65] J. Swift, *A Letter to a Young Gentleman, Lately enter'd into Holy Orders* (London, 1721).

[66] Cic. *de Orat.* 2.195.

[67] Cic. *de Orat.* 2.199–200 (abbreviated).

[68] Cic. *Brut.* 140.

[69] Cic. *de Orat.* 2.23; cf. 3.5, 3.33; Tac. *Dial.* 18.

[70] ap. Cic. *de Orat.* 2.225–6, fr. 43 Malcovati.

[71] Cic. *de Orat.* 3.171–2.

[72] Cic. *Brut.* 162; *Orat.* 223.

[73] Cic. *Orat.* 226; *de Orat.* 3.190; Norden, *Kunstprosa*, 1.174. Some of Crassus' rhythms were criticised as poetical: *Orat.* 222; Quint. *Inst.* 9.4.109.

[74] Cic. *Orat.* 214.

[75] Cic. *Brut.* 158.

[76] Cic. *Brut.* 141; *Tusc.* 2.57.

[77] Quint. *Inst.* 10.3.21.

[78] Cic. *Tusc.* 1.5.

CHAPTER V

[1] Cic. *Top.* 1–5.

[2] Cic. *Fam.* 1.9.23 *abhorrent a communibus praeceptis atque omnem antiquorum et Aristoteliam et Isocratiam rationem oratoriam complectuntur.* F. Solmsen has drawn attention to the Aristotelian elements in *de Oratore* in *CP* 33 (1938), 390–404 and *AJP* 62 (1941), 35–50, 169–90, and H. M. Hubbell to the Isocratean in *The Influence of Isocrates on Cicero, Dionysius and Aristides* (New Haven, 1913).

[3] H. von Arnim, *Leben und Werke des Dio von Prusa* (Berlin, 1898), 97ff.; W. Kroll, *RhM* 58 (1903), 552–97; *id.*, *NJA* 11 (1903), 688–9; Gwynn, *Roman Education*, 114.

[4] Cic. *Orat.* 12.

[5] Cic. *de Orat.* 3.145; cf. *Fat.* 3.

[6] Von Arnim put forward the claims of Philo as Cicero's source, Kroll those of Antiochus. Philo did at least teach rhetoric, but all we know of his teaching is that he handled *quaestiones finitae* (Cic. *de Orat.* 3.110) and that he taught rhetoric and philosophy at different times (Cic. *Tusc.* 2.9).

[7] See L. Laurand, *De M. Tulli Ciceronis studiis rhetoricis* (Paris, 1907), which emphasises the variety of Cicero's sources and his own contribution. H. K. Schulte, *Orator: Untersuchungen über das ciceronische Bildungsideal* (Frankfurt, 1935), finds Posidonian influence. See Barwick, *Das rednerische Bildungsideal Ciceros*, for a thorough analysis of *de Oratore* and discussion of its sources. Barwick concludes that nothing points to any of the single sources that have been suggested and that Cicero's own contribution was considerable.

[8] Cic. *de Orat.* 2.40.
[9] Cic. *de Orat.* 1.47.
[10] Cic. *de Orat.* 1.5.
[11] Cic. *de Orat.* 2.75; cf. 1.105.
[12] Cic. *de Orat.* 2.162.
[13] Cic. *de Orat.* 2.139; cf. 2.77ff. Further criticism of rhetoricians occurs in 2.323, 3.54, 3.70, 3.121.
[14] See Cic. *de Orat.* 2.4 for Crassus' and Antonius' attitude towards Greek learning.
[15] Cic. *de Orat.* 2.217–18, 235.
[16] Cic. *de Orat.* 2.44–6.
[17] Cic. *Orat.* 43.
[18] Cic. *de Orat.* 1.146, 2.150.
[19] Cic. *de Orat.* 1.145, 2.356; *Brut.* 263.
[20] Cic. *Fin.* 4.10.
[21] Cic. *Orat.* 12; cf. Plut. *Cic.* 32.5.
[22] Cic. *Inv.* 1.1.
[23] Cic. *Inv.* 1.5.
[24] Cic. *Inv.* 1.2–3; cf. Isocr. *Nic.* 6.
[25] Cic. *de Orat.* 1.33, 3.55; cf. *Div. Caec.* 27, 70.
[26] Cic. *de Orat.* 1.32, 2.35.
[27] Cic. *de Orat.* 1.35ff.
[28] Cic. *de Orat.* 1.44.
[29] Quint. *Inst.* 2.17.21.
[30] Cic. *Off.* 2.51; cf. *Mur.* 59.
[31] Cic. *de Orat.* 1.47.
[32] Cic. *de Orat.* 3.122.
[33] Cic. *de Orat.* 3.66ff.
[34] Cic. *de Orat.* 3.142–3.
[35] Cic. *de Orat.* 1.5, 2.34.
[36] Cic. *de Orat.* 1.20; cf. 1.72; *Div. Caec.* 39.
[37] Cic. *de Orat.* 3.124; cf. 3.93.
[38] Cic. *Orat.* 14–16.
[39] Cic. *de Orat.* 1.219ff., esp. 223.
[40] Cic. *Orat.* 115.
[41] Cic. *Orat.* 119. The idea was probably taken from Plat. *Phdr.* 270 a.
[42] Cic. *de Orat.* 1.68.
[43] Cic. *de Orat.* 1.56; cf. *Orat.* 118.
[44] Cic. *de Orat.* 1.169, 173, 184; *Orat.* 120.
[45] Cf. Cic. *de Orat.* 1.166ff.
[46] Cic. *de Orat.* 1.249–50.
[47] Cic. *de Orat.* 1.193, 195.
[48] Cic. *Orat.* 120; cf. *de Orat.* 1.18, 256.
[49] See his remarks in *de Orat.* 2.62–4 and *Orat.* 120.
[50] Cic. *Inv.* 1.8.
[51] Cic. *Orat.* 45.
[52] Cic. *de Orat.* 2.134. Other examples follow.
[53] Cf. Cic. *de Orat.* 3.120.

54 Cic. *de Orat.* 2.178.

55 Cic. *Brut.* 89, 279; *Orat.* 128.

56 In this respect Cicero was returning to Aristotle. See F. Solmsen, *CP* 33 (1938), 390–404.

57 Cic. *de Orat.* 2.189.

58 Cic. *de Orat.* 2.191, 193. But writing as a moralist in the *Tusculans* he says *oratorem vero irasci minime decet, simulare non dedecet* (4.55).

59 Cic. *de Orat.* 2.195.

60 Cic. *Orat.* 130, 132.

61 Cic. *de Orat.* 2.216–89; cf. *Orat.* 87–90.

62 e.g. Theophrastus in his *peri geloiou* (*On the laughable*): D.L. 5.46; Athen. 8.348 a. See M. A. Grant, *The Ancient Rhetorical Theories of the Laughable: the Greek Rhetoricians and Cicero* (Madison, 1924), 24ff.

63 Cic. *de Orat.* 2.216.

64 Cic. *de Orat.* 3.52–3.

65 Cic. *de Orat.* 3.104.

66 Cic. *de Orat.* 3.124ff.

67 Cic. *de Orat.* 3.125.

68 Cic. *de Orat.* 3.145–8.

CHAPTER VI

1 Cic. *Tusc.* 4.55; cf. *Brut.* 91–3. *Red. Sen.* was written out beforehand and read (*Planc.* 74). In most cases the orator would come prepared with notes (*commentarii*), parts of which would be written out in full. These were sometimes published. See *Brut.* 164; Quint. *Inst.* 10.7.30–1.

2 Cic. *Att.* 1.13.5, 13.20.2.

3 Plin. *Ep.* 1.20.6. There is evidence for this in the text of more than one of the speeches, where the published version merely gives bare headings for certain counts in the indictment: see Cic. *Font.* 20; *Mur.* 57; *Cael.* 19.

4 This is the thesis of J. Humbert, *Les Plaidoyers écrits et les plaidoiries réelles de Cicéron* (Paris, 1925). For a more conservative treatment of the matter see Laurand, *Études*, 1–23.

5 Cic. *Flac.* 21. See Greenidge, *Legal Procedure*, 477–8. In the action against Verres Cicero dispensed with an opening speech of the normal type and produced his witnesses straightaway. In *Font.*, *Flac.* and *Scaur.*, also cases *de repetundis*, where Cicero was defending, a similar procedure seems to have been followed. See Humbert, *op. cit.* (n. 4), 217, 223ff., 237.

6 See Humbert, *op. cit.* (n. 4), 67–70.

7 Asc. 36 Clark.

8 Tac. *Dial.* 38; Plin. *Ep.* 1.20.4ff.

9 Cicero criticises this practice in *Brut.* 208–9.

10 Asc. 20 Clark. Before then, says Asconius, there had seldom been more than four; later, between the civil wars and the *lex Iulia*, there were sometimes as many as twelve.

11 *Schol. Bob.* 125 Stangl *causam plurimi defenderunt, in quis fuit Q. Hortensius, M. Crassus, C. Licinius Calvus, partibus inter se distributis quas in agendo tuerentur.*

[12] With two: *Mur.*, *Cael.*, *Balb.*; with one: *Rab. Perd.*, *Sul.*, *Flac.*, *Planc.*

[13] Cic. *Orat.* 130; *Brut.* 190.

[14] See Cic. *Sest.* 3; *Balb.* 17.

[15] Is it a coincidence that this device appears in the early *pro Roscio Amerino* and the late *pro Milone*, both speeches, for different reasons, closer to the rhetorical pattern than most of Cicero's?

[16] But parts of the argument were omitted in the published version. See n. 3 above.

[17] Cic. *Clu.* 1 *consuetudinis causa.*

[18] Cic. *Mur.* 11.

[19] See also Cic. *Balb.* 56ff. and *Rab. Post.* 6ff. for references to irrelevant charges.

[20] Cic. *Planc.* 3; *Sul.* 35.

[21] Cic. *Dom.* 93.

[22] Cic. *Mur.* 11; *Font.* 37–40.

[23] Cic. *Ver.* 3.164, 5.19. He 'passes over' the vices of Verres' early life in 1.32.

[24] Cic. *Flac.* 98.

[25] Cic. *Rab. Perd.* 2.

[26] Cic. *Mur.* 7–8.

[27] Cic. *Arch.* 1. See Kroll, *Rhetorik*, § 30.

[28] Cic. *de Orat.* 2.331 *quia neque reprehendi quae contra dicuntur possunt nisi tua confirmes neque haec confirmari nisi illa reprehendas idcirco haec et natura et utilitate et tractatione coniuncta sunt.* In the speeches the tendency is for *confutatio*, if anything, to come before *confirmatio*.

[29] See F. Solmsen, *TAPA* 69 (1938), 542–56.

[30] Cic. *Quinct.* 11ff.; *Tul.* 14ff.; *Caec.* 10ff.

[31] The rhetoricians did their best to make facts fit theory by counting as *narratio* not only a statement of the facts of the case itself but also one of the facts incidental to the case, and even an account of the accused's past life (Quint. *Inst.* 4.2.9ff.). In this sense, of course, *narrationes* can be found in Cicero's speeches.

[32] Cic. *de Orat.* 2.330.

[33] *Pro Cluentio* begins with a *divisio*; only after it come the usual topics of the *exordium*.

[34] Cic. *de Orat.* 2.105.

[35] If Rabirius had killed Saturninus he would have done rightly. But he did not kill him. See Cic. *Rab. Perd.* 18ff.; Quint. *Inst.* 7.1.16.

[36] Quint. *Inst.* 2.6.11.

[37] Probably his treatment was similar in the speech as delivered and was dictated by the prosecution. See Asc. 41 Clark.

[38] See Quint. *Inst.* 3.11.15.

[39] Cic. *Lig.* 30.

[40] See Antonius' remarks in Cic. *de Orat.* 2.120.

[41] Cic. *Mil.* 32, 36, 41, 45, 53, 61.

[42] Cic. *Cael.* 53–4.

[43] Cic. *Caec.* 65.

[44] His defence is much on the lines suggested in Cic. *Inv.* 2.142: *huic qui*

contra scriptum dicet, plurimum proderit, ex ipsa scriptura aliquid ad suam causam convertere ...; deinde ... verbi definitionem inducere et illius verbi vim quo urgeri videatur ad suae causae commodum traducere.

[45] Cic. *Caec.* 67–75.

[46] Cic. *S. Rosc.* 71–2; cf. *Orat.* 107.

[47] Cic. *Inv.* 2.48.

[48] Cic. *Font.* 21ff.; *Flac.* 6, 24; *Scaur.* 15. The *locus de quaestionibus* is to be found in *Sul.* 78.

[49] Cic. *Ver.* 5.136ff. Cicero gives an emotional tone to his recapitulation by putting it in the mouth of Verres' father, an ingenious device which aroused Quintilian's admiration (*Inst.* 6.1.3).

[50] Cic. *Planc.* 83.

[51] Cic. *Font.* 46ff.; *Flac.* 106; *Sest.* 144; *Planc.* 102.

[52] Cic. *Cael.* 79.

[53] Cic. *Mil.* 92, 95, 105.

[54] We may perhaps see a trace of the scholastic classification in the second speech on the agrarian law, when Cicero says *de commodo prius vestro dicam, Quirites; deinde ad amplitudinem et dignitatem revertar* (*Agr.* 2.76).

[55] According to Quintilian (*Inst.* 3.8.6), deliberative oratory does not always require an *exordium* of the type necessary in forensic speeches, but the beginning must bear some resemblance to an *exordium*; it should not be abrupt.

[56] Quint. *Inst.* 8.3.14.

[57] Laurand, *Etudes*, 310.

[58] The other two were *in Competitores* (*in Toga Candida*) and *in Clodium et Curionem.* Cicero's use of abusive language was not without precedent in oratorical theory and practice. One of the earliest rhetoricians, Thrasymachus, was 'unrivalled in casting aspersions and removing them on any grounds or none' (Plat. *Phdr.* 267 c–d). Cf. Süss, *Ethos*, 245.

[59] Cic. *Clu.* 58.

[60] Quint. *Inst.* 9.2.7–8.

[61] Cic. *Catil.* 1.1; cf. Quint. *Inst.* 9.3.30.

[62] Treated by Quintilian as an example of simulation (*Inst.* 9.2.26).

[63] Quint. *Inst.* 9.3.44. It might also serve as an example of self-correction; cf. *Rhet. Her.* 4.36.

[64] Cic. *Catil.* 1.3; cf. *Rhet. Her.* 4.37.

[65] Cic. *Catil.* 1.3.

[66] Cic. *Catil.* 1.18, 27. See Quint. *Inst.* 9.2.32.

CHAPTER VII

[1] Cic. *Brut.* 322.

[2] The art of digression is not particularly stressed in Cicero's theory; but see *de Orat.* 2.311–12.

[3] In the published version the interruption, if such it was, appears as '*quid ad istas ineptias abis?*' *inquies* (Cic. *S. Rosc.* 46).

[4] Cic. *Pis.* 71; *Sest.* 119; cf. *Ver.* 4.109. In *Har.* 18, Cicero finds it necessary

to explain that his literary interests do not extend to anti-religious writings.
  [5] Cic. *Pis.* 68; cf. *Mur.* 61.
  [6] Cic. *Arch.* 3.
  [7] Quint. *Inst.* 1.8.11–12.
  [8] W. Zillinger, *Cicero und die altrömischen Dichter* (Würzburg, 1911), 67.
  [9] Cic. *Cael.* 37–8.
  [10] Cic. *Scaur.* 4. He refers to the *Phaedo* in that vague manner which he adopts when wishing to avoid the appearance of exact knowledge. Compare the frequent affectation of ignorance regarding works of art in *Ver.* 4.
  [11] Cic. *Man.* 22. There are other references to Greek legend at *Ver.* 1.48, 4.106ff., 5.145ff.; *Sest.* 48; *Har.* 20, 39; *Pis.* 47.
  [12] Cic. *N.D.* 1.6.
  [13] Cic. *Mur.* 60ff.; *Pis.* 42, 59, 65. *sis licet Themista sapientior*, says Cicero at *Pis.* 63. How many of his audience would know who Themista was? Other references to Epicureanism: *Red. Sen.* 14; *Sest.* 23.
  [14] Cic. *Sest.* 47; *Cael.* 41.
  [15] Cic. *Arch.* 28–30; *Red. Pop.* 22–3; *Dom.* 107; *Planc.* 80.
  [16] Cic. *Sest.* 91–2.
  [17] Cicero's familiarity with legal matters is shown occasionally in his letters: *Att.* 1.5.6; *Fam.* 7.22 (see also *Leg.* 1.12). We can discount the mockery of the legal profession in *Mur.* 25ff.: cf. *Clu.* 139 *errat vehementer si quis in orationibus nostris quas in iudiciis habuimus auctoritates nostras consignatas se habere arbitratur.*
  [18] Cic. *Balb.* 17.
  [19] Cic. *Ver.* 3.209.
  [20] J. Russell (ed.), *Memorials and Correspondence of Charles James Fox* 4 (London, 1857), 349–50.
  [21] Quint. *Inst.* 6.3.2–3.
  [22] Quint. *Inst.* 6.3.5.
  [23] Cic. *Ver.* 1.121, 4.53, 4.57, 4.95. Quintilian defends these on the ground that Cicero attributes them to others (*Inst.* 6.3.4).
  [24] An attempt to do so has been made by Laurand, *Études*, 234–55.
  [25] Plut. *Cat. Mi.* 21.5.
  [26] Cic. *Mur.* 22ff. Quintilian gives this question as an example of a *thesis* and refers to the passage in *pro Murena* (*Inst.* 2.4.24). But Cicero's treatment is by no means free from reference to the particular question concerned.
  [27] Cic. *Cael.* 39ff.
  [28] See Kroll, *Rhetorik*, § 30.
  [29] Cic. *de Orat.* 2.312.
  [30] Cic. *Ver.* 2.2ff., 4.106ff.
  [31] Quint. *Inst.* 4.3.13. H. V. Canter (*AJP* 52 (1931), 351–61) gives an 'approximately complete' list of Cicero's digressions, numbering fifty-five in all. But it is not easy to decide what should be classed as a digression, nor is it highly important.
  [32] Cic. *Ver.* 1.75, 5.62; cf. Quint. *Inst.* 4.2.113–14.
  [33] Cic. *Ver.* 3.64, 81–2, 130–1, 137ff., 207–8. In Quintilian's day some theorists still forbade appeals to emotion in *narrationes* (*Inst.* 4.2.111). Others squared theory with Cicero's practice by regarding the outbursts in the

Verrines as quasi-perorations (*Inst.* 6.1.54–5).

[34] Cic. *Orat.* 132. Once he even took up an infant child in his arms during a peroration (*Orat.* 131).

[35] Cic. *Planc.* 76.

[36] Cic. *Cael.* 60; cf. *Sul.* 92; *Rab. Post.* 48.

[37] Plut. *Cic.* 39.6.

[38] Quint. *Inst.* 8.3.4 (H. E. Butler's translation).

[39] Quint. *Inst.* 12.10.12–14; cf. Tac. *Dial.* 18.

[40] Similarly the relative good taste of the Rhodian school, which was regarded as half-way between the Attic and the Asiatic (Quint. *Inst.* 12.10.18; cf. Cic. *Brut.* 51) might be explained by the island's history of independence and democratic government.

[41] Cic. *Brut.* 325.

[42] Cic. *Brut.* 326.

[43] It is noteworthy that there is no mention of Asianism and Atticism in *de Oratore* (U. von Wilamowitz-Möllendorff, *Hermes* 35 (1900), 1–52).

[44] Ironically enough the arch-Asiatic Hegesias had considered himself an imitator of Lysias (Cic. *Orat.* 226).

[45] M. Calidius, whose lack of emotional power Cicero criticises (*Brut.* 274ff.), has often been counted among the Atticists, but, as A. E. Douglas shows (*CQ* n.s. 5 (1955), 241–7), without good reason.

[46] Cic. *Tusc.* 2.3.

[47] Quint. *Inst.* 8.3.6; Tac. *Dial.* 18; cf. Cic. *Fam.* 15.21.4.

[48] One such, it appears, was T. Annius Cimber. See Virg. *Cat.* 2; Quint. *Inst.* 8.3.29.

[49] Cic. *Brut.* 287; *Opt. Gen.* 15; *Orat.* 30. Cicero himself had in *de Oratore* 2.93 mentioned Thucydides as one of the earliest Greek orators.

[50] Cic. *Brut.* 283–4.

[51] Cicero did not in fact imitate Demosthenes to any appreciable extent. His proclamation of himself as imitator of Demosthenes is his answer to the neo-Atticists who set themselves up as followers of Lysias. See W. Kroll, *M. Tullii Ciceronis Orator* (Berlin, 1913), 9.

[52] Cic. *Brut.* 184–5, 289.

[53] Cic. *Opt. Gen.* 7–13; cf. *Att.* 15.1b.2.

[54] Cic. *Orat.* 69, 100–1. The association of the three *genera* with the three aims or functions of the orator appears to have been an innovation of Cicero: see A. E. Douglas, *Eranos* 55 (1957), 18–26.

[55] Cic. *Orat.* 23, 104; cf. *Opt. Gen.* 9–10.

[56] Cic. *Orat.* 100–3.

[57] Cic. *Orat.* 80–1; Hor. *Ars* 309.

[58] Cic. *Orat.* 162ff.; *de Orat.* 3.172–98.

[59] Cic. *Orat.* 170; Quint. *Inst.* 9.4.76.

[60] Cic. *Orat.* 168–73, 234.

[61] Cic. *Orat.* 235.

[62] Cic. *Orat.* 170, 188–9, 209, 221.

[63] Cic. *Orat.* 227.

[64] See Laurand, *Études*, 117–230, and works cited there; L. P. Wilkinson, *Golden Latin Artistry* (Cambridge, 1963), ch. 5.

[65] Cic. *Orat.* 168.

[66] Quint. *Inst.* 1.8.11. In the case of Caelius, Crassus had preceded Cicero in quoting from Ennius (*Cael.* 18).

[67] Cic. *Parad.* 1; *Catil.* 4.7; Sal. *Cat.* 51.20.

[68] Cic. *Balb.* 2.

[69] Tullius Albinovanus: Cic. *Sest.* 127; Silanus: Cic. *Catil.* 4.7; Caesar: Sal. *Cat.* 51.4–6.

[70] Cic. *Div. Caec.* 46.

[71] Asc. 20 Clark.

[72] Cic. *Sest.* 130.

[73] Tac. *Dial.* 25.

CHAPTER VIII

[1] Sen. *Con.* 1 pr. 12. The passage, which is not without its difficulties, is discussed by W. A. Edward, *The Suasoriae of Seneca the Elder* (Cambridge, 1928), xv; Gwynn, *Roman Education*, 164.

[2] Pollio and T. Labienus declaimed in private (Sen. *Con.* 4 pr. 2, 10 pr. 4). Albucius generally did (7 pr. 1). Cf. 10 pr. 3 (Scaurus). See also Quint. *Inst.* 10.7.24.

[3] One teacher of the time of Cicero, Antonius Gnipho, is recorded as having given declamations, but only once a week, whereas he lectured on rhetorical theory every day (Suet. *Gram.* 7).

[4] Juv. 7.150–4. It may well be however that when Juvenal wrote the great days of public declamation were over.

[5] And Nicetes among the Greeks (Sen. *Con.* 9.2.23).

[6] Augustus attended declamations (Sen. *Con.* 2.4.12, 10.5.21); Tiberius was a connoisseur (*Suas.* 3.7), and Nero a declaimer himself (Suet. *Rhet.* 1; *Nero* 10). Maecenas, Agrippa (Sen. *Con.* 2.4.12), Messala (*Con.* 4.8; *Suas.* 2.17) and Pollio (Sen. *passim*) attended, and we hear of declamations before M. Aemilius Lepidus (*Con.* 10 pr. 3), L. Aelius Lamia (*Con.* 7.6.22) and Sosius (*Suas.* 2.21).

[7] Albucius only opened his school to the public five or six times a year (Sen. *Con.* 7 pr. 1). Many rhetoricians seem to have done so regularly.

[8] Sen. *Con.* 1.1.22; cf. 1.3.10.

[9] Aietius Pastor declaimed when a member of the senate (Sen. *Con.* 1.3.11), Domitius Ahenobarbus after his consulship (9.4.18). Juvenal *ad mediam fere aetatem declamavit animi magis causa quam quod se scholae aut foro praepararet* (*Vita Iuvenalis*).

[10] Suet. *Rhet.* 1 *aut ex historiis trahebantur ... aut ex veritate ac re, si qua forte recens accidisset.* Bonner (*Roman Declamation*, 18) would translate 'collections of stories' rather than 'history', on the ground that there is an antithesis intended between *historiis* and *veritate ac re*. But is not the contrast between past history and recent events?

[11] Suet. *Rhet.* 1 (J. C. Rolfe's translation).

[12] All the themes which Seneca mentions as declaimed in this school are of the new type, except for the historical, or pseudo-historical, one about

Cicero and Popillius (Sen. *Con.* 7.2). Marullus himself seems to have been rather old fashioned in his style (1 pr. 22).

[13] Sen. *Con.* 1.8.11; Cic. *Brut.* 325. Some have thought Seneca's Aeschines a different person from Cicero's. See *RE* 1.1062–3.

[14] Sen. *Con.* 1.4.7. Crispus, an *antiquus rhetor*, is recorded as having declaimed a *controversia* of the same type (7.4.9).

[15] Tac. *Ann.* 3.55.

[16] Unless Seneca's prejudice against Greeks makes him give a false impression.

[17] Sen. *Con.* 9.3.13.

[18] Sen. *Con.* 10 pr. 13.

[19] Sen. *Con.* 9.6.16 *ex Asia*; but some would read *ex Asianis*.

[20] Sen. *Con.* 1 pr. 13–17.

[21] Vibius Gallus (Sen. *Con.* 2.1.25).

[22] Seneca (*Con.* 1.7,15) characterises Fulvius Sparsus as *hominem inter scholasticos sanum, inter sanos scholasticum*.

[23] Sen. *Con.* 9 pr. 3.

[24] Sen. *Con.* 3 pr. 17.

[25] Sen. *Con.* 7 pr. 6–7; cf. Suet. *Rhet.* 6.

[26] Sen. *Con.* 3 pr. 18.

[27] Tac. *Dial.* 35.4.

[28] Sometimes the character was made to speak in his own person. See Bonner, *Roman Declamation*, 53.

[29] In Seneca's collection five are from Greece and two from Rome, both the latter from recent history. Elsewhere we hear of deliberations of Hannibal (Juv. 7.160ff.), Sulla (Juv. 1.16) and Caesar (Quint. *Inst.* 3.8.19). See J. E. B. Mayor on Juv. 1.16 (edition, London, 1901).

[30] Sen. *Suas.* 7; cf. Quint. *Inst.* 3.8.46.

[31] Sen. *Suas.* 7.11.

[32] Sen. *Suas.* 7.10; cf. 6.11. Varius Geminus, according to Cassius Severus, was the only one who gave real advice.

[33] Sen. *Con.* 2 pr. 3; *Suas.* 2.10.

[34] Quint. *Inst.* 3.8.58–61.

[35] Quint. *Inst.* 3.8.70.

[36] Sen. *Con.* 1.1.

[37] Sen. *Con.* 1.2.

[38] Sen. *Con.* 1.4.

[39] Sen. *Con.* 1.5.

[40] Sen. *Con.* 1.6.

[41] Sen. *Con.* 1.7.

[42] See Bonner, *Roman Declamation*, 33–9.

[43] Tac. *Dial.* 35.4.

[44] Seven of the seventy-four themes in Seneca: *Con.* 4.2, 6.5, 7.2, 8.2, 9.1, 9.2, 10.5. Two more, 3.8 and 5.3, introduce real places.

[45] Sen. *Con.* 7.2.8.

[46] N. Deratani (*RPh* (sér. 3) 3 (1929), 187) points to parallels with circumstances of the Greek world in the fourth to third centuries B.C., when the themes about tyranny originated.

[47] Sen. *Con.* 2.4.12–13.

[48] Plin. *Ep.* 2.3.6. But the rhetorician Secundus Carrinas was banished by Caligula for declaiming against tyranny (Dio 59.20). See Bonner, *Roman Declamation*, 43 n. 5.

[49] Sen. *Suas.* 6.2, 7.1; Tac. *Ann.* 3.57. See V. Cucheval, *Histoire de l'éloquence romaine depuis la mort de Cicéron* (Paris, 1893), 1.337; Caplan in Wichelns, *Studies in Speech and Drama*, 299.

[50] Bonner (*Roman Declamation*, 84–132) discusses the laws in detail, and shows that earlier views regarding the fictitious character of the declamatory laws were exaggerated.

[51] Bonner, *Roman Declamation*, 90–1, 95–6.

[52] Quint. *Inst.* 7.4.11.

[53] Sen. *Con.* 7 pr. 8.

[54] Sen. *Con.* 3 pr. 12, 10.5.12; Quint. *Inst.* 4.2.29, 5.13.50, 7.1.38.

[55] Quint. *Inst.* 3.8.51 *paucissimas controversias ita dicunt ut advocati.* The declaimer would choose whether to take the part of an advocate or not (Quint. *Inst.* 4.1.46). He would do so if the character concerned was a woman, or if there was something discreditable about him (Quint. *Decl.* 260 (*sermo*); cf. 313 (*sermo*) and 331 (*sermo*)).

[56] Sen. *Con.* 1.1.13.

[57] Sen. *Con.* 2.3.12–13.

[58] See Quint. *Inst.* 8.5.30.

[59] Sen. *Con.* 1.2.16.

[60] W. Peterson on Quint. *Inst.* 10.1.116 (edition, Oxford, 1891).

[61] Sen. *Con.* 1.6.9–10.

[62] Sen. *Con.* 7.3.7, 7.3.8.

[63] Sen. *Con.* 1.7.18.

[64] Sen. *Con.* 1.1.16, 1.1.21, 1.4.7, 2.1.33, 7.7.15; Quint. *Inst.* 4.2.94.

[65] Sen. *Con.* 9 pr. 1.

[66] See Bornecque, *Les Déclamations et les déclamateurs*, 95–6.

[67] Quint. *Inst.* 8.5.2–3.

[68] Quint. *Inst.* 8.5.14.

[69] Sen. *Con.* 1.5.1, 1.5.2, 1.5.9.

[70] Note the jingle of like-sounding words, characteristic of Gallio (cf. Tac. *Dial.* 26.1).

[71] A favourite type. Cf. Sen. *Con.* 1.1.17 *quaeritis quid fecerim? quod solebam.*

[72] Cf. Sen. *Con.* 7.4.10.

[73] Sen. *Con.* 1 pr. 10 *sententias a disertissimis viris dictas in tanta hominum desidia pro suis dicunt.*

[74] Sen. *Con.* 1.5.1.

[75] Sen. *Con.* 2.1.28.

[76] See Sen. *Con.* 7.5.12–13.

[77] Sen. *Con.* 1 pr. 18, 10.1.8.

[78] Sen. *Con.* 1 pr. 23.

[79] Sen. *Suas.* 1.9; *Con.* 2.1.10ff.

[80] Quint. *Inst.* 3.8.51.

[81] Sen. *Con.* 7.4.10.

[82] Quint. *Inst.* 2.2.9–12; cf. Sen. *Con.* 1.1.21, 2.3.19, 9 pr. 5.

83 Sen. *Con.* 2.2.8, 10.1.14; Petr. 6.1–2; Tac. *Dial.* 20.4.

84 Sen. *Con.* 9.6.12.

85 Petr. 3.2.

86 Petr. 1.3.

87 Tac. *Dial.* 35.

88 Sen. *Con.* 3 pr. 12.

89 Quint. *Inst.* 2.10.4–12.

90 ap. Sen. *Con.* 9 pr. 1–2, 5.

91 T. Sprat, *The History of the Royal Society of London, For the Improving of Natural Knowledge*, (ed.) J. I. Cope and H. Whitmore Jones (St Louis and London, 1959), 112.

92 Plin. *Ep.* 2.3.5–7. St Jerome however had less pleasant recollections of declamation (*contr. Ruf.* 1.30).

CHAPTER IX

1 Cornelius Severus ap. Sen. *Suas.* 6.27.

2 Virg. *Aen.* 6.849.

3 An old theory, on which see T. Zielinski, *Cicero im Wandel der Jahrhunderte*[3] (Leipzig and Berlin, 1912), 279–80.

4 Suet. *Aug.* 86.

5 Tac. *Dial.* 5–7; Plin. *Ep.* 4.16.

6 Tac. *Dial.* 8.

7 e.g. Junius Otho (Tac. *Ann.* 3.66).

8 Juv. 7.197–8.

9 Plin. *Ep.* 4.11.2.

10 Cf. the discussion on lawyers' fees reported in Tac. *Ann.* 11.5–7, and Martial's *dives eris si causas egeris* (2.30.5). See Parks, *The Roman Rhetorical Schools*, 56–9.

11 Suet. *Aug.* 33; Dio 57.7.2; Sen. *Apoc.* 7; Tac. *Ann.* 11.5.1; Suet. *Claud.* 14–15.

12 Tac. *Ann.* 3.11–12.

13 Quint. *Inst.* 9.2.68.

14 Tac. *Dial.* 36.4–5.

15 Tac. *Dial.* 37.4.

16 Tac. *Dial.* 38–9.

17 His son also treats this theme in *Ep.* 114, esp. 11.

18 Tac. *Ann.* 1.74.

19 Tac. *Ann.* 4.52; cf. 4.66. Tacitus describes Cassius Severus as *sordidae originis maleficae vitae sed orandi validus* (*Ann.* 4.21) and Mamercus Scaurus as *insignis nobilitate et orandis causis vita probrosus* (6.29).

20 P. H. Stanhope, *Life of the Right Honourable William Pitt*[3] (London, 1879), 3.414.

21 Tac. *Dial.* 36 *magna eloquentia sicut flamma materia alitur et motibus excitatur et urendo clarescit.* This fine sentence is, strangely enough, derived from a trite comparison of the schools: Sen. *Con.* 2.2.8 *memini Latronem . . .*

dicere, quod scholastici quasi carmen didicerant: non vides ut immota fax torpeat, ut exagitata reddat ignes? Cf. Plin. *Ep.* 4.9.

22 Tac. *Dial.* 36–41.

23 Sen. *Con.* 1 pr. 7. The same idea is found in Vell. 1.17.6.

24 Tac. *Dial.* 19–20.

25 Cf. Quint. *Inst.* 10.1.118.

26 Plin. *Ep.* 1.5.11–13.

27 It should however be said that Quintilian, for all his admiration of Cicero, did not approve of mere imitation and believed in the possibility of progress: see *Inst.* 10.2.4–13.

28 The most important controversy that agitated the professors in the early empire was that between the followers of Apollodorus, Augustus' master, and those of Theodorus, who taught Tiberius (see Quint. *Inst.* 3.1.17–18). Apollodorus was a dry pedantic writer (Tac. *Dial.* 19ff.) who believed in maintaining the full rigour of the rules (every speech, for instance, must contain proem, *narratio*, proof and peroration in the correct order) whereas Theodorus and his followers allowed some latitude. (For further details see *RE* 1.2886–94.) The ordinary man had some difficulty in understanding what the controversy was about (Str. 13.4.3), and it is unlikely that it had much influence on practice. See Quintilian's remarks in *Inst.* 5.13.59, and his story in 2.11.2.

29 Quint. *Inst.* 9.2.81.

30 Quint. *Inst.* 5.8.1; cf. Sen. *Con.* 9 pr. 2.

31 Sen. *Con.* 9 pr. 1; Quint. *Inst.* 4.2.122, 4.3.2.

32 Quint. *Inst.* 8.5.22, 8.5.31. See also Seneca on Votienus Montanus, *Con.* 9.5.15.

33 Quint. *Inst.* 5.12.17–20, 8.3.23.

34 Sen. *Con.* 2.1.34–6. Note the esoteric jokes about Apollodorus and Theodorus.

35 Quint. *Inst.* 4.2.29.

36 Quint. *Inst.* 5.13.42, 5.13.46; Sen. *Con.* 9 pr. 2; cf. Quint. *Inst.* 7.2.54.

37 Quint. *Inst.* 6.1.42.

38 Sen. *Con.* 3 pr. 12–15.

39 Tac. *Dial.* 19.1.

40 Sen. *Con.* 3 pr. 1–7; Quint. *Inst.* 10.1.116–17.

41 *Gravitas*: Quint. *Inst.* 10.1.116. But see Sen. *Con.* 3 pr. 4.

42 Tac. *Dial.* 26.5.

43 Sen. *Con.* 10 pr. 2; cf. 9.2.25 (Vibius Rufus).

44 Quint. *Inst.* 10.1.118. But Tacitus implies that he was very different from Cicero.

45 *Anth. Lat.* 1.405 Riese; Quint. *Inst.* 6.1.50, 10.1.24.

46 Quint. *Inst.* 10.1.122.

47 Plin. *Ep.* 2.14.

48 Plin. *Ep.* 2.14.9–12.

49 Plin. *Ep.* 4.16.

50 Plin. *Ep.* 1.2.6, 6.11.

51 e.g. the defence of Julius Bassus (Plin. *Ep.* 4.9).

52 Plin. *Ep.* 2.11, 4.9, 5.13.3, 6.5.4.

53 Plin. *Ep.* 1.2.2–4.

54 Plin. *Ep.* 7.30.4–5; cf. 9.26.8.

55 Plin. *Ep.* 7.9.1–6; cf. Cic. *de Orat.* 1.154–5.

[56] Plin. *Ep.* 7.9.8.
[57] Plin. *Ep.* 3.13.3.
[58] Cic. *de Orat.* 2.120; cf. Quint. *Inst.* 8 pr. 13.
[59] Plin. *Ep.* 3.18.1–2.
[60] It is unnecessary to go to Menander the rhetorician, as do J. Mesk, *WS* 32 (1910), 241ff. and 33 (1911), 72ff.; M. Durry, *Pline le Jeune: Panégyrique de Trajan* (Paris, 1938), 27–8.
[61] Quint. *Inst.* 3.7.10.
[62] Quint. *Inst.* 3.7.12. Pliny touches on Trajan's bodily endowments incidentally (*Pan.* 4.7, 55.11).
[63] Quint. *Inst.* 3.7.15.
[64] In details there are of course agreements with rhetorical precepts, e.g. Plin. *Pan.* 7.1 *o novum atque inauditum ad principatum iter*; cf. Quint. *Inst.* 3.7.16 *gratiora esse audientibus quae solus quis aut primus aut certe cum primis fecisse dicetur*. One reason for Pliny's frequent comparisons of Trajan with Domitian was *nihil non parum grate sine comparatione laudatur* (*Pan.* 53.1).
[65] Plin. *Ep.* 3.18.2.

CHAPTER X

[1] Quint. *Inst.* 1 pr. 1–2.
[2] Quint. *Inst.* 3.1.22; cf. 2.15.38.
[3] See Quint. *Inst.* 3.1.7, 3.4.12.
[4] Quint. *Inst.* 3.1.20.
[5] Quint. *Inst.* 7.3.8.
[6] Quint. *Inst.* 3.1.7.
[7] Quint. *Inst.* 2.13.1, 2, 7, 15.
[8] e.g. Quint. *Inst.* 1 pr. 24, 2.15.37, 3.11.21, 5.14.27, 5.14.31.
[9] Quint. *Inst.* 3.3.1–3.
[10] Quint. *Inst.* 1 pr. 22.
[11] Quint. *Inst.* 3.7, 3.8.
[12] Quint. *Inst.* 6.2; cf. 3.9.7, 4.2.111ff., 6.1.9–55.
[13] Quint. *Inst.* 6.2.4–6.
[14] Quint. *Inst.* 6.2.25.
[15] J. Cousin (*Études sur Quintilien* (Paris, 1936), 1.323) points out that the comparison with fire in *Inst.* 6.2.28 is derived from Cic. *de Orat.* 2.190.
[16] Quint. *Inst.* 6.2.36.
[17] Quint. *Inst.* 6.3.6.
[18] Quint. *Inst.* 6.3.28.
[19] Quint. *Inst.* 6.3.35.
[20] Quint. *Inst.* 12.2.26.
[21] Quint. *Inst.* 12.2.30.
[22] Quint. *Inst.* 1 pr. 11–17, 10.1.35, 12.2.5, 8, 9.
[23] Quint. *Inst.* 1 pr. 15, 5.11.39, 11.1.33, 11.1.35, 12.2.6–9.
[24] Quint. *Inst.* 12.3.12.
[25] I cannot agree with R. G. Austin, who in his edition of Book 12 ((Oxford, 1948), xvi) attributes jealousy rather to the philosophers and

suggests that they were afraid of losing their traditional status in the world of education. It was the rhetoricians not the philosophers who had the traditional status, a status enhanced by Vespasian's founding of state chairs of rhetoric at Rome.

[26] There are good reasons for dating the publication of the *Institutio* to the very end of Domitian's reign, after the expulsion of philosophers in 93.

[27] Quint. *Inst.* 12.2.7.

[28] Quint. *Inst.* 1 pr. 10 *vir ille vere civilis et publicarum privatarumque rerum administrationi accommodatus.*

[29] Quint. *Inst.* 8 pr. 13–16.

[30] Quint. *Inst.* 8 pr. 3.

[31] Quint. *Inst.* 8 pr. 20.

[32] Quint. *Inst.* 8 pr. 8.

[33] Quint. *Inst.* 8 pr. 22–3.

[34] Quint. *Inst.* 8 pr. 31.

[35] Quint. *Inst.* 8 pr. 24–6.

[36] Quint. *Inst.* 8 pr. 28–30.

[37] Quint. *Inst.* 10.3.15.

[38] Quint. *Inst.* 1 pr. 9, 2.15.1, 2.16.11, 2.16.31, 2.16.43, 2.20.4, 2.21.12.

[39] Quint. *Inst.* 12.1.1. It is interesting to note that Cato's definition is nowhere quoted by Cicero.

[40] See Cousin, *op. cit.* (n. 15), 1.739ff. for Stoic elements in Quintilian. Gwynn (*Roman Education*, 232–4) criticises earlier attempts to find Stoic sources for Quintilian's ideas. See also Austin, *op. cit.* (n. 25), xix–xx.

[41] Quint. *Inst.* 12 pr. 2–4.

[42] Quint. *Inst.* 1 pr. 9. See M. Winterbottom, *JRS* 54 (1964), 90–7 for a discussion of Quintilian's idea of the *vir bonus* in relation to the oratorical successes of the *delatores*.

[43] Quint. *Inst.* 2.15ff.

[44] It is interesting to note that one of Quintilian's Roman predecessors, Celsus, was on the non-moral side (Quint. *Inst.* 2.15.32, 3.7.25).

[45] Quint. *Inst.* 2.15.38. He does not identify his definition with that of the Stoics, *scientia recte dicendi*, though he admits that this comes to much the same as his (2.15.35). Other authorities ascribe to the Stoics the definition *episteme tou eu legein* ('science of speaking well'). See H. von Arnim, *Stoicorum Veterum Fragmenta* (Leipzig, 1903–5), 2.293, 294.

[46] Quint. *Inst.* 2.15.34.

[47] Quint. *Inst.* 2.16.1–6, 10.

[48] Quint. *Inst.* 2.16.11.

[49] Quint. *Inst.* 2.17.31.

[50] Quint. *Inst.* 12.1.1.

[51] Quint. *Inst.* 12.1.1, 3, 4ff.

[52] Quint. *Inst.* 12.1.11.

[53] Quint. *Inst.* 12.1.12.

[54] Quint. *Inst.* 12.1.33–5.

[55] Quint. *Inst.* 2.17.29.

[56] Quint. *Inst.* 2.17.36.

[57] Quint. *Inst.* 12.1.42–3.

⁵⁸ Quint. *Inst.* 12.1.36–7; cf. 2.17.26–7.

⁵⁹ R. Whately, *Elements of Rhetoric*⁷ (London, 1882), 5. For a critical estimate of Quintilian see G. A. Kennedy, *AJP* 83 (1962), 130–46.

⁶⁰ Quint. *Inst.* 12.1.19–21; cf. 10.2.9.

⁶¹ Quint. *Inst.* 12.1.24–6.

⁶² See pp. 134–5.

CHAPTER XI

¹ Quint. *Inst.* 1 pr. 4–5. But Pliny the elder may have done something of the sort in those six volumes *quibus oratorem ab incunabulis instituit et perfecit* (Plin. *Ep.* 3.5.5).

² Suet. *Vesp.* 18.

³ Plin. *Ep.* 2.18.1.

⁴ Quint. *Inst.* 2.1.1–3. Things had not gone so far in the Greek schools, according to Quintilian. But his Greek contemporary Theon has a similar complaint to make (*Prog.* 1).

⁵ Quint. *Inst.* 2.1.4–6.

⁶ Fables, *sententiae, chriae, ethologiae*, short stories from poets (Quint. *Inst.* 1.9.2–6).

⁷ Quint. *Inst.* 2.4.2, 18, 20, 21, 22–5, 33–40.

⁸ Quint. *Inst.* 2.7.1–3.

⁹ Quint. *Inst.* 1.10.1.

¹⁰ Quint. *Inst.* 1.10.11, 22, 29, 33.

¹¹ Quint. *Inst.* 1.10.36, 37, 46.

¹² Quint. *Inst.* 1.10.3–4, 1.12.12. Quintilian himself appears to have studied under a *geometres* (see his reminiscence in *Inst.* 1.10.39). In general the subjects belonging to the *encyclios paideia* ('general education'), other than grammar and rhetoric, tended to be neglected; cf. Theon *Prog.* 1.1 'they pay no attention whatsoever to the so-called general education, but throw themselves at oratory'. If this was true of the Greek-speaking world, it would probably be all the more so of the Latin. In the fourth century St Augustine taught himself the liberal arts 'out of school': *omnes libros artium quas liberales vocant ... per me ipsum legi et intellexi, quoscunque legere potui* (*Conf.* 4.16.30). See Marrou, *Saint Augustin*, 226.

¹³ Quint. *Inst.* 2.5.1, 3.8.67. In both cases historians are coupled with orators.

¹⁴ Quint. *Inst.* 10.1.31.

¹⁵ Quint. *Inst.* 10.1.34.

¹⁶ Quint. *Inst.* 12.4. Gwynn (*Roman Education*, 221–4) regards this and the two previous chapters as hurried afterthoughts dealing with those parts of Cicero's theory with which Quintilian was least in sympathy. R. G. Austin in his edition of Book 12 ((Oxford, 1948), xxx) explains the inadequacy of ch. 4 as due to lack of final revision.

¹⁷ Quint. *Inst.* 12.3.

¹⁸ Quint. *Inst.* 12.3.7–8. Gwynn (*Roman Education*, 224) comments on the lack of personal enthusiasm in this chapter. But law had always been

neglected in the rhetorical schools, and one would not expect a professional rhetorician like Quintilian to show much enthusiasm for it. At least he makes his point adequately.

[19] Quint. *Inst.* 12.2.

[20] At a later date however Augustine came across the *Hortensius* of Cicero *usitato more discendi* (*Conf.* 3.4.7). Was this used in the school of rhetoric to illustrate the *quaestio infinita*? See Mart. Cap. 5 (454 Halm).

[21] Quint. *Inst.* 2.5.4. In Greek schools this form of teaching was entrusted to an assistant (2.5.3).

[22] Quint. *Inst.* 2.5.1ff.

[23] Quint. *Inst.* 2.5.14–16.

[24] Quint. *Inst.* 2.5.18.

[25] Quint. *Inst.* 10.1.

[26] Quint. *Inst.* 10.1.4.

[27] Quint. *Inst.* 10.1.1ff.

[28] Quint. *Inst.* 10.2.1.

[29] Quint. *Inst.* 2.10.1–3, 10.5.14, 11.2.39.

[30] Quint. *Inst.* 2.10.4–6.

[31] Quint. *Inst.* 2.10.6, 9.

[32] Quint. *Inst.* 2.10.7, 10.

[33] Quint. *Inst.* 2.10.12, 14.

[34] Sen. *Ep.* 106.12. Quintilian writes in one place: *quamvis enim omne propositum operis a nobis destinati eo spectet ut orator instituatur, tamen ne quid studiosi requirant, etiamsi quid erit quod ad scholam proprie pertineat, in transitu non omittemus* (*Inst.* 2.10.15).

[35] Quint. *Inst.* 3.8.30, 46, 47; cf. 3.8.16, 7.1.24, 7.4.2.

[36] Quint. *Inst.* 3.8.58ff.

[37] Quint. *Inst.* 3.8.70.

[38] e.g. Quint. *Inst.* 4.1.47, 7.1.29.

[39] Quint. *Inst.* 7.4.21.

[40] See the elaborate analysis of a *controversia* in *Inst.* 7.1.42–62. On nature as guide see 7.1.40, 46, 49; cf. 7.3.30ff.

[41] Though the declamations ascribed to Quintilian by Lactantius (*Inst.* 1.21, 5.7) may have been in the missing part of the collection.

[42] F. Leo, *NGG* (1912), 117–18.

[43] Quint. *Inst.* 1 pr. 7.

[44] C. Ritter, *Die quintilianischen Deklamationen* (Freiburg im Breisgau and Tübingen, 1881), 217 and his Teubner edition (Leipzig, 1884), v; Gwynn, *Roman Education*, 212.

[45] Quint. *Inst.* 1 pr. 7 *duo iam sub nomine meo libri ferebantur artis rhetoricae*; cf. 3.6.68. See F. H. Colson's edition of Book 1 (Cambridge, 1924), xix n. 2.

[46] See Ritter, *op. cit.* (n. 44), 224ff.; Leo, *op. cit.* (n. 42), 117–18; Gwynn, *Roman Education*, 215–16; N. Deratani, *RPh* (sér. 2) 49 (1925), 106ff.

[47] *Decl.* 349: *Inst.* 4.2.90 (a theme also found in Sen. *Con.* 2.3).

[48] *Decl.* 268: cf. *Inst.* 7.1.38, 7.4.39; *Decl.* 283: cf. *Inst.* 4.2.30; *Decl.* 284: cf. *Inst.* 5.10.104. In all three cases the slight difference between the version in Quintilian and that in the declamations is significant.

[49] *Decl.* 316, second *sermo*.

[50] *Decl.* 337, *sermo.*

[51] Not that *sententiae* are entirely lacking, or *colores.* In *Decl.* 297, 352, 355, 362, 363 and 364 there is some degree of *color*, that is, motives are attributed to the actors which are not in the theme.

[52] *Decl.* 270, *sermo.* For definition cf. 246, 247, 308, 349, 350.

[53] *Decl.* 316.

[54] *Decl.* 333, *sermo.*

[55] See p. 115.

CHAPTER XII

[1] SHA *Hadr.* 16.8, 10; Philostr. *VS* 1.25 (532–3); Gel. 13.22.1; Modest. *dig.* 27.1.6.1. These privileges were shared with other professors. Subsequent emperors continued the policy, which was incorporated in the Code of Justinian (*cod. Just.* 10.52). See Marrou, *Education in Antiquity*, 301–2.

[2] Philostr. *VS* 2.9 (582–3), 2.7 (577), 2.10 (589).

[3] Dio 72.31.3; Philostr. *VS* 2.2 (566–7), 2.10 (588–9).

[4] Philostr. *VS* 1.8 (490–1), 2.10 (589).

[5] Philostr. *VS* 1.8 (491), 2.10 (589).

[6] Gel. 1.2.6, 9.2, 20.1. See Norden, *Kunstprosa*, 1.362–3.

[7] Postumius Festus, mentioned in Gel. 19.13, was *oratorem utraque facund. maximum* (H. Dessau (ed.), *Inscriptiones Latinae Selectae* (Berlin, 1892–1916), no. 2929).

[8] e.g. Isaeus in A.D. 97 (Plin. *Ep.* 2.3; Juv. 3.74).

[9] Unless Julius Severianus belongs to this period, as suggested by L. Radermacher, *RE* 10.805–11.

[10] Cic. *de Orat.* 2.45.

[11] Quint. *Inst.* 3.7.2.

[12] Cic. *de Orat.* 2.341.

[13] This is implied by Cic. *de Orat.* 2.341.

[14] Quint. *Inst.* 3.7.4.

[15] Quint. *Inst.* 3.7.6–18, 26.

[16] On Fronto see M. D. Brock, *Studies in Fronto and his Age* (Cambridge, 1911), esp. ch. X.

[17] Fro. *ad M. Caes.* 3.16.1 (1.104–6 Haines).

[18] Fro. *Laud. Fum. et Pulv.* 2 (1.40 Haines) *nullum huiuscemodi scriptum Romana lingua extat satis nobile.*

[19] Fro. *Laud. Fum. et Pulv.* 2, 3, 6 (1.40–4 Haines).

[20] Fro. *ad Verum Imp.* 2.1.8 (2.138 Haines).

[21] Fro. *ad Verum Imp.* 2.1.5 (2.136 Haines).

[22] Fro. *de Eloqu.* 1.5 (2.58 Haines).

[23] Fro. *de Eloqu.* 3.3, 5 (2.74, 76 Haines).

[24] Fro. *de Eloqu.* 1.2 (2.54 Haines).

[25] Fro. *ad M. Caes.* 4.3.2–3 (1.4–6 Haines).

[26] Fro. *ad M. Caes.* 3.11 (1.12 Haines); cf. 5.59 (1.54 Haines).

[27] Fro. *ad M. Caes.* 3.7 (1.34 Haines).

[28] Fro. *ad M. Caes.* 3.8.1 (1.36 Haines).

²⁹ Fro. *ad M. Caes.* 3.15.1 (1.100 Haines).
³⁰ Fro. *ad M. Caes.* 4.13 (1.216–18 Haines).
³¹ Fro. *de Eloqu.* 1.10 (2.62 Haines).
³² *ibid.*
³³ Fro. *de Eloqu.* 1.11–12 (2.62–4 Haines).
³⁴ Fro. *de Eloqu.* 1.18 (2.70 Haines).
³⁵ Fro. *de Eloqu.* 3.4 (2.74 Haines).
³⁶ Fro. *de Eloqu.* 4.3 (2.82 Haines).
³⁷ Fro. *ad Ant. Imp.* 1.2.4, 1.2.10 (2.38–40, 46 Haines).
³⁸ M. Ant. 1.11 (A. S. L. Farquharson's translation).
³⁹ M. Ant. 1.7, 1.17.4.
⁴⁰ There is one reference to a controversial theme: *ad M. Caes.* 5.22 (1.210 Haines).
⁴¹ In the MSS they have the heading *Incipiunt ex Calpurnio Flacco excerptae. Excerpta X rhetorum minorum.* It thus appears that the extracts from Calpurnius Flaccus came from a larger collection in which nine other rhetoricians were represented.
⁴² External evidence before the fourth century is dubious. SHA *Tyr. Trig.* 4.2 refers to Quintilian's declamations, but the date is doubtful.
⁴³ Calp. *Decl.* 12 = Sen. *Con.* 9.6; *Decl.* 40 = *Con.* 6.6; *Decl.* 42 = (nearly) *Con.* 8.1; [Quint.] *Decl.* 17 = *Con.* 7.3.
⁴⁴ Calp. *Decl.* 5; Sen. *Con.* 10.1.13.
⁴⁵ This was traditional; cf. Petr. 48.5.
⁴⁶ [Quint.] *Decl.* 13.
⁴⁷ Calp. *Decl.* 11.
⁴⁸ Calp. *Decl.* 17.
⁴⁹ Sen. *Con.* 1.5.
⁵⁰ Calp. *Decl.* 51.
⁵¹ Calp. *Decl.* 10.
⁵² See p. 94.
⁵³ [Quint.] *Decl.* 17; Sen. *Con.* 7.3.7.

CHAPTER XIII

¹ Edited by K. Halm (Leipzig, 1863). For Fortunatianus, Julius Victor, Sulpitius Victor and Martianus Capella see A. Reuter, *Hermes* 28 (1893), 73–134.
² Part of his *de Nuptiis Mercurii et Philologiae.*
³ Apart from Capella, whose literary pretensions are confined to his introductory passage.
⁴ Julius Rufinianus (38 Halm). Alexander Numenius, an epitome of whose work survives, probably flourished in the second century A.D.
⁵ Sulpitius Victor (313 Halm).
⁶ *C. Iulii Victoris Ars Rhetorica Hermagorae, Ciceronis, Quintiliani, Aquili, Marcomanni, Tatiani* (371 Halm).
⁷ He refers to the five-fold division, but rejects it, with the words *sed nos a Graecis tradita, ut coepimus, persequamur* (Sulpitius Victor 4, = 315 Halm).

[8] Reuter, *op. cit.* (n. 1), 133. Reuter finds that Fortunatianus and Julius are nearest to one another, Capella is further off and Sulpitius is further still.

[9] Quint. *Inst.* 3.1.7.

[10] Julius Severianus 1 (355 Halm).

[11] Even though they may not have written for school purposes. Sulpitius Victor writes for his son-in-law (313 Halm).

[12] Can we, asks Fortunatianus (2.20, = 113 Halm), sometimes begin with a *narratio*, without an *exordium*? We can, he answers, in certain circumstances. 'But this is only the case in the forum. Can it be done in school declamations? By no means.' Cf. Julius Victor 3.9 (382 Halm), 4.4 (389 Halm).

[13] See Marrou, *Education in Antiquity*, 301–2. The exemptions were shared with other classes.

[14] *Paneg.* 9.14.

[15] For the thought cf. Vitr. 6 pr. 4.

[16] Jul. *Ep.* 42 Hertlein, = 36 Wright; Amm. 22.10.7, 25.4.20; Aug. *Conf.* 8.5.10.

[17] *cod. Theod.* 13.3.11.

[18] Cic. *Rep.* 4.3.

[19] *cod. Theod.* 14.1.1 *literatura quae omnium virtutum maxima est*; cf. *Paneg.* 9.8.

[20] See Marrou, *Education in Antiquity*, 310–12.

[21] *Paneg.* 6.23; cf. 9.8.

[22] Aus. *Prof.* 1.9–10. Victorinus was a teacher of many noble senators (Aug. *Conf.* 8.2.3).

[23] Aus. *Prof.* 15.18, 17.13. Ausonius and Exuperius owed their positions to having been tutors to future emperors.

[24] Aug. *Conf.* 6.11.19.

[25] See T. J. Haarhoff, *Schools of Gaul: a Study of Pagan and Christian Education in the Last Century of the Western Empire* (Oxford, 1920), 140–1.

[26] Aug. *Conf.* 6.6.9.

[27] Aus. *Prof.* 1.13.

[28] Of the panegyrists Nazarius (an author of the fourth century) is otherwise known as a famous rhetorician (Aus. *Prof.* 14.9; Jer. *Chron.* A.D. 324), and the authors of *Paneg.* 5 and 8 declare themselves members of the profession (5.1, 8.1). For Eumenius see p. 142.

[29] Juv. 15.110–12.

[30] Plut. *Sert.* 14.

[31] Tac. *Agr.* 21.

[32] Tac. *Dial.* 10, 20.

[33] R. Thouvenot, *Essai sur la province romaine de Bétique* (Paris, 1940), 668.

[34] The father of Bonosus (third century). He called himself a rhetorician, but others said he was only an elementary school teacher (SHA *Firm. Sat. Proc. Bon.* 14.1). See R. G. Collingwood in T. Frank (ed.), *An Economic Survey of Ancient Rome* 3 (Baltimore, 1937), 69.

[35] Sen. *Suas.* 2.18; *Con.* 10 pr. 15–16. Lucan's grandfather on his mother's side was a distinguished advocate in Spain (*Vita Lucani* 334 Hosius). For Spanish rhetoricians see H. de la Ville de Mirmont, *BH* 12 (1910), 1–22; 14

(1912), 11–29, 229–43, 341–52; 15 (1913), 154–69, 237–67, 384–410.

[36] Mart. 9.73.

[37] Aus. *Prof.* 23; *Paneg.* 2.4. An inscription from Gades records a Greek rhetorician (*CIL* 2.1738). *CIL* 2.354 is an inscription to an orator.

[38] Juv. 7.148–9.

[39] Stat. *Silv.* 4.5; Suda s.v. Cornutus.

[40] SHA *Diad.* 8.9.

[41] *CIL* 8.5530; H. Dessau (ed.), *Inscriptiones Latinae Selectae* (Berlin, 1892–1916), nos. 7742c, 7744, 7747, 7761. See E. S. Bouchier, *Life and Letters in Roman Africa* (Oxford, 1913), ch. III.

[42] Apul. *Fl.* 20. See F. Schemmel, *PhW* 47 (1927), 1342–4.

[43] Aug. *Conf.* 2.3.5, 5.8.14. Tertullian (*adv. Valent.* 8) mentions a *frigidissimus rhetor* of the Carthaginian schools called Phosphorus.

[44] Juv. 15.111; cf. Jer. *Comm. Ep. Gal. II* pr.

[45] Suet. *Gram.* 3.

[46] Claudius Quirinalis: Jer. *Chron.* A.D. 44; Julius Gabinianus: *Chron.* A.D. 76; Tac. *Dial.* 26; Jer. *in Esaiam* 8 pr.; Julius Florus: Quint. *Inst.* 10.3.3; Sen. *Con.* 9.2.23; Statius Ursulus: Jer. *Chron.* A.D. 56; Domitius Afer: *Chron.* A.D. 44; Quint. *Inst.* 5.7.7.

[47] Suet. *Cal.* 20.

[48] Str. 4.1.5. Two Massilian rhetoricians, Moschus and Agroetas, are mentioned by Seneca (*Con.* 2.5.13, 2.6.12).

[49] Tac. *Ann.* 3.43; *Paneg.* 9.

[50] Bordeaux: Aus. *Prof. passim*; Toulouse: Symm. *Ep.* 9.88; Aus. *Prof.* 16.9–12, 17.7, 19.4; Narbonne: Aus. *Prof.* 17.8–11, 19.12; Lyons and Besançon: Aus. *Grat. Act.* 7; Trèves: Aus. *Mos.* 403; Poitiers: Aus. *Epigr.* 10; Angoulême: Aus. *Ep.* 11.21; Saintes: Aus. *Ep.* 4.3, 4.12. Other places are known to have been the home of schools, but not necessarily of rhetorical schools. See Marrou, *Education in Antiquity*, 297; M. Roger, *L'Enseignement des lettres classiques d'Ausone à Alcuin* (Paris, 1905), 3ff.

[51] Aus. *Prof.* 16.9–12, 19.4, 1.4.

[52] Aus. *Prof.* 23.

[53] Alethius (Aus. *Prof.* 2.7), Delphidius (5.15–18) and Ausonius himself (*Praef.* 1.17).

[54] Aus. *Prof.* 5.19–33.

[55] E.g. Alethius (Aus. *Prof.* 2.7), Luciolus (3.3–4) and Delphidius (5.5–12).

[56] Aus. *Prof.* 1.17–18, 17.4–6.

[57] See Roger, *op. cit.* (n. 50).

CHAPTER XIV

[1] Jer. *Ep.* 22.30.

[2] Aug. *Doctr. Christ.* 2.13.19.

[3] Aug. *Conf.* 3.5.9.

[4] Lact. *Inst.* 5.1; cf. Aug. *Catech. Rud.* 9.13. See P. de Labriolle, *Histoire de la littérature latine chrétienne*[3] (Paris, 1947), 22ff.

⁵ See Labriolle, *op. cit.* (n. 4), 10ff.

⁶ The poets, who with their stories of the gods and their sexual laxity offered a more obvious target, belonged to the *grammaticus* rather than the rhetorician.

⁷ In what follows I am much indebted to Marrou, *Saint Augustin.*

⁸ Aug. *Conf.* 1.18.28–9.

⁹ Aug. *Conf.* 4.2.2.

¹⁰ Aug. *Conf.* 3.3.6; cf. 6.6.9–10.

¹¹ Aug. *Conf.* 9.2.2; *Ep.* 101.2; cf. Prud. *Praef.* 8–9.

¹² Aug. *Conf.* 1.9.14; cf. 1.12.19.

¹³ Aug. *Conf.* 6.6.9.

¹⁴ Aug. *Discipl.* 11.12.

¹⁵ Aug. *Conf.* 3.4.7.

¹⁶ Aug. *Conf.* 9.4.7; cf. *Doctr. Christ.* 2.13.20, 4.7.14.

¹⁷ The fourth book of *de Doctrina Christiana* was written in 427, most of the earlier books thirty years earlier.

¹⁸ See C. S. Baldwin, *Medieval Rhetoric and Poetic to 1400* (New York, 1928), ch. II. The question has been discussed whether Augustine's programme is for the clergy only or for laymen as well. Clearly he has the clergy in mind; on the other hand he has nothing to say about a different kind of education for the layman. He is in the tradition of Cicero and Quintilian, neither of whom has any idea of different kinds of education for different professions. As they ignore all but the orator-statesman, so Augustine ignores all but the Christian teacher.

¹⁹ Aug. *Doctr. Christ.* 4.2.3; cf. *contr. Cresc.* 1.2.

²⁰ Aug. *Doctr. Christ.* 2.26.54.

²¹ Aug. *Doctr. Christ.* 4.1.2. Augustine did shortly after his conversion begin a *Rhetoric*, which may or may not be that which survives under his name.

²² Aug. *Doctr. Christ.* 4.3.4, 4.2.21.

²³ See p. 53.

²⁴ Aug. *Doctr. Christ.* 4.12.27ff.

²⁵ Aug. *Doctr. Christ.* 4.14.31; cf. 4.25.55.

²⁶ Aug. *Doctr. Christ.* 4.14.31: Cypr. *ad Don.* 1 *petamus hanc sedem; dant secessum vicina secreta; ubi dum erratici palmitum lapsus nexibus pendulis per arundines baiulas repunt viteam porticum frondea tecta fecerunt.* Cf. the opening of an anonymous sermon on the marriage of Cana: *inter aestuosa et ripis tumentia flumina quibus avida terrarum viscera fecundantur siccus noster palpitat sensus* (quoted by Marrou, *Saint Augustin*, 528). It is worth remembering that Augustine had at first attended Ambrose's sermons for their manner rather than their matter (*Conf.* 5.13.23).

²⁷ Aug. *Doctr. Christ.* 4.17.34.

²⁸ Aug. *Doctr. Christ.* 4.18.35, 4.19.38.

²⁹ Aug. *Doctr. Christ.* 4.26.56–8.

³⁰ Aug. *Doctr. Christ.* 4.27.59.

³¹ Aug. *Doctr. Christ.* 4.11.24; cf. *Ord.* 2.13.

³² Aug. *Doctr. Christ.* 4.4.6.

³³ Aug. *Doctr. Christ.* 4.6.10.

[34] Aug. *Doctr. Christ.* 4.6.10; cf. 3.29.40.

[35] Aug. *Doctr. Christ.* 4.7.11. He forbears to illustrate at length the tropes and figures to be found in the scriptures (3.29.40, 4.6.10, 4.7.14). This was later done by the Venerable Bede.

[36] Aug. *Doctr. Christ.* 4.7.12.

[37] Aug. *Doctr. Christ.* 4.7.16.

[38] Aug. *Doctr. Christ.* 4.20.41. Whether this was due to the translations or the original he is unable to say.

[39] Aug. *Doctr. Christ.* 4.20.39–4.21.50.

[40] Aug. *Doctr. Christ.* 2.19.29ff.

[41] Aug. *Doctr. Christ.* 2.42.63.

[42] Tert. *Idol.* 10.

[43] Jul. *Ep.* 42 Hertlein, = 36 Wright.

[44] Jul. *Ep.* 42 Hertlein, = 36 Wright 'Now all who profess to teach anything whatever ought to be men of upright character, and ought not to harbour in their souls opinions irreconcilable with what they publicly profess' (W. C. Wright's translation). This suggests that Christian teachers kept their religion to themselves in school.

[45] Aug. *Ep.* 135.1. See Marrou, *Saint Augustin*, 90–1.

[46] Cassiod. *Var.* 9.21.

[47] Cassiod. *Inst. Div.* pr.

[48] Cassiod. *Rhet.* 16 (500 Halm).

[49] Cassiod. *Inst. Div.* 27.

[50] Cassiod. *Var.* 6.5.

[51] He professed to give up such studies on ordination, but did not live up to his resolve. See F. Vogel's edition (Berlin, 1885), viii.

[52] This presumably descends from the progymnastic exercise *ethopoiia* or *prosopopoiia.*

[53] Ennod. *Dict.* 21 (363 Vogel).

[54] There is also evidence of declamation in fifth-century Gaul: see Sid. *Ep.* 5.5.3, 9.7.1; Claud. Mam. *Ep.* 2.

[55] Ennod. *Opusc.* 6 (452 Vogel).

Chapter XV

[1] E. Renan, *Discours et conférences*[10] (Paris, 1935), 130.

[2] Quint. *Inst.* 10.7.26.

[3] Quint. *Inst.* 10.3.12, 10.3.16; cf. 8 pr. 27, 8 pr. 31.

[4] Quint. *Inst.* 8 pr. 23–6.

[5] Quint. *Inst.* 8.2.18. Quintilian records this on the authority of Livy.

[6] Quint. *Inst.* 8.2.21.

[7] Suet. *Aug.* 86.3.

[8] Quint. *Inst.* 8.3.23.

[9] Quint. *Inst.* 7.3.76 (H. E. Butler's translation).

[10] Quint. *Inst.* 3.8.70.

[11] See L. Petit de Julleville, *L'École d'Athènes au quatrième siècle après Jésus-Christ* (Paris, 1868), 105.

12 Quint. *Inst.* 2.20.3.
13 Jul. *Ep.* 55 Hertlein, = 3 Wright.

BIBLIOGRAPHY

Adamietz, J., 'Quintilians "Institutio oratoria"', *ANRW* 2.32.4 (1986), 2226–71.

Albrecht, M. von, *Masters of Roman Prose from Cato to Apuleius: Interpretative Studies*, tr. N. Adkin (Leeds, 1989).

Atkinson, J. M., *Our Masters' Voices: the Language and Body Language of Politics* (London and New York, 1984).

Bartsch, S., *Actors in the Audience: Theatricality and Doublespeak from Nero to Hadrian* (Cambridge, Mass. and London, 1994).

Barwick, K., *Das rednerische Bildungsideal Ciceros* (Abhandlungen der sächsischen Akademie der Wissenschaften zu Leipzig, philologisch-historische Klasse; 54.3 Berlin, 1963).

Berry, D. H., and Heath, M., 'Oratory and declamation', in S. E. Porter (ed.), *A Handbook of Classical Rhetoric* (Leiden, forthcoming).

Bonner, S. F., *Roman Declamation in the Late Republic and Early Empire* (Liverpool, 1949).

Bonner, S. F., 'Roman oratory', in M. Platnauer (ed.), *Fifty Years of Classical Scholarship* (Oxford, 1954), 335–83 (reprinted in *Fifty Years (and Twelve) of Classical Scholarship* (Oxford, 1968)).

Bonner, S. F., *Education in Ancient Rome from the Elder Cato to the Younger Pliny* (London, 1977).

Bornecque, H., *Les Déclamations et les déclamateurs d'après Sénèque le père* (Lille, 1902).

Brink, C. O., 'Quintilian's *de Causis Corruptae Eloquentiae* and Tacitus' *Dialogus de Oratoribus*', *CQ* 39 (1989), 472–503.

Bryant, D. C. (ed.), *Ancient Greek and Roman Rhetoricians: a Biographical Dictionary* (New York, 1968).

Burgess, T. C., *Epideictic Literature* (Chicago, 1902).

Caplan, H., 'The decay of eloquence at Rome in the first century', in H. A. Wichelns *et al.* (eds), *Studies in Speech and Drama in Honor of Alexander M. Drummond* (Ithaca, 1944), 295–325.

Clark, D. L., *Rhetoric in Greco-Roman Education* (New York, 1957).

Clarke, M. L., 'Ciceronian oratory', *G&R* 14 (1945), 72–81.

Clarke, M. L., 'Rhetorical influences in the *Aeneid*', *G&R* 18 (1949), 14–27.

Clarke, M. L., 'The *thesis* in the Roman rhetorical schools of the republic', *CQ* n.s. 1 (1951), 159–66.

Clarke, M. L., '*Non hominis nomen, sed eloquentiae*', in T. A. Dorey (ed.), *Cicero* (London, 1964), 81–107.

Clarke, M. L., 'Quintilian: a biographical sketch', *G&R* 14 (1967), 24–37.

Clarke, M. L., 'Cicero at school', *G&R* 15 (1968), 18–22.

Clarke, M. L., *Higher Education in the Ancient World* (London, 1971).

Clarke, M. L., 'Quintilian on education', in T. A. Dorey (ed.), *Empire and Aftermath: Silver Latin II* (London, 1975), 98–118.

Classen, C. J., *Recht-Rhetorik-Politik: Untersuchungen zu Ciceros rhetorischer Strategie* (Darmstadt, 1985).

Cole, T., *The Origins of Rhetoric in Ancient Greece* (Baltimore and London, 1991).

Craig, C. P., *Form as Argument in Cicero's Speeches: a Study of Dilemma* (A.P.A. American Classical Studies 31; Atlanta, 1993).

Crook, J. A., *Legal Advocacy in the Roman World* (London, 1995).

Curtius, E. R., *European Literature and the Latin Middle Ages*, tr. W. R. Trask (London, 1953).

D'Alton, J. F., *Roman Literary Theory and Criticism: a Study in Tendencies* (London and New York, 1931).

Dalzell, A., 'C. Asinius Pollio and the early history of public recitation at Rome', *Hermathena* 86 (1955), 20–8.

David, J.-M., *Le Patronat judiciaire au dernier siècle de la république romaine* (Bibliothèque des Écoles Françaises d'Athènes et de Rome 277; Rome, 1992).

Davies, J. C., 'Molon's influence on Cicero', *CQ* n.s. 18 (1968), 303–14.

Dingel, J., *Scholastica Materia: Untersuchungen zu den Declamationes Minores und der Institutio Oratoria Quintilians* (Untersuchungen zur antiken Literatur und Geschichte 30; Berlin, 1988).

Douglas, A. E., 'A Ciceronian contribution to rhetorical theory', *Eranos* 55 (1957), 18–26.

Douglas, A. E., '*Clausulae* in the *Rhetorica ad Herennium* as evidence of its date', *CQ* n.s. 10 (1960), 65–78.

Douglas, A. E., 'Hellenistic rhetoric and Roman oratory', in D. Daiches and A. Thorlby (eds), *The Classical World* (London, 1972), 341–54.

Fairweather, J., *Seneca the Elder* (Cambridge, 1981).

Greenidge, A. H. J., *The Legal Procedure of Cicero's Time* (Oxford, 1901).

Grube, G. M. A., 'Educational, rhetorical, and literary theory in Cicero', *Phoenix* 16 (1962), 234–57.

Grube, G. M. A., *The Greek and Roman Critics* (London, 1965).

Gwynn, A., *Roman Education from Cicero to Quintilian* (Oxford, 1926).

Heath, M., 'The substructure of *stasis*-theory from Hermagoras to Hermogenes', *CQ* n.s. 44 (1994), 114–29.

Heath, M., 'Zeno the rhetor and the thirteen *staseis*', *Eranos* 92 (1994), 17–22.

Heath, M., 'Invention', in S. E. Porter (ed.), *A Handbook of Classical Rhetoric* (Leiden, forthcoming).

Jones, A. H. M., *The Criminal Courts of the Roman Republic and Principate* (Oxford, 1972).

Kennedy, G. A., 'An estimate of Quintilian', *AJP* 83 (1962), 130–46.

Kennedy, G. A., *The Art of Persuasion in Greece* (Princeton, 1963).

Kennedy, G. A., 'The rhetoric of advocacy in Greece and Rome', *AJP* 89 (1968), 419–36.

Kennedy, G. A., *Quintilian* (New York, 1969).

Kennedy, G. A., *The Art of Rhetoric in the Roman World, 300 B.C.–A.D. 300* (Princeton, 1972).

Kennedy, G. A., *Classical Rhetoric and its Christian and Secular Tradition from Ancient to Modern Times* (Chapel Hill and London, 1980).

Kennedy, G. A., *Greek Rhetoric under Christian Emperors* (Princeton, 1983).

Kennedy, G. A., *A New History of Classical Rhetoric* (Princeton, 1994).

Kroll, W., 'Rhetorik', *RE* Suppl. 7 (1940), 1039–1138.

Laughton, E., 'Cicero and the Greek orators', *AJP* 82 (1961), 27–49.

Laurand, L., *Etudes sur le style des discours de Cicéron*[4], 3 vols (Paris, 1936–8).

Lausberg, H., *Handbuch der literarischen Rhetorik*, 2 vols (Munich, 1960).

Leeman, A. D., *Orationis Ratio: the Stylistic Theories and Practice of the Roman Orators, Historians and Philosophers*, 2 vols (Amsterdam, 1963).

Ludwig, W., and Stroh, W. (eds), *Éloquence et rhétorique chez Cicéron* (Entretiens sur l'antiquité classique 28; Geneva, 1982).

MacCormack, S., 'Latin prose panegyrics', in T. A. Dorey (ed.), *Empire and Aftermath: Silver Latin II* (London, 1975), 143–205.

MacKendrick, P., *The Speeches of Cicero: Context, Law, Rhetoric* (London, 1995).

Marrou, H.-I., *A History of Education in Antiquity*, tr. G. Lamb (London, 1956).

Marrou, H.-I., *Saint Augustin et la fin de la culture antique*[4] (Paris, 1958).

Martin, J., *Antike Rhetorik* (Munich, 1974).

May, J. M., *Trials of Character: the Eloquence of Ciceronian Ethos* (Chapel Hill and London, 1988).

Neumeister, C., *Grundsätze der forensischen Rhetorik gezeigt an Gerichtsreden Ciceros* (Munich, 1964).

Nisbet, R. G. M., 'The speeches', in T. A. Dorey (ed.), *Cicero* (London, 1964), 47–79.

Norden, E., *Die antike Kunstprosa*[2], 2 vols (Leipzig and Berlin, 1909).

Parks, E. P., *The Roman Rhetorical Schools as a Preparation for the Courts under the Early Empire* (Baltimore, 1945).

Rohde, F. J. A., *Cicero, quae de Inventione praecepit, quatenus secutus sit in orationibus generis iudicialis* (Königsberg, 1903).

Russell, D. A., *Greek Declamation* (Cambridge, 1983).

Solmsen, F., 'Aristotle and Cicero on the orator's playing upon the feelings', *CP* 33 (1938), 390–404.

Solmsen, F., 'Cicero's first speeches: a rhetorical analysis', *TAPA* 69 (1938), 542–56.

Solmsen, F., 'The Aristotelian tradition in ancient rhetoric', *AJP* 62 (1941), 35–50, 169–90.

Stroh, W., *Taxis und Taktik: die advokatische Dispositionskunst in Ciceros Gerichtsreden* (Stuttgart, 1975).

Sumner, G. V., *The Orators in Cicero's* Brutus: *Prosopography and Chronology* (*Phoenix* Suppl. 11; Toronto, 1973).

Süss, W., *Ethos: Studien zur älteren griechischen Rhetorik* (Leipzig and Berlin, 1910).

Sussman, L. A., *The Elder Seneca* (*Mnemosyne* Suppl. 51; Leiden, 1978).

Vasaly, A., *Representations: Images of the World in Ciceronian Oratory* (Berkeley etc., 1993).

Vickers, B., *In Defence of Rhetoric* (Oxford, 1988).

Volkmann, R., *Die Rhetorik der Griechen und Römer*[2] (Leipzig, 1885).

Weische, A., *Ciceros Nachahmung der attischen Redner* (Heidelberg, 1972).

Winterbottom, M., 'Quintilian and the *vir bonus*', *JRS* 54 (1964), 90–7.

Winterbottom, M., 'Quintilian and rhetoric', in T. A. Dorey (ed.), *Empire and Aftermath: Silver Latin II* (London, 1975), 79–97.

Winterbottom, M., *Roman Declamation* (Bristol, 1980).

Winterbottom, M., 'Schoolroom and courtroom', in B. Vickers (ed.), *Rhetoric Revalued* (Medieval & Renaissance Texts & Studies 19; New York, 1982), 59–70.

Winterbottom, M., 'Quintilian and declamation', in *Hommages à Jean Cousin* (Paris, 1983), 225–35.

Winterbottom, M., 'Cicero and the middle style', in J. Diggle, J. B. Hall and H. D. Jocelyn (eds), *Studies in Latin Literature and its Tradition in Honour of C. O. Brink* (*PCPS* Suppl. 15; Cambridge, 1989), 125–31.

Wisse, J., *Ethos and Pathos from Aristotle to Cicero* (Amsterdam, 1989).

INDEX